Serving Homeschooled Teens and Their Parents

Recent Titles in Libraries Unlimited Professional Guides for Young Adult Librarians

Teen Library Events: A Month-by-Month Guide
Kirsten Edwards

Merchandizing Library Materials to Young Adults
Mary Anne Nichols

Library Materials and Services for Teen Girls
Katie O'Dell

Serving Older Teens
Sheila Anderson

Thinking Outside the Book: Alternatives for Today's Teen Library Collection
C. Allen Nichols

SERVING HOMESCHOOLED TEENS AND THEIR PARENTS

Maureen T. Lerch and Janet Welch

Libraries Unlimited Professional Guides for Young Adult
Librarians Series
C. Allen Nichols and Mary Anne Nichols, Series Editors

LIBRARIES
U N L I M I T E D
A Member of the Greenwood Publishing Group
Westport, Connecticut • London

Library of Congress Cataloging-in-Publication Data

Lerch, Maureen T.
 Serving homeschooled teens and their parents / by Maureen T. Lerch and Janet Welch.
  p. cm.—(Libraries Unlimited professional guides for young adult librarians)
 Includes bibliographical references and index.
 ISBN 0–313–32052–7
 1. Libraries and families—United States. 2. Libraries and teenagers—United States.
 3. Home schooling—United States. 4. Public libraries—Services to teenagers—United
 States. 5. Libraries and education—United States. I. Title: Serving home schooled teens
 and their parents. II. Welch, Janet, 1953–. III. Title. IV. Series.
 Z711.92.F34L47   2004
 027.6—dc22   2004046518

British Library Cataloguing in Publication Data is available.

Library of Congress Catalog Card Number: 2004046518
ISBN: 0–313–32052–7
ISSN: 1532–5571

First published in 2004

Libraries Unlimited, 88 Post Road West, Westport, CT 06881
A Member of the Greenwood Publishing Group, Inc.
www.lu.com

Printed in the United States of America

The paper used in this book complies with the
Permanent Paper Standard issued by the National
Information Standards Organization (Z39.48–1984).

10 9 8 7 6 5 4 3 2 1

Copyright Acknowledgments

Article by Carter McNamara, "Basics of Conducting Focus Groups," www.mapnp.org/
library/evaluatn/focusgrp.htm used with permission of the author.

CONTENTS

Series Foreword   ix

Introduction   xi

1 Who Are These Kids and Why Are They in My Library on
Tuesday Morning?   1

2 What Makes Them Tick: A Short Course in Adolescent
Development   13

3 Getting Your Ducks in a Row: The Game Plan for Serving
Homeschoolers   25

4 Hitting the Target: Giving Homeschoolers the Services They
Want and Need   39

5 Construction Zone: Building a Collection to Serve
Homeschooled Teens   53

6 Success Depends on How You Bait Your Hook: Great
Programs for Homeschooling Teens   85

7 The Marketing Mambo: Yes, We Can Teach You to Dance   131

8 From Soup to Nuts: Resources for Librarians,
Homeschooled Teens, and Their Parents   163

Appendix   219

LSTA Grant Application: Johnsburg (IL) Public Library District
Homeschool Resource Center   220

Index   235

SERIES FOREWORD

We firmly believe in young adult library services and advocate for teens whenever we can. We are proud of our association with Libraries Unlimited and Greenwood Publishing Group and grateful for their acknowledgment of the need for additional resources for teen-serving librarians. We intend for this series to fill those needs, providing useful and practical handbooks for library staff. Readers will find some theory and philosophical musings, but for the most part, this series will focus on real-life library issues with answers and suggestions for frontline librarians.

Our passion for young adult librarian services continues to reach new peaks. As we travel to present workshops on the various facets of working with teens in public libraries, we are encouraged by the desire of librarians everywhere to learn what they can do in their libraries to make teens welcome. This is a positive sign since too often libraries choose to ignore this underserved group of patrons. We hope you find this series to be a useful tool in fostering your own enthusiasm for teens.

Mary Anne Nichols
C. Allen Nichols
Series Editors

INTRODUCTION

We assume you've picked up this book because you want to know more about the homeschoolers who are starting to appear more and more often in your library. Perhaps you are curious about why they've opted out of traditional public or private schools. Maybe you've already been thinking about ways to reach out to this group or you've been approached with requests for special privileges and are still sorting out how best to respond. And, having received those requests, you may be wondering why you should target library services specifically to homeschoolers.

The primary reason for providing service for homeschoolers is that there is no compelling reason not to. Homeschoolers using the library represent a "market segment" of your population in the same way that children coming for story hour, seniors requesting large print books, and companies utilizing your business reference collection also represent market segments. Libraries serve a wide variety of "publics" in just that way, by targeting materials and services to specific age groups or user interest/need groups. By viewing homeschoolers as simply another market segment of your population, you'll see that services geared to them can be nothing more elaborate than a rearrangement of your collection; inclusion of homeschool associations when sending out information about programs; or the extension of privileges already in place, such as teacher loans, to include homeschooling parents.

Serving Homeschooled Teens and Their Parents was written for any library staff member (professional or support staff) that may be involved in the planning of programs, collections, or services. We hope that the ideas presented in this book will help not only with planning for serving homeschooled teens, but with general library services as well. For example, programming planning sheets and checklists, program ideas, and marketing ideas may be applied to many situations in your library, not just when working with homeschoolers.

The book is organized in a way we feel is a natural progression for planning for a new service population. First you'll read about the history and background of the homeschooling movement, followed by information on the developmental and social needs of teens and how those needs may be met in the public library setting. Planning library services for this newly targeted service population can be a daunting endeavor, so the third chapter will offer advice on preparing to serve homeschooling teens. Next, we will describe services many homeschooled teens and their families request from their public libraries. Because our collections are at the heart of our libraries, we will give pointers for collection development with homeschoolers in mind. We'll share ideas for programs—many suggested by homeschoolers themselves—and then make suggestions for ways to market what your library has to offer. Finally, we'll provide you with lists of resource materials that will help you better serve the home-educated teen and his parents.

Many of the ideas presented in this book have been in practice at public libraries around the country, and other ideas are suggestions from homeschoolers themselves. While preparing for this project, we e-mailed several homeschooling discussion lists and generated ideas on what the ideal library would offer to homeschooling teens. Many of the warm responses we received from our inquiry reinforced our feelings that libraries are treasured by homeschoolers and that many homeschooling families value the services we offer. In order to honor the wishes of several of our survey respondents, we have chosen not to publish their responses to ensure their privacy.

This book is the collaboration between a young adult librarian and the parent of a once-homeschooled teen. We felt that it was essential for both perspectives to be reflected here; through better understanding, the relationship between libraries and homeschoolers can be a rewarding one for all concerned.

ONE PERSPECTIVE: THE YOUNG ADULT LIBRARIAN *(MAUREEN LERCH)*

Before I began working on this book, I admit that I had very limited knowledge of homeschooling. I thought I knew plenty, but as with any good research process, I found that the more I learned, the more I needed to discover.

When, over eight years ago, I entered the field of public librarianship, I knew instantly that I wanted to work with young adults. I thoroughly enjoyed YA literature and felt my rapport with the teens themselves was very satisfying. Looking back to my first job, I realize that I cannot recall a single homeschooled teen. I knew they existed, but either they weren't easily identified, or I just wasn't very effective at connecting with them. For whatever reason, I began noticing that over the years, more and more of my teen library patrons were homeschoolers.

As I became acquainted with homeschooled teens, my assumptions about homeschoolers were shattered. Before I began working with home-schooled teens, I assumed they were all made in the same mold. I thought that homeschooled teens were taught at home their entire lives and their parents taught them at home because of strong religious convictions. I also pictured them getting up at 7 A.M. every morning and reporting to a home classroom complete with a desk, attendance records, and a stay-at-home mom. Although this is surely the reality for some homeschooled teens, I have yet to meet one.

My assumptions were, of course, rooted in inexperience and igno-rance. Those assumptions were relatively harmless in comparison to the wealth of prejudices and misconceptions that I discovered when I began investigating the relationship between homeschoolers and the public library. I admittedly struggle with some of these biases, but feel that the more I learn about homeschooling the more able I am to move past them.

So how do some librarians view homeschoolers and how do prejudices affect service? First, many librarians believe that homeschoolers are ultra-conservative and will cause "trouble" by challenging library materials. Indeed, many are conservative and some have asked for library materials to be removed from collections. In reality, there is a wealth of conservative customers who use our collections who would never dream of challeng-ing materials that they find objectionable. Challenges occur, and it's the library's responsibility to deal with each challenge fairly and justly. Why waste the energy fretting over the possibility that a group of homeschoolers might pick up a copy of *Annie on My Mind*? It would be more useful to make sure that our collections are balanced and that those conservative library users are aware of available materials that suit their tastes. Furthermore, not all homeschoolers are conservative—some are very liberal-minded.

Another misconception that I have encountered is the opinion that a parent is unable to properly teach their children. Once the children reach junior high age, we begin to wonder if the parent could possibly have the knowledge required to tackle specialized subjects like biology and chemistry. It wasn't until I began researching the many ways homeschooling families approach difficult subjects that I realized the wealth of options available to homeschooled teens. Distance learning and correspondence courses offer a variety of options, not to mention the child's own ability to be self-taught. Instead of worrying if the teen in front of you can comprehend the calculus text he is checking out, you could let him know about videocassettes in your collection that teach advanced mathematics.

The last and possibly more dominant prejudice that I have encountered is the belief that homeschoolers want too much from the public library. If they don't want a teacher loan card, then they are demanding specialized programming, or requesting too many interlibrary loans. In some libraries, homeschooling families are offered the same privileges as teachers, but this is the exception to the rule. I am not suggesting that libraries should *always* offer the same privileges to homeschool parents as they do to teachers, but isn't it true that we would probably jump through hoops to plan a program suggested by the high school English teacher? Why are we so happy when the school invites us into their classrooms and so inconvenienced when homeschoolers request library instruction?

It's important to acknowledge that these assumptions and prejudices exist, even if we do not personally espouse them. It's important because even though our own libraries may offer extraordinary services to the homeschooling population, chances are that the homeschoolers who have experienced these prejudices in other arenas are expecting some resistance when they walk through our doors.

Now that I have left the arena of public librarianship and have entered the world of the academic library, I hope to see some of my former library patrons move on from homeschooling to college, correspondence universities, the military, or some sort of continuing education. Regardless, I hope that each of them has made the connection that the library is a place that will be there for them, no matter where their paths take them.

THE OTHER SIDE OF THE STORY: THE HOMESCHOOLER *(JANET WELCH)*

It's tough to step away from the status quo. The day I came home with an armload of books on homeschooling was just the first day of many when I would be challenged to pull together a cogent, articulate "mission statement" about why I wanted to homeschool my teenage son. As I shared my vision with my husband, my mother, my minister, my best friend, my boss, and my coworkers and, as I answered a battery of questions, all beginning with "But...", I realized that to make our homeschooling experience work was going to take an incredible amount of energy. Not only was I going to need to figure out my son's learning style and the best ways to "teach" to that style, I was also going to have to defend my choice. And I was lucky; some homeschooling parents in the early days of the movement had to defend their choice in courts of law. I was only dealing with the court of public opinion.

Another reason I was lucky is because I work in a public library. My coworkers supported my efforts by making sure I knew about relevant new titles or articles from the professional journals. I was blessed with a library director whose area of interest and experience was in young adult services; it was he who told me about Grace Llewellyn's wonderful books on homeschooled teens. More importantly, he listened and offered ideas as I struggled to design a curriculum. I think he may have been the only person who never asked a question that began with "But...".

But being different is still tough. No kid likes to be thought of as "different" and, let me tell you as a parent, no adult likes it much, either. We want the support of our social circle, but when you're the only one following a particular path, it takes a lot of courage. I was glad that Maureen was so forthcoming about her preconceived ideas regarding homeschoolers. Some of us may have really had to fight with our local school districts to get them to follow the law regarding homeschooling.

Consider the homeschool parents. We may have only recently removed our children from a classroom situation that we deemed academically substandard and emotionally damaging. We've arrived in your library, seeing it as a haven for those who want to learn. We may be defensive and we may seem demanding. Unfortunately, up until now, this may have been the only way we could get what we needed for our children. But all we really want is exactly what the public library has to offer: a wealth of resources and the opportunity to learn in any fashion and on any schedule we choose (assuming we renew our books on time!).

A 1997 study by Brian D. Ray and the Home School Legal Defense Association explored public library use by homeschoolers, kindergarten through grade 12. On average, homeschoolers as a group visit their library 3.8 times a month. More than 53 percent visit 1 or 2 times, while 47 percent are there even more often. The National Home Education Research Institute calculates that between 1.3 million and 1.7 million children, K-12, are homeschooled (1999–2000), and that figure grows at a rate of 7 to 14 percent annually. Put those statistics together and you see that homeschoolers, including homeschooled teens, are a growing part of your user base.

There's something special about working with homeschooled teens that really sets the experience apart from what you've known with their age-peers and other library users. Armed with this book, we hope you'll embrace the experience with enthusiasm. Make your library a welcoming and indispensable place, and you'll be nurturing library advocates for life.

1

◇ ◇ ◇

WHO ARE THESE KIDS AND WHY ARE THEY IN MY LIBRARY ON TUESDAY MORNING?

It's mid-morning and you are sitting at your desk in the reference department. Between helping patrons, you've gradually become aware that there are several teens gathered around a worktable, each quietly reading or taking notes from the books piled in front of them. You know school is in session and these really don't look like truants, so what are they doing here in the middle of the day?

Most likely these are homeschoolers, children whose parents have opted to educate them at home. These parents have made the deeply personal decision that their children are better served when learning within the family circle. They may have particular religious beliefs that they wish to instill as part of the education of their children. They may not be able to afford private or parochial school or may not live near enough to one. They may have memories of negative school experiences of their own and have vowed that things will be different for their children. They may fear that negative peer influences will lead their children to alcohol and drug abuse. They may fear violence in their neighborhood public school. They may believe that the academic quality of public schools is sub-par. The reasons are as varied as the families themselves.

Chris Cardiff, writing for *The Freeman* in 1998 says that homeschooling is a bit of a misnomer:

[T]he word conjures up a vision of mom instructing her kids around the kitchen table....The reality is far different...the flexibility and range of homeschooling encourages an enormous variety of alternative educational models...child-led, interest-based learning...the traditional classroom model with professional teachers...distance learning, cooperative teaching...commercial learning centers, and subject-specific tutors.[1]

As we see from Cardiff's description, not only is the decision to homeschool a very individual one but so, too, is the choice of how to go about it.

If you visit with "traditional" homeschoolers, you're likely to find a portion of the home set aside as a classroom. The child/student follows a set curriculum—the more prominent ones will be listed in the collection development chapter—and the parent/teacher makes assignments and grades papers aided by the accompanying teacher's manuals. The experience itself still looks like "school" but without the negative aspects of public schools that these families perceive.

Although not exclusively the domain of "traditional" homeschoolers, distance learning institutions are also available for those who feel the need for structure. These schools-by-mail (or, for that matter, "virtual" schools via e-mail and real-time chat), provide a curriculum, maintain records, and may even issue a high school diploma. Among the better-known are Clonlara in Ann Arbor, Michigan and American School in Lansing, Illinois. Some traditional universities also offer high school courses by correspondence, including the University of Nebraska at Lincoln, Indiana University, Brigham Young, and Texas Tech. These university-based programs are fully accredited and usually follow the requirements of their states in terms of credit hours or units needed for graduation. They also confer diplomas. It takes a highly motivated teen with well-developed study habits to follow through on correspondence studies. The flexibility in both course selection and scheduling still makes this an attractive alternative for homeschooled teens.

"Unschooling," as Cardiff indicates, refers to those home learners who devise their own curriculum. And they would define that word *curriculum* loosely, for their course of study and the means they use may only vaguely resemble that of traditional homeschoolers or the average public or private high school. Unschoolers view the experience of homeschooling as an opportunity to learn what they want, when they want, and how they want. Unschooling teens create their own learning experiences by following their own interests. Libraries become especially important places for these learners, because the average collection, in its breadth and depth, allows them to delve deeply into nearly anything that interests them. The teen who is starting a home-based business may make use of titles on small business, marketing, and advertising. That research may, for instance, lead the reluctant math student into working with numbers in a way that for him is completely practical and therefore of interest.

Other experiences for unschoolers may include travel, paid employment, volunteering, teaching younger students, apprenticeships, writing, designing web sites—the possibilities are limitless because unschoolers see and use the learning opportunities in the world around them.[2]

Another term that arises when reading about homeschooling is "deschooling." Deschooling can be thought of as a time of decompression, a transitional period after a child who has been in the traditional school environment leaves to begin the homeschool journey. It's usually a space of time—weeks or months, depending on the individual child and how long they were in a traditional school—during which he or she shakes off the practices of the school setting. To parents, grandparents, neighbors, and the teen's peers, deschooling may look like world-class time-wasting. The teen may sleep more, play video games, spend more time at the computer, or simply sit staring into space. The "downtime" is part of the process, though. For the child for whom traditional school had involved negative peer situations or other stresses, the deschooling period can be a time to regain emotional health. For others, it's simply the chance to find their own rhythms and interests, a time to think without interruption, even a time for solitude. Whatever character this transitional period takes, it impacts the entire family; the student who is accustomed to highly directed, top-down learning and the parent who must be willing to follow the teen's interests toward a goal of self-directed learning.[3]

Back to those teens in your reference department. One of them could be Debbie's son:

I have two sons, ages 21 and 18. Both have graduated from high school. We began homeschooling the oldest in seventh grade and the youngest in fourth grade. I wish I had started the older one earlier, but it took me two years of research before I felt comfortable with the idea. We lived in an affluent area of San Diego and, honestly, there weren't any families we knew who homeschooled.

We homeschooled because we felt our kids were being cheated out of a good education....Textbooks were outdated, days were too long, teachers didn't seem to care or had too many discipline problems to really teach, bullies on the playground; the list goes on and on.

Debbie's e-mail goes on to cite year after year of frustration. Finally, homeschooling became the only and obvious answer:

> We gave the system a happy kid, who loved to learn, who enjoyed life, who thought he was unique and smart. We got back a kid who couldn't read, write, do math, and who was very depressed. (At home), my oldest went from a fourth-grade reading level to an eighth-grade reading level in about six months. He learned to write, he learned to do math.
>
> The (David and Micki) Colfaxes' book, *Homeschooling for Excellence* really says it all: We homeschooled for control over "content, method, timing, influence, efficiency, autonomy, and creativity." To that I would add socialization and family time.[4]

Now you know a bit more about homeschoolers, but you're still a little suspicious of those teens in your reference department. Relax! Go over to the table and see what your newly discovered homeschoolers are working on. Maybe one is researching college scholarships. Another may be learning the ins and outs of starting his own small business. Still another has seen Zeffirelli's "Romeo and Juliet" and is now engrossed in reading the play. How about that? They're just like all of your other patrons! They're using your library for research, for pleasure, and for learning. The only real difference is that they're in your library at a time of day when their age-peers are not.

It could be Shirley's daughter searching for those college scholarships:

> We first homeschooled her for seventh and eighth grade because the middle school was so overcrowded. She wanted to go to public high school in the ninth grade because she missed her friends. During her sophomore year, she was having pain in her ankles and we took her to the doctor frequently....When she returned to school with her doctor's note of explanation for her absence, her math teacher refused to help her on one homework problem out of the entire week's worth of work. The teacher's reply was, "I don't do that sort of thing."
>
> Our daughter was so stressed out that she was hating school. We asked her if she wanted to return to homeschooling. She did.[5]

HISTORICAL BACKGROUND

Shirley and Debbie's stories may have left you thinking that homeschooling is a new phenomenon, the baby-boomers' response to perceived inadequacies in the public school system. But historically there is nothing particularly novel or unusual about home-based education. For hundreds of years, children learned outside of a formal school setting, even when schools were available.[6] The children living on the Carter's Grove plantation in colonial Virginia were instructed by a live-in tutor. Pioneering families settling the Ohio Valley instilled in their children the skills for survival. Alaskan homesteaders taught their children at home out of geographic necessity. Where it was practical, more formal means of education did exist. Schooling in the early days of colonial America included the teaching of religion and the laws of the colony. Later, Latin grammar schools were established to prepare young men for Harvard where they would be trained for the ministry or government service. Parochial schools of various denominations thrived, as did commercial trade schools. As America moved toward independence, leaders like Franklin, Webster, and Jefferson urged the formal education of the citizenry, citing the need for an educated electorate in a participatory democracy. Education for citizenship became more important than education for personal salvation.[7]

Home-based education might have continued unchallenged to the present day had it not been for the Industrial Revolution and America's large immigrant population. The perceived need for a cohesive, uniformly educated workforce, stripped of ethnic individuality and trained in state-supported schools "grounded in a common Christian morality" resulted in the creation of "common schools."[8] Coupled with compulsory attendance laws, these common schools were the basis for the public school system that we know today.

Yet universal, compulsory schooling is still a relatively new phenomenon. It wasn't until the nineteenth century that state legislatures began requiring local governments to build schools and parents to enroll their children. Even then, school was only compulsory for a few months of the year. It wasn't until the mid-twentieth century that universal high school graduation was considered the norm.[9] By 1970, every state had enacted compulsory attendance laws, save Mississippi where compulsory school attendance was not in place until 1983.

The contemporary homeschool movement actually began as a liberal, not conservative alternative to public school. A handful of families in the late '50s and early '60s felt that schools were too conservative and rigid.[10] They were all too happy to embrace the philosophies of education reformer John Holt who believed that children actually learned best without a curriculum and with the encouragement of their parents. As he worked with students in his classroom and as he observed the young children of relatives, Holt became increasingly convinced that the very best way to educate children was through child-centered or guided instruction. His contention was that children would naturally learn what they needed and wanted to learn on a timetable appropriate for them. In the introduction to his book *Teach Your Own*, considered a classic in homeschool literature, Holt says, "At first I did not question the compulsory nature of schooling. But by 1968 or so I had come to feel strongly that the kinds of changes I wanted to see in schools, above all in the ways of teachers related to students, could not happen as long as schools were compulsory."[11]

Holt began a newsletter, *Growing Without Schooling*, that provided support and guidance for parents who subscribed to his belief that children learned best through unstructured, real-life experiences. Holt's ideas were a good fit for those who espoused the counterculture lifestyle of the '60s and '70s. Rather than re-creating the classroom environment at home or relying on traditional textbooks or curriculum packets, these first "unschoolers" adopted a more relaxed attitude toward learning, believing that education is a natural process. With no schedule or set curriculum, parents could allow their children to decide what and when they wanted to learn.

At about the same time that Holt was introducing the idea of child-led learning, Dr. Raymond Moore, a former Department of Education employee and Christian missionary, and his wife, Dorothy, a former teacher, began questioning whether institutionalized education was the best way to help young children learn, and at what age that education should begin. Their studies, based on developmental theories about the age-appropriateness of formal education, coupled with their perceptions about the negative influences of peers in the public school setting led the Moores to become advocates for home-based education. It was with their guidance that many parents made the decision to homeschool based on religious beliefs. The continued growth of this segment of the homeschool movement has changed it from a revolution against the establishment to a revolt against a secular culture.[12]

Like other revolutions, the homeschool movement has not been without its firefights. Early in the movement some families found themselves defending their homeschool decision in court, necessitating the creation of the Home School Legal Defense Association in 1983. Parents were threatened with jail and the removal of their children from their homes. Some families homeschooled "underground," not taking their children out of the house until after the bell at the public school had rung in the afternoon. Others would hide their children on the backseat of their cars while running errands during the school day. Still others refused to register the birth of their children. Through the 1970s and early 1980s, parents continued to fight within their local school districts and in the courts for the right to teach their own children. Finally, by 1986, all fifty states ruled that homeschooling was a legitimate option for the education of children. The degree to which the local school districts have oversight of the process varies from state to state.

Despite its legal acceptance in the United States, homeschooling is not without its critics. Public school system administrators and staff often see homeschooling as a threat, not only because of the loss of state per-pupil funding, but because of the social threat perceived. Some public educators say that the erosion of parental confidence in public schools undermines support and makes it difficult to pass tax levies. In addition, many educators are concerned about the loss of the most affluent and articulate parents from the system, people whose strengths could contribute to improvements in the public school system.[13]

Pediatricians are also not generally supportive of homeschooling. Their concern centers on the educational achievement and social maturity of homeschooled children. In addition, they see an important role for public schools to play in screening for a variety of childhood medical conditions including tuberculosis and scoliosis and in providing sex education and information about sexually transmitted diseases. Finally, schools are seen as environments where abuse and neglect can be identified and addressed.[14]

Despite opposition and the concerns of public educators, homeschooling continues to grow at a rate of 15 to 20 percent each year. Basing her estimates on states with reliable information, researcher Patricia Lines suggests that the number of homeschoolers tripled in the five years from 1990–91 to 1995–96 when there were, by best estimate, 700,000 homeschoolers. With an anticipated growth rate of better than 15 percent, Lines estimated a homeschooling population of 1.5 to 2 million children by 2000–01 or around 3 to 4 percent of all school-aged children.[15]

Definitive numbers are hard to obtain, in part because data gathering and reporting requirements differ from state to state and also because some homeschooling parents refuse to cooperate with state-mandated reporting.[16] However, there can be no doubt that the option to educate children at home is being embraced by a segment of the population that is increasingly diverse. While religiously conservative homeschoolers continue to be the most organized branch of the homeschool movement, more and more parents are today making the homeschool decision based on secular concerns like school safety and academic quality. Carolyn Kleiner and Mary Lord, in an article for *US News and World Report* in October, 2000, describe the shift:

> [T]he present-day home-schooling phenomenon dates back to the 1960s and '70s when counterculture types—inspired by educational reformers like John Holt...pulled their kids out of school for pedagogical, not ideological reasons.... Now, after several decades of explosive growth due to religious considerations, more and more families—including a rising number of African-Americans and Hispanics—are once again choosing to home-school for academic reasons: They are concerned about the quality of public and private schools, as well as their kids' safety, and skeptical that reforms like charter schools and vouchers will make a timely difference.[17]

Despite this increasing diversity, there are some similarities among the families that homeschool. Surveys confirm that the typical homeschooling family is religious, conservative, Caucasian, middle-income, and better educated than the general public.[18] Eighty percent are two-parent households; 47 percent of homeschooling parents have a bachelor's degree or higher.[19]

Those generalizations being made, you must still resist the temptation to "stereotype" homeschoolers as Caucasian conservatives. As Kleiner and Lord indicate in their *US News* article quoted above, more racially and religiously diverse families are opting to homeschool, as witnessed by an increase in book titles, Web sites, and newsletters specifically addressed toward African-American, Muslim, Jewish, and Roman Catholic homeschoolers.

Mothers typically assume the largest portion of teaching responsibilities. Families following a more traditional model of homeschooling tend to give mother and father traditional roles; mother as teacher and father as principal and disciplinarian. In some families—Lines estimates as many as 10 percent—circumstances may favor dad serving not only as primary caregiver, but as homeschool teacher as well. Jim Dunn, writing in a column for *Home Education Magazine*, thinks those dads are rarities, in large part because of cultural expectations.

> For a man to place himself in the home on a full-time basis turns cultural assumptions on their head, but for him to take on the task of full-time homeschooling forces him to re-evaluate his own assumptions. The processes of the home replace his role as breadwinner, and as homeschooling itself will, his new work brings into question the reality of his old world.[20]

Not surprisingly, the decision to homeschool can have a considerable impact on family finances. This is the point at which the services and programs of the public library can also have the most impact. Contemplate for a moment, as homeschooling mother Gail Thorsen did, on the value of the public library:

[T]o homeschool on a shoestring budget, we need to find free or inexpensive ways to educate.... Can your local libraries provide the answer? Yes, they can!.... The sky's the limit on (what) you can save (with) a weekly trip to the library...there is always something new.... New books...movies...new magazines...it's great.[21]

Those unfamiliar with homeschooling tend to assume that it is only appropriate for those who are academically advanced. In fact, students at all levels of achievement can and are learning at home successfully, including those who are mentally or physically challenged. Tom Bushnell, president and director of the National Challenged Homeschoolers Associated Network (NATHHAN), estimates that some 30,000 children with disabilities are homeschooled in the United States. Membership in NATHHAN, an information and resource network for families homeschooling special-needs children, numbered 4,100 families in 1996. Bushnell says parents turn to homeschooling for many different reasons. Some want control over curriculum and its religious and moral content. Others feel a regular school doesn't provide a safe environment for their special-needs child or doesn't provide enough protection against "school-yard bullying" by other, nondisabled students. Some parents resent the labeling of their children. Still others turn to homeschooling after confrontations with public school officials over how best to educate their child.[22] In some cases—autism, for example—homeschooling may even be preferred because of the quiet, stable structure of the home in contrast to the school classroom.[23]

More visible, perhaps, than homeschoolers with challenges are those whose academic achievements have been making headlines across the country. A homeschooled student won the 73rd Scripps Howard National Spelling Bee. Second and third place also went to homeschoolers. At the age of twenty-four, Jedediah Purdy, a Harvard graduate and Yale law school student, published his first book, *For Common Things: Irony, Trust, and Commitment in America Today*. What makes Purdy remarkable was not his youth, but the fact that he was homeschooled.[24]

Studies show that homeschooled students outperform public and private school students on standardized tests. In 2000, homeschooled students scored 81 points higher than the national mean on the SAT.[25] The reasons may lie not only in the self-discipline that homeschooling requires, but also in the wealth of interests that homeschoolers have time to pursue. A typical homeschooling teen may actually complete traditional high school in two or three years, not because they are necessarily smarter than their traditionally schooled peers, but because their days are not spent with the general "busywork"—passing out supplies, waiting for a teacher to discipline other students, and changing classes—that make up a public school day. With academic work streamlined, homeschooled teens have time to work, volunteer, read, and pursue individual passions.

Homeschoolers can and do go on to college, as evidenced not only by Purdy, but also by the sons of David and Micki Colfax; three of their four homeschooled sons were admitted to Harvard. The Colfaxes' book, *Homeschooling for Excellence*, made them celebrities among homeschoolers when it was published in 1988. Today, college-bound homeschoolers are not a rarity. Admissions officers everywhere report an increase in applications from homeschoolers. Some colleges are even actively recruiting homeschooled students. And at some universities, notably Stanford, homeschoolers have higher-than-average odds of getting accepted.[26]

And if not Stanford or one of the Ivy League schools, there's Patrick Henry College (Purcellville, VA), which welcomed ninety students when it first opened in October 2000. Patrick Henry has the distinction of being the first college in the country specifically targeted at homeschooled students. All of this courting of homeschoolers by institutions of higher learning and the creation of a college just for them clearly demonstrates that, after decades of struggle, homeschooling has finally gained acceptance as a viable educational alternative.

Remember those teens in your Reference Department? Here comes Shirley's daughter to ask for a Peterson's college guide. Go give her a hand; she'll remember your helpfulness when she gets that acceptance letter from Yale.

FURTHER READING

Holt, John. *Teach Your Own*. Norfolk, UK: Lighthouse Books, 1997.
    This classic by the leading advocate for homeschooling sets out Holt's arguments for why compulsory school attendance thwarts, stifles, and stymies children and how learning at home produces eager, independent, and self-reliant individuals. Much of the text is based upon articles in and letters from parents to Holt's newsletter *Growing Without Schooling*. This title should be part of both the librarian's and the parent's first exploration into the topic of homeschooling.

Ishizuka, Kathy. *The Unofficial Guide to Homeschooling*. Foster City, CA: IDG Books Worldwide, Inc., 2000.
A comprehensive handbook that deserves a place in any library's core collection on homeschooling. Ishizuka touches on many issues not usually covered including homeschooling the gifted and differently-abled; family finances; and homeschooling teens through high school and the transition to college. The book includes a resources directory, reading list, and details concerning laws governing homeschooling families.

Llewellyn, Grace. *The Teenage Liberation Handbook: How to Quit School and Get a Real Life and Education*. Rockport, MA: Element Books, Ltd., 1997.
This is the first book to put into the hands of teens contemplating homeschooling. As inspiration for a teen unhappy in a traditional school, it simply can't be topped. Llewellyn is a former middle school teacher who knows from personal experience the ways in which school can destroy and confuse the process of learning, and puts forth the radical notion that life can change for the better by leaving school. Llewellyn suggests practical ways of getting an education simply by engaging in real life, volunteering, or finding meaningful work.

NOTES

1. Chris Cardiff, "The Seduction of Homeschooling Families," *The Freeman* (March 1998), 139–144.

2. Grace Llewellyn, *The Teenage Liberation Handbook: How to Quit School and Get a Real Life and Education* (Rockport, MA: Element Books, Ltd., 1997).

3. Kathy Ishizuka,. *The Unofficial Guide to Homeschooling* (Foster City, CA: IDG Books Worldwide, Inc., 2000), 316–317.

4. Debby C. Personal e-mail (Winter 2001).

5. Shirley B. Personal e-mail (Winter 2001).

6. Patricia Lines, "Homeschooling Comes of Age," *Public Interest* (Summer 2000), 74. (Retrieved from InfoTrac April 23, 2003).

7. "American Education, Chapter 4 Summary," Little Rock: University of Arkansas College of Education. http://www.ualr.edu/~coedept/ae/2300/chapters/unit1/ch4.html

8. J. Kirchner, "The Shifting Roles of Family and School as Educator: A Historical Perspective," in J. Van Galen and M. A. Pitman (eds.), *Home schooling: Political, Historical, and Pedagogical Perspectives* (Horwood, NJ: Abex Publishing Corporation, 1991).

9. Lines.

10. Ibid.

11. John Holt, *Teach Your Own* (Norfolk, VA: Lighthouse Books, 1997).

12. Deborah Grubb, "Homeschooling: Who and Why?" (Paper presented at the annual meeting of the Mid-South Education Research Association, New Orleans, LA, 1998.)

13. John Cloud and Jodie Morse, "Home Sweet School," *Time.Com*, August 27, 2001. http://www.time.com/time/education/article/0,8599,171832,00.html (April 14, 2003).

14. Randal Rockney, "The Home Schooling Debate: Why Some Parents Choose It, Others Oppose It," *The Brown University Child and Adolescent Behavior Letter* 18 (February 2000), i2.

15. Lines, p. 1.

16. Grubb, p. 9.

17. Carolyn Kleiner and Mary Lord, "Home School Comes of Age," *US News and World Report* 129, (October 16, 2000), 52–54.

18. Lines.

19. "It's All Homework," *American Demographics* (November 1, 2001), 25.

20. Jim Dunn, "When Dad Homeschools: From Breadwinning to Baking," *Home Education Magazine,* May–June 1998. http://www.home-ed-magazine. com/HEM/HEM153.98/153.98_art_dad.html (June 4, 2001).

21. Gail Thorsen, "The Link Librarian," *The Link Homeschool Newspaper* 6, no. 2. http://www.homeschoolnewslink.com/articles/vol6iss2/linklibrarian.html (September 16, 2002).

22. J. Beales, "How the Private Sector Serves Difficult-to-Educate Students," Policy Study #212, *Reason Public Policy Institute,* 1996. http://www.rppi.org/ps212.html. (July 21, 2001).

23. Posting to listserv AUT-2B-HOME. http://www.paulbunyan.net/users/Academy/autism01.htm (July 22, 2001).

24. David Gergen, "No Place Like Home," *US News and World Report* 128, no. 24, June 19, 2000. http://usnews.com/usnews/issue/00619/19edit.htm (March 5, 2001).

25. Kleiner and Lord,

26. Mary Lord, "Home-Schoolers Away From Home," *US News Online,* November 16, 2000. http://www.usnews.com/usnews/issue/001016/homeschool.b.htm (March 3, 2001).

2

◆ ◆ ◆

WHAT MAKES THEM TICK: A SHORT COURSE IN ADOLESCENT DEVELOPMENT

Librarians do not necessarily need an extensive background in adolescent psychology to do their jobs well, but an understanding of what's going on between the ears of young adult patrons may make regular interactions and service planning more successful. Since an in-depth discussion of adolescent development is beyond the scope of this book, we will instead focus on the aspects of development that relate to library services to homeschooled teens. If this discussion whets your appetite for the fascinating world of adolescent development, be sure to check out some of the books listed as further reading at the end of this chapter.

The teen years can be quite complicated. When you think of how many changes a child goes through between the ages of eleven and eighteen, it's no surprise that we hardly recognize the same teenager from one day to the next. Would any of us really want to go back and live those years again? Not likely. Besides, we vicariously get our fill of the adolescent experience every day in our libraries.

Even though every teenager is an individual, they all go through the same stages of development. They may experience those different stages at different ages than their peers, but the progression toward adulthood beats out the same path, no matter what age the journey begins. Our young adult patrons will all struggle with the physical growth spurts, the sexual changes, and the moral and emotional challenges. Throw in social and intellectual development and we can certainly understand the potential for some adolescent angst to go with "the best years of their lives."

A NOTE ABOUT "GRADE" LEVELS

Before we get into a discussion of what to expect from patrons experiencing adolescence, it's essential to note a big difference between homeschool patrons and traditional school patrons. Our homeschooled patrons do not go to school. Since they do not go to school, they are not in a particular "grade." They do not get together with twenty to thirty kids of the same age each day and learn the same thing. The reason we mention this difference is because in a discussion of developmental stages, it is easy to group characteristics by "grade level." It has been our experience that librarians tend to see their patrons more at a "grade level" than a particular age. For example, we often ask our patrons what grade they are in during reference transactions or during program registrations in an attempt to identify grade-appropriate materials, determine a specific assignment, or to satisfy statistical reports.

Most homeschoolers will volunteer a grade level based on what grade they might be in if they did attend traditional school. Some homeschoolers will tell you a grade level determined by the reading or skill level of the materials they are currently studying. Therefore, asking our homeschooled patrons their grade is practically useless. To better understand where they are in their development, an actual age is much more useful.

AGES AND STAGES

The period of human development that is referred to as "adolescence" usually begins around the age of 11 to 13 and lasts until the age of 18 to 21.[1] This period can be further divided into early (11 to 15) and late adolescence (16 to 21). Because many changes happen during this stage of life, it's even possible to divide adolescence into early, middle, and later adolescence. No wonder it can be such a challenge planning programs and services for an age group that seems to change characteristics every few years!

PUBERTY

Even though puberty and sexuality are at the center of adolescent development, thankfully they do not overtly affect our interactions on a daily basis. Just keep in mind that dramatic hormonal changes during puberty do affect much of a young adult's behavior.

We probably witness the hormonal changes in our teen patrons in the usual way: moodiness. One day a young adult patron will be a pleasure to talk to, and the next day be a major discipline problem. In addition to the moodiness, we might notice some "pubescent posturing" when groups of teens congregate in our libraries. This behavior can range from the very subtle (flirting, teasing, following each other around the library) to the downright disruptive (fighting, abusive language, vandalism).

As librarians, we, of course, have no control over a teen's hormones. Instead, we can be understanding as we enforce the rules of our libraries and make our best effort to have a balanced collection of materials on human sexuality and adolescent development available. Quality books and videos may help some of our young adult patrons better understand what is going on with their bodies and let them know that they are not alone.

Since many homeschooled teens do not have the health and sex education classes that their age-peers have in school, the library's health collection is very important to them. Be sure to include materials that offer religious and moral perspectives on sexuality, as well as the more "mass market" alternatives. (See below for collection resources for Christian teens.) Many homeschoolers like to include videos in their studies, so try to include some educational videos dealing with human anatomy and physiology, as well as some "real-life" documentaries about teens dealing with sexuality.

Armed with an understanding of puberty and a collection of materials for your teen patrons, those occasional glimpses of hormonal behavior may not seem too uncomfortable.

Dating/Sexuality Resources for Christian Teens

Videos:

The Myth of Safe Sex. 52 min. Colorado Springs, CO: Focus on the Family Films, 1993. (Part of the *Life on the Edge* video series.)

No Apologies...The Truth about Life, Love, and Sex. 30 min. Colorado Springs, CO: Tyndale Entertainment, 1998.

Sex, Lies, and the Truth. 30 min. Colorado Springs, CO: Focus on the Family Films, 1993.

Books:

Anderson, Neil T. *Purity under Pressure.* Eugene, OR: Harvest House Publishers, 1995.

(continued)

(continued)

Johnson, Greg, and Susie Shellenberger. *Getting Ready for the Girl/Guy Thing: Two Ex-Teens Reveal the Shocking Truth about God's Plan for Success with the Opposite Sex.* Ventura, CA: Regal Books, 1991.

Johnson, Greg, and Susie Shellenberger. *What Hollywood Won't Tell You about Sex, Love, and Dating.* Ventura, CA: Regal Books, 1994.

Smith, Michael W. *Old Enough To Know: What Teenagers Must Know about Life and Relationships.* Nashville: Tommy Nelson, 2000.

White, Joe. *Pure Excitement: A Radical, Righteous Approach to Sex, Love, and Dating.* Colorado Springs, CO: Focus on the Family, 1996.

IDENTITY IN EARLY ADOLESCENCE

When folks talk about an "identity crisis," don't we usually picture middle-aged people in red convertibles? In reality, the first true identity crisis occurs during adolescence.

Psychoanalyst Erik Erikson dedicated much of his writing to adolescence and identity. In his book, *Childhood and Society*, Erikson suggested that rapid body growth, sexual changes, and looming adulthood responsibilities confront adolescents with an identity crisis. Among the eight stages of humans, adolescence is the fifth and possibly most essential developmental stage. Erikson believed that the essential task for adolescents is to figure out who they are and where they fit in the world around them. It's not just important to know how they feel about things, but also to know what others think about them. Without an established identity, a young adult may experience role confusion, which could affect future success as an adult.[2]

According to the American Academy of Child and Adolescent Psychiatry, young teens struggle with identity as they move toward independence. Moving toward independence also means moving *away* from the influence of parents. The void is quickly filled by the teen's friends, whose influence over dress, physical appearance, interests, and behavior becomes more important.[3]

Young teen patrons often start coming to the library without their parents or, when accompanied by a parent, seem irritated when the parent tries to do the talking for them. When a group of young teens comes to the library together, they may not ask for our help, so as not to risk looking "stupid" in front of their friends.

As they begin to experiment with more independence, young teen patrons may start exploring other collections, moving out of the children's department and into the young adult and adult collections. Even though they will still occasionally visit the children's department, rarely will we see them congregate in groups. They would much prefer to be seen as older and more mature than the children who use the juvenile collections.

It's refreshing to find that some of our homeschooling patrons are less concerned about what their peers think (at least when it comes to the library). Young teen homeschooling patrons may start coming to the library without their parents or family, but they more often continue with the same family library schedule. Many homeschooling teens take on the added responsibility of helping with younger siblings, but still find ways to assert independence during their library visits. By the time homeschooling patrons reach early adolescence, they are probably already familiar with the young adult and adult collections in the library. Because their schooling is more self-directed than their age-peers, they often demonstrate more curiosity toward subjects that will take them all over the library. We have also noticed that our homeschooling teen patrons have no problems hanging out in our children's departments. If they frequent the library during normal school hours, there's little risk of being seen among the children's collections by anyone other than adults, children, or other homeschooling teens.

Interestingly, some homeschooled girls actually may not experience the same struggle for identity as do their age-peers in a traditional school setting. In the book *A Sense of Self: Listening to Homeschooled Adolescent Girls,* Susannah Sheffer interviewed fifty-five homeschooled girls between the ages of eleven and sixteen. Sheffer found the girls she interviewed had a very strong sense of identity. The power to guide their own learning has led to assertiveness, self-respect, and the ability to stand up for themselves.[4] Although our experience is limited, and the group studied in this book was only a small one and did not include boys, we agree that many of the homeschooled teens we've encountered as patrons seem to have a solid grasp of identity. Just like any population, though, there are exceptions. There will be homeschooled teens on the other end of the spectrum, for whatever reason, who truly struggle with the sense of self. Keep in mind that these homeschooled patrons may need the library the most as they attempt to find their place in the world. Whether it is through books or at our programs, our homeschooled patrons may find many opportunities to discover their likes, dislikes, and a sense of identity.

IDENTITY IN LATER ADOLESCENCE

By the time teen patrons reach later adolescence, they will have a stronger, more cohesive sense of identity.[5] As they continue the journey toward independence, we may start seeing them less and less often as they become involved in activities that truly match their interests. We may also see them less frequently because they are more able to find what they need without our assistance.

Older homeschooled teens, like those in a traditional school setting, will start looking toward the future and to where they will fit into society as adults.[6] Our libraries have the potential to play an integral role in this process by making college and career materials readily and clearly available. Remember that homeschooled teens do not have the benefit of high school guidance counselors to announce upcoming test dates, scholarship opportunities, or even entrance requirements for colleges. This kind of information and referral falls outside of the traditional job description of young adult librarians, but if you have access to this kind of information, the homeschooling community does appreciate any information you can pass on to them. It may be sufficient to have a strong college catalog collection (much of which is now available online), but many of our older homeschooling patrons appreciate receiving some direction as well. In addition to the traditional materials, don't forget to have information about some of the alternatives to college including correspondence schools, the military, and the Peace Corps.

Even though older teens may not frequent the library as much as they used to, when they do come in to use our resources, chances are they have a very important reason to be there. It may be enough to simply "touch base" with them, but many of them may also need us to go that extra mile so that they have the same benefits and future opportunities as teens from the traditional schooling environment.

SOCIALIZATION

One of the biggest criticisms homeschooling families face is the belief that their children do not have the same opportunities for socialization as children who are in the traditional school setting. While it is true that adolescents should be exposed to social situations with peer groups to achieve healthy development, schools are certainly not the best or only agent for socialization. Many people confuse "socialization" with age-peer group interaction. Most homeschooled teens develop their own peer groups, at times consisting of other homeschoolers, neighbors, people at church and other organizations, as well as online. These peer groups, along with the other agents of socialization (family, church, etc.) offer many opportunities for homeschooled teens to learn the acceptable behaviors of society.

Richard G. Medlin examined the existing research on the socialization of homeschoolers and found that there are few solid studies.[7] Fortunately, some studies are worth looking at, including Rudner[8] and Chatham-Carpenter.[9] Medlin sorted through the research findings with the following questions in mind:

1. Do homeschooled children participate in the daily routines of their communities?
2. Are homeschooled children acquiring the rules of behavior and systems of beliefs and attitudes they need?
3. Can homeschooled children function effectively as members of society?[10]

When socialization is examined with these questions in mind, we realize that socialization is larger than attending classes, spending time with friends, and going to school dances. Even if some homeschooled teens will not ever attend a prom or participate in a pep rally, it doesn't mean they are not getting "socialized."

According to Medlin, the existing research shows that homeschoolers are not only actively involved in the social routines of their communities, but they also are learning appropriate social behavior, forming healthy attitudes about themselves, and becoming adults with exceptional social and leadership skills.[11]

These conclusions will probably surprise many of the homeschooling skeptics. The idea that homeschoolers might actually be better off socially than children who go to school may seem like an impossible concept. But there are many of us who deal with homeschoolers on a regular basis who are not surprised at all by these findings. We know that a homeschooler's schedule is much more open and flexible than kids who go to school, and this flexibility affords them many more opportunities for social activities like volunteering, jobs, church functions, and hobbies. We also may notice that our homeschooling patrons have more contact with people of all ages, not just kids their own age. Both of these factors can be potentially beneficial to librarians when trying to find teen volunteers, teen board members, or paging staff. A homeschooled teen may be ideal in any of these situations. Don't be surprised when a homeschooled teen steps into leadership roles among other teens in your library. Keep in mind, though, that some of our homeschooled teen patrons may be advanced in dealing with adults and younger children, but at times may need some guidance when interacting with groups of teens their own age.

What should we think, then, when we hear the teens complain that they feel at times isolated and lonely because of their homeschooling? We, of course, could offer opportunities for interacting with teens their own age. But keep in mind that feeling isolated and lonely is not unusual for many teenagers. Many teens attending traditional schools would also confess to feeling isolated even though they spend at least seven hours a day with twenty to thirty other kids their age. Sometimes all of the social interaction in the world will not erase an adolescent's desire to truly connect with another human being. The library can offer social opportunities, and the librarian can be supportive and listen to their feelings when they care to share them. There is little we can do to completely eliminate the feeling of loneliness many teens experience—it's a part of adolescence, whether the teen is homeschooled or not.

DEVELOPMENTAL NEEDS

When the many facets of adolescent development are combined, the result is a complicated picture. As important as it is for young adult librarians to understand the different parts of development, it may be difficult to keep track of them all. Because many of us like things organized and in checklists, a list of essential developmental needs may be helpful when designing programs and services for teens. When you are targeting homeschooled teens, you may want to concentrate on those needs that would normally be met in the traditional school setting.

In *The Middle Grades Assessment Program User's Manual*, Gayle Dorman presents seven developmental needs encompassing the many sides of healthy young adolescent development.[12] Keeping these needs in mind will help create a strong strategy for serving the homeschooled teen population, as well as your entire young adult community.

Dorman first suggests that adolescents need to have "diverse learning experiences."[13] Homeschooled teens are probably already experiencing a variety of learning experiences due to their freedom to design their own studies. Library programs that offer abstract thinking, hands-on activities, and opportunities to interact with diverse groups of people may give homeschoolers chances to explore learning in ways they may not have tried yet. If you want to meet this developmental need, avoid falling into the rut of instruction followed by a hands-on activity. The more you can mix things up and add variety, the more likely that our patrons will keep coming back for more, just to see what happens next!

Adolescents also need experiences that allow "self-definition and self-exploration."[14] Book discussion groups offer wonderful opportunities for teens to think about who they are, what they believe, and then bounce these ideas off of other people. Creative writing programs and books on journal writing can also support this need.

Third, adolescents need opportunities for "meaningful participation in school and community."[15] Include homeschooled teens in your library focus groups, teen boards, and volunteering programs. In addition, maintain a collection of books about volunteerism and community service opportunities to offer ideas for teens not interested in library service.

Closely related to the need for meaningful participation is the need for "positive social interaction with both peers and adults."[16] Again, volunteering and participation on a teen board allows a teen to work toward a common goal with other teens and library staff. You can extend this to positive interaction with children by having homeschooled teens help out with children's programs. This is an area where many homeschooled teens excel if they are already involved in their church or other community groups.

You may find it more difficult to meet "the need for physical activity."[17] The traditional library setting is, of course, meant to be a quiet and relaxed place to read and study. Most of our successful programs, though, have included some element of physical activity. Scavenger hunts, water balloon fights, and relay races have all allowed teen patrons to get some exercise while visiting the library. With enough warning to other patrons, chances are most folks will enjoy seeing teenagers come together in a program and enjoying themselves, even if it does interfere with normal library operations! Homeschooled teens may especially be looking for physical activities to help meet physical education requirements to graduate. Advertisements for sporting leagues and programs from the local YMCA and Boys and Girls Clubs can help them discover new opportunities.

Adolescents also need opportunities for "competence and achievement."[18] Volunteer recognition should be a regular occurrence at libraries that use volunteers, but there are other ways that you can provide homeschooled teens with a sense that they have accomplished something and that they are truly good at it. Judged events, like art and writing contests, allow teens to shine. Creating certificates for participants who complete a series of programs or participate in a reading program can be valuable additions to a homeschooler's portfolio.

Finally, adolescents need "structure and clear limits."[19] Although some homeschoolers need more structure than others, this may not be too much of a problem for most homeschooled teens. Many homeschooled teens have self-imposed structure in their lives, but some may also struggle with limits. By letting your teen patrons know what to expect from you and what is expected of them while they are at the library and attending programs, you are allowing them to test limits and understand consequences. The best thing you can do is to establish rules of conduct and enforce them. By doing this you let them know you care about their safety and want them to be strong, responsible young adults.

DEVELOPMENTAL ASSETS

In addition to identifying an adolescent's developmental needs, it is also helpful to determine the developmental assets a teen has already achieved. An excellent resource on developmental assets that is readily available via the Internet is from the Search Institute (http://www.search institute.org). Many communities are turning to the Search Institute's developmental assets approach to better understand child and adolescent development and find ways for the entire community to support the needs of its youth. Although the Search Institute's research and recommendations focus on adolescents who attend traditional schools, many of the recommendations may also apply to homeschooled teens.

The Search Institute, a nonprofit organization "dedicated to the well-being and positive development of children and youth," has created a list of forty developmental assets that encompass the physical, intellectual, emotional, social, and moral growth of children and teens. These assets are defined as "the building blocks of healthy development that help young people grow up healthy, caring, and responsible."[20] According to the research, the more assets a young person acquires, the less likely that child or teen will take part in unhealthy behaviors like sexual activity, violence, drug or alcohol use, smoking, or reckless driving.[21] The approach is more proactive than reactive, intending to provide opportunities for asset building before a child or teen takes part in these destructive behaviors.

Probably the most helpful feature of this program is that the forty assets provide a framework to measure what a teen has achieved and identify areas that might need attention. Especially when working with home-schooled teens, you can focus attention through programming and services on those assets that may be missed by not being in traditional schools. For example, one of the developmental assets for teens is "achievement motivation."[22] While many traditionally schooled teens have ample opportunities for winning contests and scoring well on tests, a homeschooled teen may lack those same experiences. By working achievement and accomplishment into your programs through prize giveaways, reading incentives, or certificates of completion, your library can provide access to one of the developmental assets.

You might find that many of your homeschooled teen patrons are well ahead of their school-going peers when it comes to developmental assets. But keeping a checklist of developmental goals in mind when planning collections, programs and services will benefit not only homeschooled teens, but all young adult library patrons.

PUTTING IT TOGETHER

Although there is still more to know about adolescent development to be the best possible young adult librarian, this is a start. One of the most important things to keep in mind is that regardless of what the research says, each teenager is an individual. It is helpful to consider all of the developmental tasks, needs, and assets while planning services for your homeschooled teen patrons, but it is certainly not the only thing to be thinking about.

The next chapter offers ideas and advice on where to go from here. Armed with a basic understanding of what might be going on in the heads of our homeschooling teen patrons, you can now go forward and start planning how to approach a comprehensive plan of service.

FURTHER READING

Benson, Peter L. *What Kids Need to Succeed: Proven, Practical Ways to Raise Good Kids.* Minneapolis, MN: Free Spirit Publishing, Inc., 1998.
   Based on the Search Institute's developmental assets, this book suggests specific activities that help build each asset.
Head, John. *Working with Adolescents: Constructing Identity.* London: Falmer Press, 1997.
   Discusses identity development as it affects an adolescent's social world, behavior, and relationships. Chapters include: perspectives on adolescence; acquiring a sense of identity; the social world of adolescents; diversity among adolescents: the case of gender, sexual behavior, and relationships; entering the world of work; beliefs and values; the schooling of adolescents; and in conclusion: adolescents today.
Holmes, George R. *Helping Teenagers into Adulthood: A Guide for the Next Generation.* Westport, CT: Praeger Publishers, 1995.
   Discusses three possible prevention tools for many of the problems associated with adolescence: information, communication, and education.
Moshman, David. *Adolescent Psychological Development: Rationality, Morality, and Identity.* Mahwah, NJ: Lawrence Erlbaum Associates, Publishers, 1999.
   Presents a constructivist approach to the development of adolescent rationality, morality, and identity from adolescence into adulthood.

NOTES

1. J. W. Santrock, "Adolescence," in *Encyclopedia of Psychology*, Vol. 1 (New York: John Wiley & Sons, 1994), 23–24.

2. Erik H. Erikson, *Childhood and Society* (New York: Norton, 1950).

3. American Academy of Child and Adolescent Psychiatry, "Normal Adolescent Development: Middle School and Early High School Years," 1997. http:// www.aacap.org/publications/factsfam/develop.htm (March 27, 2003).

4. Susannah Sheffer, *A Sense of Self: Listening to Homeschooled Adolescent Girls* (Portsmouth, NH: Heinemann, 1995).

5. American Academy of Child and Adolescent Psychiatry, "Normal Adolescent Development: Late High School Years and Beyond," 1997. http://www. aacap.org/publications/factsfam/develop2.htm (March 27, 2003).

6. Ibid.

7. Richard G. Medlin, "Home Schooling and the Question of Socialization," *Peabody Journal of Education* 75 (2000): 107–123.

8. Laurence M. Rudner, "Scholastic Achievement and Demographic Characteristics of Home School Students in 1998," *Education Policy Analysis Archives, 7,* March 23, 1999. http://epaa.asu.edu/epaa/v7n8/ (May 28, 2001).

9. A. Chatham-Carpenter, "Home Versus Public Schoolers: Differing Social Opportunities," *Home School Researcher* 10 (1994): 15–24.

10. Medlin, 110.

11. Ibid., 119.

12. Gayle Dorman, *The Middle Grades Assessment Program User's Manual* (Minneapolis, MN: Search Institute, 1995).

13. Ibid., 20.

14. Ibid., 21.

15. Ibid., 22.

16. Ibid., 22.

17. Ibid., 22.

18. Ibid., 22.

19. Ibid., 23.

20. The Search Institute, "40 Developmental Assets," 1997. http://www. search-institute.org (May 2, 2001).

21. The Search Institute, "Raising Caring and Responsible Children and Teenagers," 2000. http://www.search-institute.org (May 2, 2001).

22. The Search Institute, "40 Developmental Assets."

3

◇ ◇ ◇

GETTING YOUR DUCKS IN A ROW: THE GAME PLAN FOR SERVING HOMESCHOOLERS

Any librarian who has attempted to target a specific segment of the community for new programs and services knows that this cannot be accomplished without a great deal of thought and planning. Many have tried to jump into serving a new population without taking the time and energy to research the needs of that population or by relying on personal perceptions. While some may have achieved success using this approach, the odds of a new service or new program succeeding and achieving longevity are greatly increased by employing a more ordered methodology.

CLEARLY IDENTIFY THE GROUP THAT IS CURRENTLY UNDERSERVED

It wasn't very long ago that librarians needed to be very aggressive in presenting their case for targeted services specifically to young adults. Now that many libraries have succeeded in creating special programs, services, and collections for the young adult population, librarians are attempting to reach out to even more specific groups that may be overlooked, underserved, and in need of specialized attention. For your community it might be a minority group, an immigrant population, or perhaps teen parents. If you are reading this book, it's likely that you have already discovered the need to extend programs and services to the home-schoolers in your community.

ENVIRONMENTAL SCAN

In order to clearly define your new target population, you may need to perform an environmental scan, a patron survey, or perhaps collect patron comments and suggestions. These tools can also assist you in identifying how many people you will be attempting to serve and how this group is being served by other organizations or agencies in your community. Homeschooling teens may already be served in ways that you were planning to serve them. Why duplicate services that will only drain your library's resources and take up your valuable time if another agency is already doing it? Perhaps a community center is allowing homeschooling associations to reserve a meeting space for their monthly meetings or for invited speakers. A local church may have a library that allows home-schoolers to trade used curriculum books. As you consider ways other agencies or organizations serve some homeschoolers, be sure to determine how accessible these services are. If only church members are allowed to exchange curriculum, many homeschoolers could be excluded. This still might be a viable service to offer at your library to ensure that all home-schooling teens have equal access.

The following questions may assist you in locating areas that are already being covered in your community:

- *What do your local schools (public and private) offer to homeschoolers?* Talk to school administrators, even if homeschoolers say that the schools do not offer services. Perhaps the homeschoolers you have spoken to were not aware of a physical education credit because they were only interested in joining the band. Use your teacher contacts in your search for answers. As you search you may be able to spark interest and set the foundation for future collaboration.
- *What do your local churches offer?* You may find that churches offer many more services to homeschoolers than you thought. If there is a church library, speak to the librarian or library volunteer. They would have a good idea of how many homeschoolers take advantage of church-based services to homeschoolers.
- *What does your local community college or university offer?* Be sure to look into continuing education opportunities, postsecondary options (high school students being allowed to take college courses for credit), as well as homeschool-specific programs

that may be offered. Some community colleges have begun to offer physical education courses specifically for homeschooling families.

- *What do your local community centers offer?* A YMCA or Boys and Girls Club may not have programming specifically for homeschoolers, but may provide programs that fill a gap in a homeschooling teen's curriculum. Programs that these organizations offer, like arts and crafts, sports, and recreation may be difficult or too expensive for the library to provide. As previously noted, don't drain your library's resources trying to produce programs that are offered somewhere else in the community. However, programs that are not prohibitively expensive for the library to fund may be very welcome to homeschooling families for whom the fees at community center programs create financial hardship. If your library can offer an arts program at no cost to participants, you will have made some friends for life!

- *What do local businesses or organizations offer?* Many car dealerships offer car care courses. The American Red Cross often offers babysitting clinics. Again, keep in mind any costs that are associated with these programs. You may also want to consider ways that these businesses or organizations can cooperate on programs, perhaps with the registration fee being paid by a grant.

Once you have an idea of how homeschooling teens are already being served in your community, try to get a clearer idea of how many teens are actually being homeschooled. While you are doing your environmental scan, you can ask your local churches, community groups, and organizations how many homeschooling teens they serve. When you have an idea of how many people may be considered part of this group and what areas are not yet already being offered in your community, you will have a better idea of how much time and resources will be needed to put your plan into action.

REVIEW YOUR LIBRARY'S MISSION STATEMENT

Before you embark on a mission of your own, you will need to spend time reviewing your library's mission statement, goals, vision, and long-range planning documents. Make sure you have the most up-to-date versions of these documents (they may have been revised since you started working at your library) and review them to see where your ideas for serving homeschooled teens fit into the overall picture.

Many public library mission statements include the support of educational and recreational endeavors in the community. Certainly serving homeschoolers fits into this part of the mission statement. What homeschooled teens want most from their libraries is support for their educational goals and their recreational interests, which are usually very closely related.

Long-range planning documents may specify what activities are to take place during the next several years to reach the library's goals. Although these plans may not include specific mention of homeschoolers, you may be able to argue the case that homeschoolers should be included in any plans that focus on students who are educated in the more traditional ways. For example, if your long-range plans include offering library orientations to high school students, you can provide a credible argument for also offering these sessions to homeschooled teens.

CREATE A PLAN

Behind every great program is a great plan. If you're accustomed to using a program planning sheet for individual events, going through the steps to create a new overall program of service should not seem very foreign. On the other hand, if you don't use a program planning sheet, it's not too late to start! (See samples of programming planning sheets in chapter 6.)

GOALS

The first part of your plan is to determine the program's goals. These goals will help you to determine what kinds of individual programs and services to offer. These goals should reflect the goals of your library. When thinking about your goals, you may want to ask yourself the following questions:

- Should the library aid families in the decision to homeschool and/or the decision to continue homeschooling through high school?
- Should the library assist families with starting the homeschooling process?
- Should the library help families with the de-schooling process?
- Should the library provide curricular materials and resources? If so, how much and in what areas?
- Should the library offer homeschooled teens opportunities for social interaction?

- Should the library offer homeschooled teens opportunities for leadership?
- Should the library extend the same services and privileges to homeschooling families that are offered to teachers?
- Should the library provide spaces for homeschoolers to meet on their own?
- Should the library offer opportunities for the assessment of learning?
- Should the library provide connections to other services in the community?

By examining these questions with your library's mission in mind, you can gain a better idea of what direction to take. Perhaps you will start with one goal and choose another goal once the first is accomplished. Or you may decide to accomplish several goals simultaneously, with the assistance of your colleagues.

BUDGET

Once you have determined your goals, you need to examine your financial resources. Look at your budget realistically and see how much money is available or perhaps where money can be reallocated. Keep in mind that the most logical place to find money may not be out of a young adult services line item. Other departments may have unused funds in their materials budgets that could be used to purchase books for a homeschooling collection. Perhaps there is already a line item in the budget to purchase materials for a parent-teacher collection. This would be an ideal place to look for money to purchase curricular materials for homeschooling teenagers.

After determining how much money is available, estimate how much is actually needed to meet your goals. Try to determine what costs will be immediate for starting up the program and what costs will be ongoing. For example, when building collections, the start-up cost is usually higher than the cost of sustaining the collection for years to come.

Because seed money tends to be high in comparison to the continuation of funding, starting to serve a new population is an ideal time to seek out grants. Many grants aim to provide seed money only, with a percentage of match or promise of continued funding from the institution. Therefore, if you have found some money in your budget, but not enough, a grant may be the ideal solution. For inspiration, read about the success of the Johnsburg (IL) Public Library District, which utilized a grant to fund a library-based homeschool resource center. Their story, plus more information on Library Services and Technology Act grants is found in chapter 4.

If a grant is not an option, perhaps fundraising is. If your library has a Friends organization, it would be worthwhile to present your case to them. If you don't have a Friends organization, consider approaching your local homeschooling organizations to see if they have any upcoming events that could raise funds for the library. A teen advisory board may also be able to raise funds for your project.

Even after all of these options have been investigated, you may discover that you just do not have the funds to meet all of your goals. If this is the case, review your goals and prioritize them. You may not have the funding to meet all of your goals, but there may be enough money to meet the one you've chosen as most important.

STAFF TIME

Another cost that you need to consider is the amount of staff time needed to begin and sustain your project. Again, start-up usually requires the greatest investment of time and attention. That time and attention can decrease as the program moves beyond the start-up phase. Before you determine how much staff time will be needed, identify the key players at your library. You may want to ask the following questions:

- *Which department will be the main contact/sponsor for serving home-schooling teens and their parents?* Even though you may be the person presenting the plan, where will your homeschooled teen patrons most likely seek out assistance? Make sure that the department with the most contact with homeschooling teens has a role in designing and implementing the plan.
- *Who will be responsible for which tasks?* Although you may decide what materials will become the core of a homeschooling collection, who will keep the collection current by locating reviews and reading homeschooling literature? You may have compiled the information for the library's homeschooling resources guide, but who will keep this information current? Also, who would be the best candidate to coordinate any homeschooling teens who want to volunteer? Take a look at each of your goals and determine who on your staff would be the best candidate to achieve these goals. At your library you may be the only person who is equipped to meet your goals, but there may be powerful allies who can act as liaisons or take on tasks that are more appropriate for their skills.
- *Will you enlist volunteers?* Volunteers can be powerful assets for a library, but can also create more work than anticipated. If your

library already has a functioning volunteer program, this question may not be difficult to answer. For the library without an existing volunteer program, your plan may come to fruition by using volunteers, but it may also be hindered if the volunteers are not coordinated properly. If you decide to use volunteers for the project, you should decide ahead of time who will supervise the volunteers, what tasks are appropriate for them, and which tasks should only be performed by library staff.

Once you have determined who will be involved with your project, the more difficult task is to figure out how much time will be needed to make it happen. It may be helpful to think in terms of hours per week. You may also want to take into consideration what tasks can be performed while staffing a service desk, if that is allowed at your library. For example, you may want to spend one hour per week compiling information for a home-schooling resources guide while working at the reference desk. You may also need to find an hour a week off the desk to be used to make contacts in the community or to track down a speaker for an upcoming event. However you decide to account for the amount of time needed to make your project work, try to be reasonable and allow enough time to meet your goals. Librarians often schedule too much to do in a single hour, which sometimes means tasks go unfinished or have to be taken home to be completed.

ALLIES

One sure key to success is to have allies on whom you can depend. Make a list of people on the library staff and in the community who you feel would want to see this project become successful. These people may or may not be directly involved in your plan, but they should be people who you could call for advice or guidance. Staff allies may include anyone who is supportive of homeschooling, or is close to someone who homeschools. Allies in your community will likely include homeschooling families, but may also include teachers, clergy, or business leaders. Your allies can suggest program ideas, speakers for events, or possibly write a letter of support for a financial grant.

While you are determining your allies, you may also want to make a mental list of people who may stand in your way. (It would be best not to write this list down anywhere!) As much as we all hope that our programs will be supported by the staff and the community, there are usually naysayers who would not be disappointed to see our programs fail. You probably won't have the time or energy to try to "convert" these people, but mentally identifying them will at least keep you from being surprised when they voice opposition.

SPACE

In order to meet some of your goals, you will need to assess what space may be available for the project. Start by asking the following questions (some questions may not be applicable, depending on your stated goals):

- *Is there currently an appropriate place for programming?* If you don't have a community room, you may be able to make occasional use of your library's story time space. Some events are better suited to the outdoors. Is there space outside? Is there a space that can be used at a nearby location like a church or community center? These are questions that may need to be asked regularly if space is an issue at your library.
- *What do policies say about how space can be used in your library?* Most libraries with community rooms have policies that determine who can use the space and how they can arrange for its use. See if your goals are supported by the policies before you plan to use this space for your project.
- *Is there space for a collection of homeschooling materials?* If your goals include building a collection of materials, where do you plan to shelve them? There may be shelf space that is currently under-utilized that would be appropriate for the homeschooling collection. If your library already has special collections (career guides, parent-teacher materials, test preparation guides) these collections may be expanded to include homeschooling materials.
- *Is there work space for volunteers?* You may not have a designated area for volunteers. The ideal situation would be a volunteer station equipped with a phone, computer, and essential supplies. If this is not an option at your library, volunteers may adapt by working on projects at home or at a table in the children's area. It may also be convenient to schedule volunteers at times when a staff member is at a service desk, making a station or office available for a volunteer to work.
- *Is there a quiet place where patrons would be able to take a test or work on a project?* Some libraries offer homeschoolers the valuable service of test proctoring. If this is one of your goals, do you have a place where a homeschooler can take a test without distraction or interruptions?

TIME TABLE

Setting the timetable for your new project might seem deceivingly simple. However, many librarians set timelines that attempt to accomplish too much too soon. If you have been realistic with your plans for funding and available time, you should have an idea of what is possible. You may decide that only one goal can be met within the first fiscal year, so try to pace yourself. If your primary goals include establishing programs for homeschooling teens, you will need to figure out how many programs you can produce within a given time, making sure that current programming does not suffer. You may even decide to plan a single event and then assess its success before taking on another event. The following questions may assist in determining your timeline for implementation of your project:

- Do you need time for fundraising or grant writing before your project can begin?
- Do you need time to enlist volunteers?
- How much time does it usually take to have ideas approved by the administration?
- How much time is required to properly market your new programs or services?
- How much time does it usually take to acquire new materials and have them available on the shelves?
- How much time is required to book meeting spaces in the library?

CLEAR YOUR IDEAS WITH YOUR ADMINISTRATION

Wherever you may fall on your library's organizational chart, there are usually administrative officials who should be informed of changes in programming or services. Any decision that may affect public services should be cleared all the way up to the library board of trustees.

You may have been asked by your director to implement a plan of action for serving homeschooled teens (or possibly homeschoolers in general). If that is the case, you simply need to articulate your specific plans on how you want to reach out to this new group. If you are going to present an unsolicited proposal to your administration, you should try to anticipate questions or concerns that may arise. Come prepared with supporting documents and statistics that you can leave with your proposal to be pondered at a later time or with other members of the administrative team. These documents can include survey results, patron comment cards, or statistics from your local homeschooling association. Be prepared to indicate how much staff and volunteer time will be involved, which departments and staff members will be involved, and what kinds of resources—financial or otherwise—will need to be allocated. (Be sure to include any ideas for fundraising or grants that may assist with the resource allocation.) You may also want to indicate what kinds of evaluative tools you intend to use to determine the success of the plan. All of this may sound like overkill, but a well thought-out plan is more likely to get approved than an idea without a backbone. Even if your administration is not interested in all of your supporting materials, they will recognize that you've done thorough research to support your project.

STAFF COMMUNICATION AND TRAINING

Once you get the administration on board, you'll need to take steps to ensure that the rest of the staff is supportive of your homeschooling project. The best approach is proactive communication with the entire staff, from the part-time shelvers to the top administrators.

Methods of communication with staff should be part of your overall plan. Think about how your coworkers best communicate with each other. If most people prefer communicating by e-mail, that may be an ideal way to keep them informed of your progress. If there are members of your staff that do not have ready access to e-mail, then you may need to also post information in staff mailboxes, a staff bulletin board, or in a break room. However you choose to communicate with the staff, there are several things that you will want to share with them.

First, once your plan is approved by the administration, make sure to inform any staff that will be directly affected by your project. A meeting of all involved parties would be an excellent step.

Second, other staff members that may be affected in any way (which usually means the entire staff) should be informed. As many of us have learned, we cannot always count on supervisors to spread the word to all of the people they supervise, so try your best to make some kind of contact with all staff yourself.

Once the staff is aware of your plans, keep them informed of your progress, even if it seems like the program isn't progressing the way you would have liked. Don't hesitate to let staff know when you've hit barriers. Your coworkers may step up to offer assistance or suggestions. Don't feel as if you should communicate successes only.

Because communication works both ways, be open to suggestions, ideas, and constructive criticism. Keep your ears open for dissension among staff. A nonsupportive staff can sabotage an otherwise successful new program. To avoid negativity among staff members, part of your overall plan should include training for all involved. Training may not convert staff members who are anti-homeschooling to homeschooling supporters, but it may make the intentions of your program clear and point out how homeschoolers fit into your library's mission.

Staff training need not take up a great deal of time. Training can even be passive, including informational handouts and reading materials placed in staff mailboxes. Consider including materials on the history of home-schooling and the many different methods employed by homeschoolers. More active methods of training can be incorporated into staff or depart-mental meetings. You may choose to demonstrate homeschooling Web sites, or offer a brief presentation by a representative from a homeschooling organization. The more dialogue you create in support of your program, the less likely it will be that you will be surprised by unwelcome dissension from staff members.

COMMUNICATING WITH
OTHER LIBRARIES

Once you get your staff on board, you may also want to communicate your intentions with other local libraries or libraries in your consortia. Other libraries may be thinking about taking on similar projects or have homeschooling programs already underway. Networking is an excellent way to alleviate duplication and save yourself some time. If another library can learn from some of the work you've done, then they will be glad to share with you in the future.

ANTICIPATING CHALLENGES

Wouldn't it be helpful to have advance notice of an impending disaster? If you knew danger was coming, wouldn't you batten down the hatches and board up the windows before the wind started to pick up speed?

In reality, most libraries rarely encounter true disasters, although some have had their share of fires, floods, and earthquakes. Everyday chal-lenges usually do not cause lasting damage, but they can certainly derail a new project or impede its success. Even though you cannot predict all the possible problems that will arise, spending time anticipating possible difficulties can help keep your new homeschooling program on track. Think about this process as your program's individual disaster plan.

As difficult as it may be for many young adult librarians to be pessimistic, it is worthwhile to explore the "what ifs." If you find yourself too wrapped up in enthusiasm, think about enlisting a devil's advocate. Asking others what kinds of problems they think might arise will allow you to take a step back from the plan and anticipate potential worst-case scenarios.

The following are just a few of the scenarios you may encounter. Should they occur, consider yourself forewarned. By being proactive, a library can turn a possible challenge into a triumph.

- *Once you start offering special programs or services to homeschooling teens and their parents, other library patrons may complain about the special treatment or even demand the same treatment.* One way to avoid this scenario is to simply offer the same access to programs and services to all patrons, and market them to homeschoolers. This makes everyone happy. In the case of the special extended loan periods requested by many teachers and homeschoolers, though, it would not be practical to offer extended loans to every patron. Instead, the library might make it a policy to offer special extended loans on a case-by-case basis due to special circumstances or to help smooth over an angry patron.

- *Once you start offering a few special programs or services to homeschooling teens and their parents, they start making unreasonable requests.* This is the true price of success. When your program starts to take off and gain energy, chances are the homeschooling community will suggest more ways the library can support their efforts. Many times these requests and suggestions will be possible, but sometimes they just aren't. The best approach to this situation is honesty. If you are up front with your patrons and tell them how much time and effort is currently being expended, chances are they will understand. A beneficial byproduct of this situation is that you might become partners trying to make the impossible, possible. Make lemonade from lemons—turn that unhappy homeschooler into a new volunteer!

FURTHER READING

Jones, Patrick. *Connecting Young Adults and Libraries: A How-to-do-it Manual.* New York: Neal-Schuman Publishers, 1998.
   An excellent start-up guide for young adult services, the training toolkit will be especially helpful when implementing services and gaining support from library staff.

Jones, Patrick, and Joel Shoemaker. *Do It Right: Best Practices for Serving Young Adults in School and Public Libraries.* New York: Neal-Schuman Publishers, 2001.
   Packed with valuable case studies, customer service techniques are provided with young adult patrons in mind.
Mondowney, JoAnn G. *Hold Them in Your Heart: Successful Strategies for Library Services to At-Risk Teens.* New York: Neal-Schuman Publishers, 2001.
   This is a title in Neal-Schuman's *Teens @ the Library* series and includes chapters on strategies for gaining support; conducting a needs assessment; planning, evaluation, and obtaining funding; and a case study from the San Francisco Bay Area.
Nichols, Mary Anne, and C. Allen Nichols. *Young Adults and Public Libraries: A Handbook of Materials and Services.* Westport, CT: Greenwood Press, 1998.
   Chapters offer advice from practitioners in the field of young adult librarianship on topics including: adolescent development, genre literature, trends in YA literature, collection development, marketing and merchandising, reader's advisory, technology, programming, partnerships, intellectual freedom, and training for young adult staff.
Vaillancourt, Renee. *Managing Young Adult Services: A Self-Help Manual.* New York: Neal-Schuman Publishers, 2002.
   Truly encompassing the many hats a librarian might wear, Vaillancourt focuses on the young adult specialty. The first section focuses on leadership including basic management principles, and approaches to managing young adults, staff, teachers, and volunteers. The second section offers valuable insight into the administration of a young adult department: collections, programming, paperwork, planning, budgeting, etc. This section also includes ideas on how to manage time, manage stress, and achieve a balanced work/home life.
Waddle, Linda, ed. *New Directions for Library Service to Young Adults.* Chicago: American Library Association, 2002.
   A new road map for planning, implementing, and evaluating services to young adults.
Walter, Virginia A. *Output Measures and More: Planning and Evaluating Public Library Services for Young Adults.* Chicago: American Library Association, 1995.
   Learn about the various ways young adult services can be evaluated at your library. Includes information on conducting a needs assessment, developing a plan for services for young adults, developing mission and vision statements, and how to use both qualitative and quantitative methods of evaluation.

4

◇ ◇ ◇

HITTING THE TARGET: GIVING HOMESCHOOLERS THE SERVICES THEY WANT AND NEED

We've all encountered library users whose demands seem excessive and beyond the scope and budget of a public library. And we won't deny that at times, homeschoolers may seem to be part of this needy crowd. It is not our contention that you must at all times bend over backward to provide for any of your users, whether homeschoolers or not. However, we suggest that there are services that the library can and should provide that may require nothing more than a change in policy or a shift in thinking. Such changes may not only benefit your homeschoolers, but other library users as well. Don't be afraid to say "no" when it is appropriate, but don't be afraid to try new approaches, either.

The intent of this chapter is to share some practical ideas for implementing new or re-designed services for your homeschoolers. Obviously not everything described will work in every library setting. The services discussed in this chapter were suggested by homeschoolers answering a survey designed by the authors of this book. A copy of the survey is included in chapter 7. We've also included some of the services that are in use at our individual libraries.

WHAT DO HOMESCHOOLERS WANT?

Each community's needs are different, depending upon economics, geography, and a host of other variables, so you may want to begin as we did by surveying your homeschoolers. Use our survey as a template for your own research, changing questions as appropriate. Review the chapter on marketing to determine the best ways to reach homeschoolers with your survey. You will have to "target-market" your survey, just as you will with the services and programs you design. Contact local homeschooling groups directly to solicit their input or consider including your survey in any information packets provided to homeschoolers by their local board of education. If you are able to identify homeschoolers when they visit your library, ask them to participate in your survey.

Beyond a simple questionnaire, you might also put together a focus group comprised of homeschooling library users, both parents and teens. Typically, focus groups are best facilitated by someone other than library staff, but in this case, staff involvement in dialogue with homeschoolers may yield more valuable information. Through conversation within the focus group setting, you may be able to more fully explore homeschoolers' requests for services and programs, separating true needs from "it would be great if…" Prioritizing in this manner will help you communicate budgetary realities and the mission and role of the library while honoring reasonable requests from your homeschoolers. As you brainstorm together, don't be surprised if your homeschoolers come up with ways to make things happen that you hadn't considered! Strive for a spirit of teamwork and cooperation. You may find that your homeschoolers' future requests are delivered to you with greater understanding of the library's mission and ability.

So what services do homeschoolers want your library to provide? Here are some ideas:

Teacher Loan Cards

Grocery store chains tout the savings benefit of carrying and using "power" cards, but for library users the true power card is the one that gives them access to your materials collection. There are ways to boost the wattage of your "power" card for homeschoolers that can be implemented easily through the use of teacher loan cards.

Teacher loan cards allow teachers to flesh out their classroom library with materials from your collection that fill a specific curricular need. Privileges under a teacher loan card may include extended borrowing periods beyond your customary time length, freedom from fines, and removal of borrowing limits on the number or dollar value of items checked out. Establish rules for teacher loan cards that discourage abuse of the extended privileges. For example, cards should expire at the end of each school year, necessitating renewals each fall. Those who are no longer teaching would no longer be eligible. Request lists of teachers from your school board office, or ask the teacher to show a copy of a current contract or letter of intent. Require that teacher loan cards only be used for classroom, not personal materials. Do make teacher loan cards fine-free, but also require payment for lost and damaged books. Finally, extend the teacher loan card option to your homeschoolers. In most cases, you should be able to request a copy of documentation they received from the local school superintendent or building principal that indicates your home-schooling user is exempt from public school. This helps you to be certain that those applying for extended privileges through teacher loan cards are, in fact, teaching.

Library Tours/Research Instruction

Give library tours to your homeschoolers that cover the basics of navigating the library, and also offer instruction in using resource materials. Consider having your teen homeschoolers submit questions to your reference staff in advance, then invite them to the library to be shown the steps used to find the answers.[1] The programming chapter in this book gives additional ideas about creating library orientation/research instruction activities, plus tips for planning an open house event for homeschoolers.

Meeting/Study Rooms

Many communities have a real shortage of public meeting space, making your library's meeting rooms a hot commodity. (If you want to make a lot of new friends and thrill your voters, add multiple meeting rooms to your new library building plans.) Your homeschoolers are no different from other community groups in their desire for space where they can gather for programs, small group instruction, and presentations. One of the realities of homeschooling is that it can be very isolating. By meeting in groups, homeschoolers can replace some of the social interaction that may be missing from their school day. This can be particularly important for teens who are moving toward independence and away from the influence of parents. The ability to meet in groups with other teens helps them figure out who they are and how they fit into the world. By making your library's meeting space available, you provide a welcoming environment for this essential interaction.

Invite your local homeschooling association to use your rooms for their regular meetings. This can provide you the perfect opportunity to address the group about library services, ask questions about their needs, or even conduct a tour of the library collection.

Before you become overwhelmed by requests for use of your meeting rooms, whether by homeschoolers or others, plan to create a meeting room policy. Things to consider for inclusion in your policy are: whether your rooms will be available to both nonprofit and commercial groups; whether the library will charge a fee; if food and beverages will be permitted; if you want to place limitations on the number of times per month or year that a single group may use the rooms; and how scheduling will be handled. Proceed with caution when defining room use by religious or political groups. Some library meeting room policies have come under fire for excluding these groups. You may wish to have your library's legal counsel or local prosecutor review your policy for compliance.

In addition to meeting and study space, homeschoolers also appreciate space where they can display art or science projects. Make tables available for homeschoolers' science projects when public schools in your community hold their science fairs. Artwork can be displayed on bulletin boards, in your library's showcases, or in your reading lounge. If your library has a gallery space that hosts local artists, invite homeschoolers to organize a gallery show of their own.

Museum Passes

A museum pass program will be welcomed not only by homeschoolers, but by your other customers as well. Depending on the cooperative arrangement established with local museums, library users may get free or reduced admission by using the pass that the library provides. The passes are typically not free to the library, but require the purchase of an annual membership. Look to your library's Friends group or Foundation, if you have one, for funding the pass program. Some museums have a reciprocity agreement that allows visitors to use a pass from one museum to visit another; such an arrangement will help expand your pass program offerings.

Set up a reservation system and determine a reasonable loan period for the museum passes; a three-day loan is usually sufficient.

For a look at how other libraries manage their museum pass program, check the Web sites for Falmouth (MA) Public Library (http://www.

falmouthpubliclibrary.org/museumpass.htm) and Fairfield (CT) Public Library (http://www.fairfieldpubliclibrary.org/museum.htm). Both offer passes to an excellent array of museums and other exhibits in their respective areas.

Book Sales/Book Fairs/Curriculum Exchange/New Collections

It can be an expensive proposition to homeschool a child. The texts and materials required—those items typically included without additional fees in the public school—must be purchased by the homeschool family. Granted, not all homeschoolers are spending thousands of out-of-pocket dollars to educate at home; in fact, many seek out ways to curtail costs through hands-on learning, apprenticeships, bartering, and self-designed curriculum that leans heavily on your library's collection.

Those who prefer to follow a more structured learning style typically invest in some kind of curriculum. There are many different curriculum packages for homeschoolers on the market and they are not inexpensive. Unless a family is able to hand down the materials from child to child, they may find themselves with a home library of little value once the individual course of study has been completed. Your library can fill an important role for both the structured homeschooler and the unschooler.

Curriculum Exchange

Repeatedly, those we surveyed requested that the library organize curriculum exchanges. This could be accomplished in a number of ways. The goal is to make used curricula available to others. This gives borrowers the chance to review curricula before purchasing elsewhere or to use and return for others to use. A simple means of creating a curriculum exchange is to invite homeschoolers to donate used materials to a collection you establish in a filing cabinet or on designated shelving. Consider minimal cataloging or no cataloging at all. If you do enter the items into your database, restrict their use to your patrons only.

Alternately, schedule a "Curriculum Exchange Fair" either in the late spring or late summer, and invite your homeschooling families to bring their used materials for sale or trade. All you'll need to do to prepare is to set up tables in your meeting room and create a display of materials and handouts available for your homeschoolers. The curriculum fair is also a great opportunity to schedule a concurrent library resources tour.

Should your collection budget allow, include some basic curriculum packages in your purchases. Since you are dealing with a relatively narrow age group, your purchases could be limited to upper-level math, civics, history, and literature, for example. Seek advice from your homeschoolers about which curriculum packages are most popular. We've included contact information for a number of curriculum publishers in chapter 5.

Book Fairs/Book Sales

It can be difficult to determine from a book catalog or online description whether a particular curriculum package meets an individual homeschooler's needs. Explore the possibility of hosting a book fair to which you invite sales representatives from various homeschool publishers, so that your homeschoolers can see and review the material in depth. If you or your library administration are uncomfortable with sales being made on the premises, request that publishers send only catalogs and sample materials; buyers can complete the purchase from home.

Book sales are another way to match up used books and those who have need of them. When marketing library services to your homeschool population, be sure to always include information about your Friends of the Library book sales. The Friends' sale can take the place of a curriculum exchange if you don't have the time or space to organize one. Ask the Friends to set aside a special sale area for used curriculum, then solicit donations from the homeschooling community. Your frugal homeschoolers are likely to be your best customers!

New Collections

Today's library is not like your father's library. Some libraries are loaning items that don't even remotely resemble books and audiovisual materials. Consider the public library that loans tools or toys. Or the one that loans "Sick at Home" kits. Now take the idea that anything can be loaned and borrowed and create a new collection for your homeschoolers.

Along with the investment in books and materials, homeschoolers frequently have need for hands-on items to enhance their study. Science study becomes particularly difficult for homeschoolers because of the need for specific equipment. Two items that come immediately to mind are microscopes and telescopes. Explore the possibility of including one or two of each in next year's budget. You might request that your Friends' group or Foundation make the purchase instead, or perhaps you'll want to research grant options. (See information about *Library Services and Technology Act* grants at the end of this chapter.)

Other science-related materials that you could consider purchasing for loan include electronic lab kits, magnet sets, optics materials, and weather lab kits. Edmund Scientifics and Radio Shack are great places to investigate for more ideas (Web addresses for Edmund Scientifics and Radio Shack are included in Chapter 8.). Finally, you will need to determine loan periods and replacement/repair policies. Review your circulating audio-visual equipment procedures for help in determining how to circulate microscopes and other science lab equipment.

Resource Lists/Homeschool Handbooks/Online Links

At its most basic, library service is about connecting people with information. Your homeschoolers' needs for information are not much different than those of your other users. Booklists, readers' advisory guidelines, and suggested reading lists are valuable to everyone.

Many of those we surveyed talked about the desire for organized lists of library materials. Specific suggestions included "what can I read next" lists located near literary classics; lists organized by genre; and recommended reading/viewing/listening titles organized by subject. To those we would add others such as the *New York Times'* best-seller list, *Library Journal's* best books of the year, and the advanced placement summer reading lists from area high schools. In addition, homeschoolers asked for lists of suggested titles provided by teachers, parents, and other homeschoolers. These lists can provide the basis for the homeschool handbook described below.

Homeschool Handbook

The goal of a homeschool handbook should be to provide "one-stop shopping" for your homeschoolers. Enlist their help in gathering some of the material; be sure to include copies of all pertinent library policies, forms, and applications as well, including your meeting room policy. Other handbook materials could include:

- Copies of catalogs from curriculum publishers; ask your homeschoolers for extras from home
- Copies of the laws and regulations governing homeschooling in your state
- Any necessary forms that homeschoolers need to register with local boards of education
- Contact information for state and local homeschool associations
- Lists of Web sites of interest to homeschoolers
- Sign-up sheet for inclusion on the library mailing list; be sure to ask for e-mail addresses that can be used for Interlibrary Loan and reserve notification and program announcements

- Lists of independent study and correspondence schools
- Local community college catalogs
- Names of tutors for specific subjects
- Names of public speakers/area speakers' bureaus
- GED information
- ACT/SAT testing information
- Community calendars of events

You may want to gather all of the materials for your homeschool handbook into a binder and/or make it part of your reference pamphlet file.

Online Links

You can also make your resource list available 24/7 by creating a homeschooling resource page on your library's Web site. Be sure to provide a clearly labeled link from your front page. Also remember to include information about your services and programs, a printable calendar of events, and contact names and phone numbers for library staff who work with the homeschoolers at your library.

A number of libraries have created detailed Web pages devoted solely to their homeschooling services. Often, building the page is only a matter of organizing existing information into logical categories that make it easy for homeschoolers to locate it. A few examples of well-designed homeschooling pages include:

Jackson County Library Services (Medford, OR)
http://www.jcls.org/jr_homeschooling.html

This nicely-organized Web page is titled "Homeschooling: A Guide to Resources." The first section suggests search terms for use in browsing the online catalog; offers several standard titles to help homeschoolers get started; gives instruction in how to search online databases for articles on homeschooling; outlines the library's material selection policy and invites suggestions for inclusion in the homeschooling collection; lists contact information for local school systems and local and state homeschooling organizations; and includes a webliography of Internet resources with Web addresses and brief descriptions.

Multnomah County Library (Portland, OR)
http://www.multcolib.org/homesch/index.html

Multnomah County Library has designed a comprehensive Web page just for homeschoolers. Some features of the page are a research guide, a compilation of booklists organized by subject including general homeschooling titles, how to develop curriculum, and teaching language arts, math, and science. From the homeschool front page, users may link to information about library services for homeschoolers, which include custom development of bibliographies, webliographies, pathfinders, and scavenger hunts; a free museum pass program to a local children's museum; educator's cards, tours, and technology training. Finally, the page provides contact information and links to national and local homeschool organizations and access to the library's online reference service.

Boise (Idaho) Public Library

http://www.boisepubliclibrary.org/Ys/ys_homeschool.shtml

While Boise's Web page is not as elaborate as the previous two, it does provide homeschoolers with useful information in a straightforward manner. Included are links to a selection of general homeschooling information (Ask ERIC; Jon's Homeschool Resource Page); a fully annotated list of books on homeschooling from the library collection; contact information for local organizations; and links to curriculum resources.

Homeschool Resource Centers

Consider setting aside a place in your library as a separate homeschooling resource center. One such center is in operation at the Johnsburg Public Library District in Illinois. Read on to see what can happen by daring to follow a library customer's dream:

A Homeschooler's Dream: The Johnsburg (IL) Public Library District

What would you get if you had a dynamic volunteer with a vision, ten active homeschool groups willing to share their wish lists, and a $55,000 grant from the Library Services and Technology Act? You might have something like the Homeschool Resource Center, operating in the Johnsburg Public Library District. Johnsburg, a town of just under 12,000 souls, is located in McHenry County, 60 miles northwest of Chicago. The library is housed in a 10,000-square-foot building and has a collection of 55,000 items. The Resource Center occupies what had been a quiet study room.

(continued)

(Continued)

Illinois does not require homeschoolers to register, making it difficult to know exactly how many have chosen this option. Basing her figures, in part, upon membership in the local homeschooling support groups, Johnsburg Library Director Maria Zawacki estimates that McHenry County has nearly 1000 homeschooling families. In addition to serving McHenry County's homeschoolers, Johnsburg Library also draws customers from at least five or more neighboring counties. During one usage survey period in 2003, 90 percent of the Homeschool Resource Center's materials were checked out to "reciprocal" or out-of-district borrowers.

While the fact that Johnsburg created a Homeschool Center is remarkable enough, it's what's inside that counts. Using the responses from surveys of area homeschool groups, plus the knowledgeable input of a dedicated homeschool mom (now the Center's onsite advocate), Johnsburg created a comprehensive collection of books and other materials that meets the needs of the most discerning homeschooling parent. The collection includes titles from recognized homeschool experts; many standard full curriculums including Sonlight, Weaver, Five in a Row, and Alpha Omega, as well as individual subject curriculums in many subject areas; and a bevy of hands-on tools including science equipment (chemistry lab glassware, telescopes, and microscopes), math manipulatives, and educational board games, kits, and software. The Center also features twenty-two homeschool periodicals and newsletters; a collection of homeschool supplier catalogs; and a pamphlet file with information about state homeschooling regulations, homeschooler support groups, local field trip information, and brochures on local points of interest.

The compact size of Johnsburg Library's homeschool center precludes them from having a continual curriculum exchange—something many homeschoolers seek—but they do offer an annual homeschool open house and mini-conference where homeschoolers may buy and sell used curriculum among themselves. The Center also accepts good, used curriculum donated for the collection and makes other donated homeschool materials available through library book sales.

The Homeschool Resource Center collection strives to seek a balance among a wide variety of theologies. In addition, much time and care has been taken to select materials that support those homeschoolers who are following different educational philosophies, with Waldorf, Montessori, Classical, and unschooling methods all represented.

Paired with its comprehensive collection for homeschoolers of all ages, the Center also boasts the services of an on-site homeschool advocate. As the homeschooling parent and fervent library supporter who originally shared the dream of an in-house homeschooling resource center, Kathy Wentz volunteers two-and-a-half hours one day each week as a resource person, answering customer questions and providing guidance to the

(continued)

(Continued)

collection. During the balance of the week, library staff handle customer questions about homeschooling; those questions they can't answer are forwarded to Wentz who returns calls from her home.

The Homeschool Resource Center also has a place of prominence on the Johnsburg Library's Web site. A rich mix of information is available at http://www.johnsburglibrary.org/hrc.htm including accelerated reader lists; instructions on how to limit online catalog searches to materials in the Resource Center; and a link to "Information Useful to Librarians," which reads like a "best practices" manual for creating a resource center like Johnsburg's.

How did this small library in rural Illinois create such a vital resource for its homeschooling families? With money from the Library Services and Technology Act (LSTA). This federal program, administered individually by each state, has, over the course of its history, done much to assist libraries in building new facilities, adding new technology, and enhancing services to customers. More information about the LSTA is included in this chapter. For the full text of the LSTA grant that funded the Johnsburg Public Library District Homeschool Resource Center, see the appendix at the back of this book.

Proctoring

There has been some debate about whether library staff should be made available to proctor exams. Those in opposition feel that proctoring goes beyond the library's mission and creates a strain on staffing resources. Others view it as a natural outreach service coming under the library's mission as a community education resource. Your administrators will need to determine what fits best with your individual library's mission; you can be on hand to remind them that proctoring fills a real need for your homeschooled teens who opt to take classes through correspondence courses. For example, the University of Nebraska-Lincoln (UNL) Independent Study High School requires a local supervisor—a qualified adult who resides near the student and who is approved by either a local school official or the Independent Study High School administration. Local supervisors are responsible for maintaining test security, establishing testing conditions, proctoring tests, and submitting completed tests. While UNL prefers a professional educator as the local supervisor, they will accept "head librarians."[2]

Volunteer Opportunities

Kathy Wentz, the volunteer who serves as homeschool advocate at Johnsburg Library's Homeschool Resource Center, is an outstanding role model for volunteers who wish to help you serve your homeschooling community. Her experience as a homeschooling parent and her understanding of the needs and interests of homeschoolers gives her the expertise for working with this unique population. Homeschooling parents are likely to feel more comfortable with someone who has been "in the trenches" and who knows her way around homeschooling curriculum, testing requirements, portfolio assessments, and public school-mandated legal forms.

If a dedicated resource center, complete with homeschooling advocate, is not in your plans, there are dozens of other opportunities that will be of interest to homeschooled volunteers. Your homeschooled teens may be particularly interested in volunteering at the library. Since their academic work rarely fills a typical school day, many homeschooled teens seek meaningful work in their communities. Volunteering at your library not only gives them a chance to serve, but also exposes them to the world of work and to the library profession. We've listed a few ideas in the programming chapter on ways to involve your homeschooling volunteers. Training volunteers can be a great investment for your library; that young man cutting out flannel board figures as a volunteer may some day come back to you as a Children's Services Librarian!

MAKING IT HAPPEN OR WHERE DO WE GET THE MONEY FOR THESE THINGS?

We've suggested elsewhere in this chapter that funding for services like museum passes and science equipment might come from your library's Friends group or Foundation. For libraries without support groups, other funding sources must be found. Pay attention to the names of businesses or corporations in your community who provide visible support for other institutions like the local schools or the hospital. Create a "wish list" of the services you want to fund and contact these community givers. Invite them to think of the library when they are making decisions about where to place their charitable dollars.

You might also follow the lead of the Johnsburg Library and apply for a grant. Conveniently, the research necessary for creating marketing plans, mission statements, and long-range plans can also be applied to grant writing. We've included a copy of the Library Services and Technology Act (LSTA) grant application from Johnsburg Library in the appendix.

Further information about LSTA grants is at the end of this chapter. We also recommend these titles for learning about grantsmanship:

Peggy Barber and Linda D. Crowe. *Getting Your Grant: A How-To-Do-It Manual for Librarians.* New York: Neal-Schuman Publishers, Inc., 1993.

Sylvia D. Hall, et al. *Grantsmanship for Small Libraries and School Library Media Centers.* Westport, CT: Teacher Ideas Press, 1999.

The Foundation Center. *Grants for Libraries and Information Services, 2002–2003.* New York: The Foundation Center, 2002.

SUMMARY

We aren't suggesting that every service discussed in this chapter be implemented in your library. Feel free to pick and choose those ideas that seem to fit your library's mission and goals. Some things may not be workable now, but could be kept on a back-burner for future consideration.

Above all, remember that whatever services you provide for your homeschooling population can also be useful to your general users. Keep an open mind when considering the requests of homeschoolers. What may sound demanding and impossible at first may actually be quite doable. Ask your homeschoolers for suggestions, not only for services, but how to bring them about. Be honest about what your library can and cannot do. Start with the small things and build on those successes. Don't be afraid to try something new!

NOTES

1. Sophia Sayigh, "Library Sweet Library," National Home Educators Network, http://www.nhen.org/librarian.

2. University of Nebraska-Lincoln Independent Study High School, http://nebraskahs.unl.edu.

The Library Services and Technology Act (LSTA)

Passed into law in 1996, this act is the most recent version of a federal program designed to stimulate a wide variety of library activities. Originally intended to support library construction and renovation, the LSTA focuses on two key priorities—information access through technology and information empowerment through special services. The LSTA is overseen by the Institute of Museum and Library Services at the federal level, but is administered individually by each state, usually through the state library.

(continued)

(Continued)

Other federal priorities that are addressed through LSTA grant-making include interlibrary cooperation and resource sharing; adaptation of new technologies for library services; and outreach to special segments of the community such as the homebound, the disabled, the elderly, those living in institutions, those with limited fluency in English, those with literacy needs, residents of Indian reservations, and children using the services of child care centers and latchkey programs.

According to the American Library Association (ALA), the reason for federal involvement in libraries is because no one individual can possess the resources necessary for personal growth, education and research, and their work and community responsibilities. Enabling libraries to provide services and materials freely, even beyond the limits of their own community or state, "increases the public good beyond what any one library could ever supply, and makes support and improvement of library services a goal in the national interest."

Source: American Library Association.

5

◇ ◇ ◇

CONSTRUCTION ZONE: BUILDING A COLLECTION TO SERVE HOMESCHOOLED TEENS

Regardless of what kind of programs and services your library is able to offer to your community, the cornerstone of the library will always be the collection. When budgets are cut and services are curtailed, the collection can continue to be what keeps your patrons coming to the library. Patrons who compare various libraries around their communities can usually tell you immediately which library has the better collection. They might attend programs at a library that offers more story hours or teen programs, but many will go to check out their books or request books from the libraries they perceive have the better collection. Because circulation figures are very important measures of success (although they are not always accurate accounts of success), it is wise to spend a good percentage of our time on collection analysis and development.

When looking at your collection with homeschooling teens in mind, you will likely find you already have plenty of resources they will enjoy and find useful. These resources might be buried in your existing collection, but with some guidance your homeschooling teens should be able to find many helpful resources. Additionally, your library probably has a selection of materials on homeschooling. As your services to homeschoolers expand, you may decide to invest a small portion of your collection budget or seek grant monies to expand your collection with additional homeschooling resources. For now, though, you can get started with what you already have in your collection.

There are several approaches to developing collections of materials for homeschoolers, so you will need to decide what would work best for your library. Some solutions employed at various libraries include:

- *Create guides to your existing collections.* If your space is limited and you do not have room for a new homeschooling collection, create pathfinders or bibliographies that highlight all or parts of your collection that would be useful to homeschoolers. This is not the most convenient way to serve your homeschooling teens, but they will appreciate the effort of highlighting important resources that may be overlooked when browsing shelves and shelves of materials. Possible bibliography topics may include biographies, career resources, college planning resources, science fair projects, or standardized test study guides (GED, ACT, SAT, etc.).

- *Create a collection of resources for homeschoolers and other educators.* Many libraries house this collection in or near the children's department and call it by a variety of names, including a homeschooling collection, a teaching/learning collection, or a parent/ teacher collection. A basic homeschooling collection would include resources describing the homeschooling process and titles written for homeschoolers, many of which are annotated in chapter 8. This collection may be expanded to include curriculum guides, activity guides, works on child and adolescent development, and actual texts for various subject areas in a range of ages. If your library has created a homeschool resource guide (see chapter 4), then this local information guide can also be added to the collection.

   Because many homeschooling collections are created and developed by the children's department, many only cover up through the sixth grade level. If your library has an existing homeschooling collection that covers these ages, then you can expand the collection to include the middle and high school levels.

   Homeschooling collections may only include general homeschooling resources, while other collections include representative nonfiction resources and fiction titles. Although many homeschooling families limit their fiction reading to inspirational fiction or gentle reading, make sure that you truly understand your own community of homeschoolers. It might be best to leave the fiction titles in the collections where they are usually held and create guides at the request of your homeschooling families.

- *Create a homeschooling resource center.* If you have an appropriate space and appropriate financial resources, you can pull materials out of your existing collection and create a special homeschooling resource center. A true homeschooling resource center would include all age ranges, both fiction and nonfiction titles, as well as a variety of formats including computer software, audiobooks, and realia.

A HOMESCHOOLING TEEN'S DREAM COLLECTION

When we surveyed families with homeschooling teens, we asked them what kinds of materials they currently use and which resources they would wish to find in their library's collection. Keep in mind that the best way to determine the wants and needs of your own community is to ask them. For ideas on surveying your community, see chapter 7.

Here are collection ideas that come directly from homeschooling families:

- *Homeschooling Books:* Any basic homeschooling collection would contain the titles about homeschooling that are designed for new homeschooling families or those considering it. There are now many excellent resources specifically addressing homeschooling teenagers. Our respondents recommended Llewellyn's *Teenage Liberation Handbook* time and time again. One respondent requested that libraries collect homeschooling success stories and testimonials. Turn to chapter 8 for an annotated listing of materials that would surely satisfy the homeschoolers' requests for appropriate materials for families who homeschool teens.
- *Textbooks:* Copies of texts used at the local public and private schools can be helpful to your homeschooling teens, as well as to traditional students who may have misplaced their copy or left it at school where it cannot be readily retrieved. You might also seek out textbooks that are being used at the local college or university for basic courses. Before you start, be sure to look carefully at your collection development policy, since many libraries specifically exclude textbooks from their collections. Textbooks can outdate very quickly and new texts are chosen on a regular basis. The cost to keep up a textbook collection is an expensive proposition, especially if they get checked out and are never returned.
- *Prepared Curricula:* Many homeschooling families prefer to design their home study using prepared curricula from a variety of vendors. Some homeschoolers use one vendor or curriculum exclu-

sively, while other homeschoolers pick and choose from several vendors depending on the topics they want to study. This can be expensive, and many parents wish there were a way they could "try out" the curricula before buying their own. Because many prepared curricula are designed for single-student use and are created with workbooks and worksheets, it is impractical for libraries to purchase these materials to lend. Instead of purchasing the curricula, though, libraries could collect donated, used curricula for patrons to evaluate the product before they purchase their own. Another option is to purchase portions of the curricula, for example, the student's text without the additional teacher's edition, workbooks, or worksheets.

- *College Preparatory Materials:* College guides and resources that help prepare for the ACT and SAT were requested by several of our respondents. Specifically, Cafi Cohen's *And What about College* and Herbert Kohl's *The Question is College* were suggested titles.
- *Curriculum Guides:* Books that guide homeschoolers to age-appropriate subject areas and unit studies are very helpful to homeschooling families. In addition, specific curriculum guides used at the local public and private schools can be collected to offer your patrons an idea of what their peers are studying and the sequence in which they are studying them. These curriculum guides will also be helpful to librarians when creating guides to the collection for homeschoolers.
- *Nonfiction:* Specific areas of interest mentioned by our survey respondents include geography, history, social science, as well as creationism. In addition to educational titles that might be used, either as a text or even for pleasure reading, many homeschooling families stated they would like to see more Christian nonfiction and biographies in their library collections.
- *Fiction:* Our respondents requested more classic fiction titles, as well as inspirational and historic fiction. Genre guides to the juvenile, young adult, and adult collections can be created with these suggestions in mind. Christian fiction authors that may be of interest to homeschooling teens include: Judy Baer, Shirley Brinkerhoff, Robin Jones Gunn, Tim LaHaye, Beverly Lewis, Gilbert Morris, Janette Oke, Frank Peretti, Nancy Rue, Patricia Rushford, and Lauraine Snelling.
- *Homeschooling Magazines:* A common request from our survey respondents was for specific homeschooling magazine titles as well as a wider variety of magazines to choose from. Your collection likely contains many periodical titles that may be of use to your homeschooling teens, so be sure to keep these in mind when creating collection guides for your patrons. Magazines like *National Geo-*

graphic, Sky and Telescope, and *Writer's Digest* are just a few titles that can be easily used to create a study topic or activity. Unfortunately, one well-loved homeschooling magazine, *Growing Without Schooling,* ceased publication with the November/December 2001 issue. Other periodicals homeschoolers may enjoy include:

Backwoods Home Magazine
http://www.backwoodshome.com/
P.O. Box 712
Gold Beach, OR 97444
Phone: (800) 835-2418
Fax: (541) 247-8600

California Homeschooler
http://www.hsc.org
Homeschool Association of California
P.O. Box 77873
Corona, CA 92877
Phone: (888) 472-4440

Education Revolution Magazine (formerly the AERO-GRAMME)
The Alternative Education Resource Organization
http://www.educationrevolution.org/aeromagazine.html
417 Roslyn Road
Roslyn Heights, NY 11577
Phone: (800) 769-4171

Home Education Magazine
http://www.home-ed-magazine.com/
Home Education Press
P.O. Box 1083
Tonasket, WA 98855
Phone: (800) 236-3278
Fax: (509) 486-2753

Home Educator's Family Times
http://www.homeeducator.com/FamilyTimes/
P.O. Box 708
Gray, Maine 04039
Phone: (888) 300-8434
Fax: (207) 657-2404

Home School Advantage
P.O. Box 8190
Phoenix, AZ 85066

Home School Court Report
http://www.hslda.org/
Home School Legal Defense Association
P.O. Box 3000
Purcellville, VA 20134
Phone: (540) 338-5600
Fax: (540) 338-2733

Home School Digest
http://www.homeschooldigest.com/
Wisdom's Gate
P.O. Box 374-www
Covert, MI 49043

Home School Researcher
http://www.nheri.org/
National Home Education Research Institute
P.O. Box 13939
Salem, OR 97309
Phone: (503) 364-1490
Fax: (503) 364-2827

Homeschooling Today
http://www.homeschooltoday.com
P.O. Box 436
Barker, TX 77413
Phone: (281) 492-6050
Fax: (281) 201-7620

Jewish Home Educator's Network Newsletter
http://www.snj.com/jhen/
J.H.E.N.
c/o Lisa Hodge Kander
2122 Houser
Holly, MI 48442

Natural Life
http://www.life.ca/
Life Media

P.O. Box 112
Niagara Falls, NY 14304
Phone: (800) 215-9574

The Old Schoolhouse Magazine
http://www.theoldhomeschoolhouse.com/
P.O. Box 185
Cool, CA 95614
Phone: (530) 823-0447

Practical Homeschooling
http://www.home-school.com
Home Life, Inc.
1731 Smizer Mill Road
Fenton, MO 63026
Phone: (800) 346-6322
Fax: (636) 225-0743

SALT Magazine
http://www.saltmagazine.com/
2131 W. Republic Road #177
Springfield, MO 65807

Teaching Home: A Christian Magazine for Home Educators
http://www.teachinghome.com/
Box 20219
Portland, OR 97294
Phone: (503) 253-9633
Fax: (503) 253-7345

Unless The Lord...Magazine
http://www.unlessthelordmagazine.com/
27959 Mellman Rd.
Hempstead, TX 77445

- *Audio Materials:* Homeschoolers seem to prefer unabridged audio-books. A well-rounded nonfiction audiobook collection paired with classics and inspirational fiction would likely please many of your homeschoolers. In addition to audiobooks, our respondents also stated that they use music CDs with their studies. A music collection featuring international music, classical music, and instrumental titles can be integrated into many areas of a teen's studies. Finally, audio materials used to learn a new language would be helpful, as well as self-help materials for personal growth, business skills, and job skills. One resource that may prove helpful in selecting and promoting audio materials to conservative Christian patrons is the magazine titled *Plugged In: Helping Parents and Youth Leaders Guide Teens through the World of Popular Youth Culture*. This title is produced by Focus on the Family and includes a "Chart Watch" that reviews CDs and evaluates genre, chart action (number of copies sold, etc.), pro-social content, objectionable content, and a summary/advisory. This review source also includes a section reviewing Christian groups, as well as reviews of movies that are "now playing" and on the "video shelf." Select reviews are available at the Web site http://www.pluggedinonline.com/.

- *Video Materials:* Educational/nonfiction videos make up a good portion of many homeschooled teen studies. Your more conservative families may also prefer classic movies to more recent movies due to content. At a time when many libraries are making the shift from videocassettes to DVDs, though, be aware that your homeschoolers may not embrace the switch. A survey of your homeschoolers may include a question about video format preferences so that materials traditionally circulated to the homeschooling community can be purchased in a format they can actually use.

- *Computer Programs:* Circulating educational CD-ROMs would be greatly appreciated by homeschooling teens. Computer software used to study a new language, learn a new skill, or brush up for tests (proficiency tests, ACT, SAT) would all be ideal packages to promote to your homeschooling teens.

- *Scientific Equipment:* Students attending traditional school have access to scientific and lab equipment that many homeschoolers never have an opportunity to use. Microscopes, slides, weights and measures, and telescopes are just a small selection of equipment that would supplement what homeschooling teens could learn using books and videos. Purchase of such equipment is another expensive proposition, but is ideal for grant opportunities.

- *Art Prints:* The illustrations that accompany art books are satisfactory for browsing, but seeing a masterpiece in a book is not ideal for in-depth study. Many homeschoolers travel to art museums for their art study, but this is not always an option for viewing many pieces of art. A collection of art prints or posters would allow homeschooling teens to view major works to study or compare.

ANTICIPATING CHALLENGES

If you decide to pursue a special collection for your homeschooling teens, it would be wise to explore any possible challenges that may arise.

If you have taken steps to keep your staff and patrons informed of your intentions to serve the homeschooling teen community, you will likely not experience any difficulties with your collection. Anticipating conflicts that might arise is only to be prepared and able to act swiftly and in your library's best interest. Depending on how you decide to organize your materials for homeschooling teens and their parents, there are some possible conflicts that you might experience:

- *If you build a special collection for homeschoolers, other groups will demand special collections.* Instead of creating a collection with just homeschoolers in mind, include materials that would be of interest to all educators. Consider calling the collection a "teaching/ learning collection" and not a homeschooling collection. Patrons will feel more comfortable with a collection that is not exclusive to a single population in your community.
- *Lending periods will be challenged.* If you offer extended lending periods to your homeschoolers, other patrons might complain about materials being unavailable for too long or demand that they receive the same extended lending periods. One possible solution would be to offer extended lending periods based on the materials, not the patron. For example, if you have textbooks in your homeschooling collection, perhaps these items could have extended lending periods regardless of who checks them out. The drawback is that if you have a small collection of materials with long lending periods your collection can be depleted rather quickly. Additionally, when you lend an item for a longer period of time you reduce the number of possible circulations on that item, thus decreasing your circulation number. You could keep the lending period the same as other materials, and instead increase the number of renewals allowed. All in all, extended lending periods would be greatly appreciated and respected by your homeschooling teens and their parents, but it may cause a conflict with other patrons when they are not allowed the same benefit or when they are waiting for those materials to be returned.
- *Budgets may not support an additional special collection.* You may decide to start your homeschooling collection by pulling out materials from your existing collections. If this is the case, how will you continue to develop this collection? Will special funds be designated for future upkeep of this collection? You may have started your homeschooling collection by obtaining a grant. Will your library be required to match a percentage of funds or earmark funds in the future in support of the collection? These are not challenges, exactly. Instead they are considerations that need

to be addressed when creating the collection. When libraries experience cuts in collection funding, they usually look to special collections to be curtailed first. How will you justify funding the collection in times when spending needs to be cut? Perhaps during times of fiscal restraint you can pursue additional grant monies or donations to keep the homeschooling collection current and thriving.

- *Homeschoolers may challenge the content of the collection.* To avoid challenges of content in the collection, try involving homeschooling teens and parents in the development of the collection. If you allow homeschooling teen participation, either by teen advisory board input, focus groups, or via a suggestion box or survey, you empower them to make some of the decisions and assume some of the responsibility for the content of the collection. Of course you cannot allow them to make all the decisions, but by allowing them to offer their opinions and suggestions you might avoid future challenges.

- *Homeschoolers will want inappropriate materials in the collection.* We have heard from other librarians that there is a concern that if a library begins to develop services and collections for homeschoolers, they will insist on having exclusively conservative and Christian materials in the collection. Additionally, homeschoolers have requested that libraries collect materials (e.g., textbooks from the 1960s, or materials that contain inaccurate or misleading information) that would be in opposition to collection development policies. Regardless of how you decide to approach developing your homeschooling collection, you will need to follow your library's collection development policy. It is that policy that will protect the collection if there are challenges or questions about what materials you decide not to add. When in doubt, you could offer to interlibrary loan the materials that are not in your collection if your homeschooling patrons insist on pursuing titles your library does not feel are appropriate for your collection.

- *Materials pulled out of the regular collection and placed in the homeschooling collection are not as available to non-homeschooling patrons.* Unfortunately, this is a common side effect of starting a special collection. Whenever you pull materials out of the existing collection and place them in a new area, those items are now lost to those who are browsing the general collection for resources. Many of our teen patrons find their materials by browsing. What could you do? Some libraries employ the use of book dummies to direct users to the special collection, but this can be cumbersome to keep up and often still leads users to dead ends (for example, if a patron is directed to the homeschooling collection only to find that an item is already checked out). The best possible solution, but not always the most efficient, is to have multiple copies of the same book, one in the general collection and one in the homeschooling collection. Since this is not a likely solution for a start-up collection, then perhaps booklists or bookmarks can be placed on the shelves of the general collection listing additional titles of interest that can be found in the homeschooling collection.

- *There just isn't enough space for an additional special collection.* This is a challenge faced by many libraries. Many young adult librarians experience difficulties justifying the space used for young adults. The last thing we want to do is give up some of that precious space for a new collection. Fortunately, you can start small. Also, consider acquiring space in the adult collection area. Because a homeschooling collection will be helpful to parents as well as their teens, and because homeschooling teens are usually already used to browsing the adult nonfiction collection, it would make sense to start with a single shelf or two in the adult nonfiction collection, perhaps near your biography collection. You might even consider starting the collection on a cart and experiment with placement to see where it gets the most attention. Either way, start small and see what happens!

COLLECTION DEVELOPMENT FOR HOMESCHOOLING TEENS AND THEIR PARENTS

Many of the same decisions and steps that went into starting a young adult collection apply to collection development for homeschooling teens and their parents:

1. *Examine your library's collection development policy.* Your collection development policy should be clear about what materials and formats can be added to the library collection. How does this relate to your ideas for developing collections with homeschooling teens in mind? How exhaustively will you collect these materials, which age levels will be included, and who will be responsible for the continued development of the resources? If this information is not currently in your policy you will need to take steps to have this information added. Without clear answers to these questions you will find it difficult to respond to challenges. Review the policy on an annual basis and make any changes that reflect changes made to the collection.

2. *Decide what materials will be included in the collection.* A basic home-schooling collection can be simple and include only resources on the history of homeschooling and homeschooling guidebooks. A more extensive homeschooling collection with teens and their parents in mind would also include age-appropriate nonfiction titles. A comprehensive homeschooling collection would also include fiction, audio and video materials, and more (see section on a Homeschooling Teen's Dream Collection for specific ideas). Most libraries will likely want to start with a core of home-schooling guidebooks, homeschooling magazines, curriculum guides, and basic textbooks. Other materials can then be high-lighted with pathfinders and bibliographies.

3. *Examine your existing collection.* What materials do you already have on homeschooling? Do you have any materials on homeschooling teenagers? These items can be the first items to be moved to your new collection. Your adult, young adult, and children's nonfiction collections may include basic materials in various topic areas (history, math, science, literature) that would make valuable resources to be promoted to your homeschooling teens.

4. *Identify sources for funding.* If you do not have resources you can rightly pull from existing collections or if you would like to start out with a new core collection, you will probably want to start looking for funds. If you're patient, you will be able to purchase items throughout the year out of the existing collections budgets, or you can request a separate allocation of funds or line item. But if your intention is to develop a core collection at once, chances are you will need to look for funds outside of your library's budget. Some options include:

   • *Donations:* Ask members of homeschooling organizations to donate used books or ask for funds to start a core collection. If you request donations of used books, though, you might not be able to add some of them to the collection due to condition or content. Asking for used books and not using them in the collection may cause a conflict. Provide patrons with a copy of your donations policy at the time they drop off donated materials.

   • *Fundraising:* A cooperative fundraising event could be held to raise funds for a core collection of materials. The library can work side by side with local homeschooling organizations to plan and implement a single fundraising event or a series of events. You will likely find that homeschooling organizations and the homeschooling community would wholeheartedly support a used book sale or car wash if it meant that the library would purchase a collection of materials with them in mind.

- *Grants:* Grants are not as hard to come by as you might think. Yes, there is a possibility that a great deal of time and effort might be spent preparing a grant proposal only to be passed over for another library or community agency. The good news is that once you've prepared the grant, it can be recycled, improved, and submitted at another time. If you first don't succeed with a grant, rewrite it and resubmit it. A single grant written to purchase inspirational fiction can be submitted to various agencies until you find a perfect match. Worthwhile grants will eventually be funded, so don't be discouraged if your first attempt doesn't reap the benefits you expected. Another consideration when writing grants is to determine the level of fund matching that will be expected by your library. Often grants require seed monies to be promised out of your library's budget, so make sure those funds are secured before you pursue these grants. Don't limit yourself to state or national grants. Often grants are readily available in your own backyard, so look to service organizations in your community. You may even have several grant-writing resources in your library collection. See the box below for possible ideas.

Resources for Library Grants

The Foundation Directory. New York: Foundation Center.
Grants for Libraries and Information Services. New York: Foundation Center.
Hoffman, Frank W., ed. *Grantsmanship for Small Libraries and School Library Media Centers.* Englewood, CO: Libraries Unlimited, 1999.
Swan, James. *Fundraising for Libraries: 25 Proven Ways to Get More Money for Your Library.* New York: Neal-Schuman Publishers, 2002.

---

5. *Identify new materials and formats to purchase.* Start out by looking through chapter 8 to identify specific titles to be added to your collection. To identify additional titles, contact the vendors listed in this chapter for catalogs, or visit their Web sites. If you have a selection of catalogs, invite your homeschooling teens and their parents to browse the catalogs and offer their suggestions about what titles might be useful to them and their peers.

6. *Create a collection of curriculum catalogs.* When parents or teens are just starting out with homeschooling, they may not be familiar with the many prepared curriculums that are available. Parents who are not new to homeschooling may find that the curricula they have used in the past only reach a certain age and they may

be looking for a curriculum to use with their older children and teens. By creating a curriculum catalog resource, whether it be in a cabinet drawer or simply a listing of Web sites and contacts, you will give them ideas about where to look for more information. It is impractical for libraries to actually collect curriculum materials to add to our collections since they usually include workbooks and worksheets that need to be completed by the homeschooler. Offering the resources to help choose a curriculum would be the next best thing.

- Many of these curriculums are Christian-oriented materials, but many non-Christian homeschoolers have been successfully purchasing only portions of curricula or just using the portions that apply to their situation.

- Many publishers have the full content of their catalogs online with online purchasing available. It has been our experience, though, that having the actual catalog makes it easier to browse and compare the publishers.

- Be sure to keep the collection of catalogs current as prices and content can change on a regular basis.

- Some standard curriculum publishers include:

A Beka Book: Excellence in Education from a Christian Perspective
http://www.abeka.com/
P.O. Box 19100
Pensacola, FL 32523-9100
Phone: (877) 223-5226
Fax: (800) 874-3590

Alpha Omega Publications
http://www.aop.com/
300 North McKemy Avenue
Chandler, AZ 85226
Phone: (800) 622-3070

American Home-School Publishing
http://www.ahsp.com/
5310 Affinity Court
Centreville, VA 20120-4145
Phone: (800) 684-2121
Fax: (800) 557-0234

Apologia Educational Ministries (science)
http://www.highschoolscience.com/
1106 Meridian Plaza, Suite 220
Anderson, IN 46016
Phone: (888) 524-4724
Fax: (765) 608-3290

Beautiful Feet Books (history through literature)
http://www.bfbooks.com/
139 Main Street
Sandwich, MA 02563
Phone: (800) 889-1978
Fax: (508) 833-2770

Bob Jones University Press
http://www.bjup.com/
Greenville, SC 29614-0062
Phone: (800) 845-5731
Fax: (800) 525-8398

Castle Heights Press, Inc. (laboratory science materials)
http://www.castleheightspress.com
2562 Montebello Drive
San Antonio, TX 78259
Phone: (800) 763-7148

Castlemoyle Books
http://www.castlemoyle.com/
P.O. Box 520
Pomeroy, WA 99347-0520
Phone: (888) 773-5586
Fax: (509) 843-3183

Catholic Heritage Curricula
http://www.chcweb.com/
P.O. Box 125
Twain Harte, CA 95383
Phone: (800) 490-7713
Fax: (209) 586-0132

Christian Liberty Press
http://ebiz.netopia.com/clpress
502 West Euclid Ave.
Arlington Heights, IL 60004
Phone: (847) 259-4444, Press 6

Core Curriculum of America (offers secular and Christian curriculum)
http://core-curriculum.com/
14503 S. Tamiami Trail
North Port, FL 34287
Phone: (888) 689-4626

The Cornerstone Curriculum Project
http://www.CornerstoneCurriculum.com
2006 Flat Creek
Richardson, TX 75080
Phone: (972) 235-5149

Curriculum Services
http://www.curriculumservices.com
26801 Pine Avenue
Bonita Springs, FL 34135
Phone: (877) 702-1419
Fax: (239) 992-6473

Hewitt Homeschooling Resources
http://hewitthomeschooling.com/
P.O. Box 9
Washougal, WA 98671
Phone: (800) 890-4097
Fax: (360) 835-8697

Judah Bible Curriculum
http://www.judahbible.com/
P.O. Box 122
Urbana, IL 61803
Phone: (217) 344-5672

Konos, Inc.
http://www.konos.com
P.O. Box 250

Anna, TX 75409
Phone: (972) 924-2712
Fax: (972) 924-2733

Math-U-See
http://www.mathusee.com/
829 Temperance Hall Road
Ringgold, GA 30736
Phone: (888) 854-6284

MeetTheMasters.com (art curriculum and art supplies)
http://www.meetthemasters.com/
15 Calle Merecida
San Clemente, CA 92673
Phone: (866) MTM-4ART
Fax: (949) 481-8566

Oak Meadow
http://www.oakmeadow.com/
P.O. Box 740
Putney, VT 05346
Phone: (802) 387-2021
Fax: (802) 387-5108

Power-Glide Foreign Language Courses
http://www.power-glide.com/
1682 West 820 North
Provo, UT 84601
Phone: (800) 596-0910
Fax: (801) 343-3912

Progeny Press (study guides for literature from a Christian perspective)
http://www.progenypress.com/
P.O. Box 100
Fall Creek, WI 54742
Phone: (877) 776-4369

Robinson Curriculum (printable curriculum books delivered on CDs)
http://www.robinsoncurriculum.com/
3321 Sesame Dr.

Howell, MI 48843
Phone: (517) 546-8780
Fax: (517) 546-8730

Rod and Staff Publishers, Inc.
http://www.anabaptists.org/ras/
P.O. Box 3, Hwy. 172
Crockett, KY 41413-0003 USA
Phone: (606) 522-4348
Fax: (800) 643-1244

Rosetta Stone (foreign language)
http://www.rosettastone.com/
135 W. Market St.
Harrisonburg, VA 22801
Phone: (800) 788-0822
Fax: (540) 432-0953

Saxon Homeschool
http://www.saxonhomeschool.com/
2600 John Saxon Blvd.
Norman, OK 73071
Phone: (800) 284-7019

Sonlight Curriculum, Ltd.
http://www.sonlight.com/
8042 South Grant Way
Littleton, CO 80122-2705
Phone: (303) 730-6292
Fax: (303) 795-8668

Sycamore Tree
http://www.sycamoretree.com/
2179 Meyer Place
Costa Mesa, CA 92627
Phone (Orders): (800) 779-6750
Phone: (714) 668-1343
Fax: (714) 668-1344

TOPS Learning Systems, Inc. (science curricula and materials)
http://www.topscience.org/
10970 S. Mulino Rd.

Canby, OR 97013
Phone (orders only): (888) 773-9755
Phone: (503) 263-2040
Fax: (503) 266-5200

TRISMS (Time Related Integrated Studies for Mastering Skills)
http://www.trisms.com/
1203 S. Delaware Place
Tulsa, OK 74104-4129
Phone: (918) 585-2778

Veritas Press
http://www.veritaspress.com/
1250 Belle Meade Drive
Lancaster, PA 17601
Phone: (800) 922-5082

Winston Grammar
http://www.winstongrammar.com/
18403 NE 111th Avenue
Battle Ground, WA 98604
Phone: (360) 687-0282
Fax: (360) 666-2511

Writing Strands / National Writing Institute
http://www.writingstrands.com/
624 W. University, #248
Denton, TX 76201-1889
Phone: (800) 688-5375
Fax: (888) 663-7855

7. *Create a collection of catalogs from independent learning schools.* As homeschoolers move beyond the elementary years, parents may begin investigating independent study schools for their teens. Create a collection of catalogs from various independent study schools or offer a list with Web sites and contact information.

- Keep in mind that not all independent study schools are accredited, so direct your patrons to pay special attention to this in order to find a good match for their individual goals.

- Keep any catalog collection current. Tuition and fees can change dramatically from year to year.

- These schools may be called many things: independent learning schools, correspondence schools, online schools, or umbrella schools. Here are some schools to include in your catalog collection:

Active Learning Academy
http://my-ala.com/
14503 S. Tamiami Trail
North Port, FL 34287
Phone: (941) 235-2077

Alger Learning Center & Independence High School
http://www.independent-learning.com/
121 Alder Dr.
Sedro-Woolley, WA 98284
Phone: (800) 595-2630
Fax: (360) 595-1141

Alpha Omega Academy
http://www.aop.com/
300 N. McKemy Ave.
Chandler, AZ 85226
Phone: (800) 682-7396
Fax: (480) 893-6112

The American School
http://www.americanschoolofcorr.com/
2200 East 170th Street
Lansing, IL 60438
Phone: (800) 531-9268

Branford Grove School
http://www.branfordgrove.com/home.html
P.O. Box 341172
Arleta, CA 91334
Phone: (818) 890-0350
Fax: (818) 890-6440

Calvert School
http://home.calvertschool.org/
10713 Gilroy Road, Suite B
Hunt Valley, MD 21031
Phone: (888) 487-4652
Fax: (410) 785-3418

Christa McAuliffe Academy
http://www.cmacademy.org/
2520 W. Washington Avenue
Yakima, WA 98903
Phone: (509) 575-4989
Fax: (509) 575-4976

Christian Liberty Academy School System (CLASS)
http://class-homeschools.org/
502 W. Euclid Avenue
Arlington Heights, IL 60004-5495
Phone: (800) 348-0899 (for information pack request)

Clonlara School
http://www.clonlara.org/
1289 Jewett
Ann Arbor, MI 48104
Phone: (734) 769-4511
Fax: (734) 769-9629

Eldorado Academy
http://www.eldoradoacademy.org/
P.O. Box 190
Nederland, CO 80466
Phone: (303) 604-2822
Fax: (303) 258-3541

Grace Academy
http://www.thegraceacademy.org/
10 Shurs Lane
Philadelphia, PA 19127
Phone: (215) 487-3700

Home School Academy
http://www.homeschoolacademy.com/
334 2nd Street
Catasauqua, PA 18032-2501
Phone: (800) 863-1474
Fax: (610) 266-7817

Home Study International
http://www.hsi.edu
P.O. Box 4437

Silver Spring, MD 20914-4437
Phone: (800) 782-4769
Fax: (301) 680-5157

Indiana University School of Continuing Studies
http://scs.indiana.edu
790 E. Kirkwood Avenue
Bloomington, IN 47405-7101
Phone: (800) 334-1011
Fax: (812) 855-8997

Keystone National High School
http://www.keystonehighschool.com
School House Station
420 West Fifth St.
Bloomsburg, PA 17815
Phone: (800) 255-4937
Fax: (570) 784-2129

Laurel Springs School
http://www.laurelsprings.com/
P.O. Box 1440
Ojai, CA 93024-1440
Phone: (800) 377-5890

Oak Meadow School
http://www.oakmeadow.com
P.O. Box 740
Putney, VT 05346
Phone: (802) 387-2021
Fax: (802) 387-5108

Seton Home Study School (Catholic)
http://www.setonhome.org/
1350 Progress Drive
Front Royal, VA 22630
Phone: (540) 636-9990
Fax: (540) 636-1602
* Site includes store to purchase standardized tests and books
used in the curriculum.

Sycamore Tree
http://www.sycamoretree.com/
2179 Meyer Place
Costa Mesa, CA 92627
Phone: (714) 668-1343
Orders: (800) 779-6750
Fax: (714) 668-1344

Texas Tech University—Extended Studies
http://www.dce.ttu.edu
P.O. Box 42191
Lubbock, TX 79409-2191
Phone: (800) 692-6877
Fax: (806) 742-7222

University of Nebraska at Lincoln Independent Study High School
http://nebraskahs.unl.edu/
P.O. Box 888400
Lincoln, NE 68588-8400
Phone: (866) 700-4747
Fax: (402) 472-1901

West River Academy
http://www.geocities.com/wracademy/
779 Jasmine Court
Grand Junction, CO 81506
Phone: (970) 241-4137

RESOURCES FOR HOMESCHOOLING COLLECTION DEVELOPMENT
Publishers of Nonfiction Titles

Barron's Educational Series, Inc.
http://www.barronseduc.com/
250 Wireless Blvd.
Hauppauge, NY 11788
Phone: (800) 645-3476
Fax: (631) 434-3723

Barron's offers titles on test preparation, college guides, career guides, language books, and many titles in their "the easy way" subject series.

Chelsea House Publishers
http://www.chelseahouse.com/
1974 Sproul Road, Suite 400
Broomall, PA 19008
Phone: (800) 848-BOOK
Fax: (877) 780-7300

From the Web site: "an abundance of biographies, social studies, health, multicultural studies, and many other types of books for children and young adults, as well as hundreds of volumes of literary criticism and references for older readers."

Chelsea House has many biography series. Other series include:

- 21st Century Health & Wellness
- Basic Domestic Pet Library
- Basic Domestic Reptiles and Amphibians
- Battles that Changed the World
- Behind the Camera (directory biographies)
- Bloom's Literary Criticism (Major Poets, Major Short Story Writers, Major Dramatists, Modern Critical Interpretations, etc.)
- Creation of the Modern Middle East (country studies)
- The G.I. Series: The Illustrated History of the American Soldier, His Uniform, and His Equipment
- Heroes of the Faith
- Insects and Spiders
- Introducing Composers
- Invertebrates
- Invisible World (biology series)
- Modern World Nations
- Natural Disasters
- Point / Counterpoint
- Popular Cat / Dog Library
- Religions of Humanity
- World Exploration

The College Board Publications
http://www.collegeboard.com/
P.O. Box 869010
Plano, TX 75074
Phone: (800) 323-7155
Fax: (888) 321–7183

Purchase test preparation guides, guides to colleges and financial aid, careers, and CLEP study guides.

Facts on File
http://www.factsonfile.com/
132 W. 31st Street, 17th Floor
New York, NY 10001
Phone: (800) 322-8755
Fax: (800) 678-3633

Publishers of the *Career Opportunities* and *Straight Talk* series; you will also find many excellent resources on nature, the arts, sciences, and history.

Grolier / Children's Press / Franklin Watts (divisions of Scholastic Library Publishing)
https://www.scholasticlibrary.com
90 Sherman Turnpike
Danbury, CT 06816
Phone: (800) 621-1115

These publishers cover a variety of nonfiction topics for grades K-12. Series include:

- America the Beautiful
- The American Religious Experience
- Armies of the Past
- Artists in Their Time
- Arts and Crafts Skills
- Cities of the World
- Documenting History
- Enchantment of the World
- Exploring Ecosystems

- Extraordinary People
- High Interest Books—Outdoor Life for Teens, Service Learning, Babysitting Smarts, Job Smarts, etc.
- In Their Own Voices
- In Their Own Words
- Lives in Science
- Native American Crafts
- Out of this World (History of NASA, Project Apollo, etc.)
- Physical Science Labs
- Projects for Young Scientists
- Science of the Past
- Speak Out, Write On (How to Write a Poem, How to Write a Term Paper, etc.)
- To the Young...(Filmmaker, Scientist, etc.)

DK Publishing
http://www.dk.com
375 Hudson St.
New York, NY 10014
Phone: (800) 788-6262
Fax: (800) 227-9604

Publisher of the much loved *Eyewitness* series; anyone familiar with DK books knows the presentation of facts is unsurpassed by any other series. Categories of titles include:

- Arts and Culture
- Business and Computers
- Food and Drink
- Health and Fitness
- History
- Home and Garden
- Maps and Atlases
- Religion and Spirituality
- Science and Nature
- Sports and Hobbies
- Travel

LifeMatters Books (a division of Capstone High Interest Books)
http://www.capstonepress.com
P.O. Box 669
Mankato, MN 56002-0669
Phone: (800) 747-4992
Fax: (888) 262-0705

From the Web site: "LifeMatters Books provide an abundance of health, wellness, and life skills information for today's teens. Each sixty-four-page book contains six to eight chapters. The text is written at a fourth- to sixth-grade reading level and has a seventh- to twelfth-grade interest level, allowing challenged readers and at-risk students to learn the same crucial life lessons as their peers."
Some of the series include:

- Career Exploration
- Careers without College
- Getting Ready for Careers
- Job Skills
- Life Skills
- Looking at Work
- Nutrition and Fitness

Christian Publishers and Resources

Bethany House Publishers / Baker Books
http://www.bethanyhouse.com/
P.O. Box 6287
Grand Rapids, MI 49516-6287
Phone: (800) 877-2665
Fax: (800) 398-3111

Christian Book Distributors
http://Christianbook.com
P.O. Box 7000
Peabody, MA 01961-7000
Phone: (800) 247-4784

Focus on the Family
http://www.family.org/resources/
8605 Explorer Drive
Colorado Springs, CO 80995
Phone: (800) 232-6459
Fax: (719) 531-3424

Moody Press
http://www.moodypublishers.org/
820 N. LaSalle Blvd.
Chicago, IL 60610
Phone: (800) 678-6928

Thomas Nelson, Inc.
http://www.thomasnelson.com/
P.O. Box 141000
Nashville, TN 37214
Phone: (800) 441-0511

Tyndale House Publishers, Inc.
http://www.tyndale.com/
351 Executive Drive
Carol Stream, IL 60188
Phone: (800) 323-9400
Fax: (800) 684-0247

Zondervan
http://www.zondervan.com/
5300 Patterson SE
Grand Rapids, MI 49530

Unabridged Audiobook Vendors

Blackstone Audio
http://www.blackstoneaudio.com
P.O. Box 969
Ashland, OR 97520
Phone: (800) 729-2665
Fax: (800) 482-9294

Books on Tape
http://www.booksontape.com/

P.O. Box 25122
Santa Ana, CA 92799-5122
Phone: (800) 88-BOOKS
Fax: (714) 825-0756

Recorded Books
http://www.recordedbooks.com/
270 Skipjack Road
Prince Frederick, MD 20678
Phone: (800) 636-3399
Fax: (410) 535-5499

Educational Video Vendors

PBS Video: Choose from award-winning films by Ken Burns, as well as titles in the American Experience series, and Frontline. PBS carries movies on history, arts, religion, culture, and much more, and all videos can be purchased with public performance rights.

http://shoppbs.org/
P.O. Box 751089
Charlotte, NC 28275
Phone: (800) 531-4727
Fax: (703) 739-8131

National Geographic Society: Choose from videos on nature, history, science, music, and more.

http://www.nationalgeographic.com
P.O. Box 10041
Des Moines, IA 50340-0014
Phone: (888) 225-5647
Fax: (888) 242-0531

Arts, Math, and Science Materials Resources

American Science and Surplus: From arts and crafts to batteries and electronics, this company offers many arts and science materials at affordable prices.

http://www.sciplus.com/
P.O. Box 1030

Skokie, IL 60076
Phone: (847) 647-0011
Fax: (800) 934-0722

Carolina Biological Supply Company: Purchase microscope sets, experiment kits, rocket kits, and more.

http://www.carolina.com/
2700 York Road
Burlington, NC 27215-3398
Phone: (800) 334-5551
Fax: (800) 222-7112

Delta Education: Purchase math and science hands-on learning kits.

http://www.delta-education.com
P.O. Box 3000
Nashua, NY 03061-3000
Phone: (800) 442-5444
Fax: (800) 282-9560

Edmund Scientifics: Purchase magnets, lab supplies, telescopes, as well as resources for anatomy, astronomy, engines, robotics, and more.

http://scientificsonline.com/
60 Pearce Ave.
Tonawanda, NY 14150-6711
Phone: (800) 728-6999
Fax: (800) 828-3299

Home Training Tools: Purchase science fair project materials, science kits, microscopes, telescopes, and curriculum materials.

http://www.hometrainingtools.com/
546 S. 18th St. W., Suite B
Billings, MT 59102
Phone: (800) 860-6272
Fax: (888) 860-2344

National Geographic Society: Purchase maps, globes, computer software, and science tools.

http://www.nationalgeographic.com
P.O. Box 10041

Des Moines, IA 50340-0014
Phone: (888) 225-5647
Fax: (888) 242-0531

Tobin's Lab, Inc.: Purchase microscopes, models, dissection kits, specimens, lab equipment, and more.

http://www.tobinslab.com
P.O. Box 725
Culpepper, VA 22701
Phone: (540) 937-7173

In addition to publishers that provide curriculum materials, there are many homeschooling book distributors. Collect these catalogs for your collection development and then make them available to homeschooling families.

Once you get onto a mailing list for a couple of catalogs you will find that other distributors' catalogs will start arriving. Some homeschooling materials distributors include:

Christian Book Distributors
http://Christianbook.com
P.O. Box 7000
Peabody, MA 01961-7000
Phone: (800) 247-4784

Critical Thinking Books & Software
http://www.CriticalThinking.com/
P.O. Box 448
Pacific Grove, CA 93950-0448
Phone: (800) 458-4849
Fax: (831) 393-3277

FUN Books
http://www.fun-books.com/
Dept. W
1688 Belhaven Woods Court
Pasadena, MD 21122-3727
Phone: (888) 386-7020

Lifetime Books and Gifts
http://www.lifetimebooksandgifts.com/

3900 Chalet Suzanne Drive
Lake Wales, FL 33859-6881
Phone (orders only): (800) 377-0390
Phone: (863) 676-6311
Fax: (863) 676-2732

Vision Forum, Inc.
http://www.visionforum.com
4719 Blanco Road
San Antonio, TX 78212-1015
Phone: (800) 440-0022
Fax: (210) 340-8577

FURTHER READING

Jones, Patrick, Patricia Taylor, and Kirsten Edwards. *A Core Collection for Young Adults.* New York: Neal-Schuman Publishers, 2003.
> Annotated listings of over 1,000 titles that make up a core collection of young adult titles. Adult and young adult titles in nonfiction, biography, and fiction, as well as Web sites and electronic formats are included.

Lewis, Marjorie, ed. *Outstanding Books for the College Bound.* Chicago: American Library Association, 1996.
> Chosen by the Young Adult Library Services Association's Outstanding Books for the College Bound Committees over the past thirty-five years, the titles listed in this book include over 1,000 annotated classic and contemporary titles broken into genre categories.

Pride, Mary, ed. *The Big Book of Home Learning.* Volume Three: Junior High to College. 4th ed. Fenton, MO: Home Life, c1999.
> This title is an excellent guide to developing a collection for homeschooling teens. Specific titles are reviewed for individual school subjects and contact information is provided for tracking down each product when available. Books, videos, audio materials and games are all included. In addition to the wealth of collection information, the appendices include a suggested course of study for junior and senior high school, a suggested classical reading list, GED requirements by state, and graduation requirements. The chapters on taking PSAT, SAT, ACT, GED, AP, and CLEP tests, as well as college and career preparation make this guide one of the most helpful for homeschooling teens and the librarians that serve them.

Walker, Barbara J. *Developing Christian Fiction Collections for Children and Adults: Selection Criteria and a Core Collection.* New York: Neal-Schuman Publishers, 1998.
> Along with helpful insights into developing collections with a special population in mind, Walker offers annotated lists of recommended titles for a core young adult Christian fiction collection. Includes a list of Christian fiction publishers.

6

◆ ◆ ◆

SUCCESS DEPENDS ON HOW YOU BAIT YOUR HOOK: GREAT PROGRAMS FOR HOMESCHOOLING TEENS

GETTING STARTED AND PROGRAM PLANNING

Programming is the most visible way to reach out to your homeschooling teen population. Unfortunately, it is also usually the most expensive and most time-consuming. Whether you plan to offer educational programs or opportunities for recreation, once you consider your time, the time of staff, marketing, and supplies (including occasional prizes), the costs can really add up. The goal with programming is to get the most bang for your buck.

Although programming in general can become a burden on your time and budget, many YA librarians find it to be the most rewarding part of their job. Programming allows you to interact with your young adult patrons, connecting the love of reading with so many other hobbies and interests. While exploring ideas for programs for teen patrons, it's not unusual for the librarian to pick up a new skill or an undiscovered talent along the way. There may be frustrations (zero attendance for the book discussion that the teen advisory board insisted they would all attend) or unexpected results (feet that were dyed red from retrieving marbles out of strawberry Jell-O). As with much of life, these occasional frustrations can be turned into learning experiences if you are willing to try again.

If this is the first time you have ventured into the world of programming for teens, there are many resources that will help you get started. (See the "Further Reading" section at the end of this chapter for ideas.) After years of experimenting, listening to experts, ignoring the experts, and "learning the hard way," here are some general tips we've learned along the way:

Use a Program Planning Worksheet and Checklist

Borrow a program planning worksheet from a colleague, or start with the examples provided in this chapter (Figures 6.1–6.3). You may want to have a planning worksheet for programs that do not include an outside speaker (Figure 6.1) and one for programs that feature an outside speaker or performer (Figure 6.2). Once you discover the steps that you must follow for your own library, you can create a worksheet of your own. A well-designed worksheet, whether it's a print copy or electronic version, will remind you of easily forgotten but essential steps of planning your program (Figure 6.3). It's so easy to forget to book the meeting room or ask the clerk treasurer to cut a check for a performer when you're arranging so many other aspects of a program. When you have several people (staff, teen board members, or volunteers) involved in the planning and implementation of your programs, the worksheet helps you keep track of individual responsibilities and deadlines. You may not need to address all of the steps for every program since each one will have various elements, so you can begin your planning by crossing out the parts of the worksheet that don't apply, creating a feeling of accomplishment before you've even lifted a finger!

Create a Program Portfolio

You may discover that you want to repeat programs on a regular basis. Keep copies of your completed program planning worksheets in a binder or on your computer so that you can refer to past programs as needed. After your program is completed, you can place copies of promotional materials, handouts, and evaluations with your worksheet and create a program portfolio.

A well-organized program portfolio can be helpful during performance appraisals, future job interviews, and while sharing ideas with other librarians. You'll create a network of grateful colleagues when you can provide examples of successful programs when needed. Even those less

Figure 6.1
Program Planning Sheet (Without Performer)

Program Title:	
Date:	Time:
Audience:	Limit:
Description:	
Support of Library's Mission:	
Location:	Room Setup:
Supplies (on hand):	Supplies (needed):
Estimated Costs: ■ Time: ■ Supplies:	Source of Funding:
Evaluation Plan:	

successful programs are worth revisiting, so be sure to keep those in your portfolio as well.

Generate Ideas

When trying to generate ideas for teen programs, you don't need to rely solely on your own ideas. There is a wealth of resources from which to pool ideas: programming manuals (interlibrary loan them if you don't

Figure 6.2
Program Planning Sheet (Featuring Performer)

Program Title:	
Date:	Time:
Audience:	Limit:
Description:	
Support of Library's Mission:	
Speaker / Performer Name:	
Phone:	Fax:
Address:	E-mail:
Contract details:	
Location:	Room Setup:

Supplies (on hand):	Supplies (from performer):	Supplies (needed):

Estimated Costs: ■ Time: ■ Supplies: ■ Performer:	Sources of Funding:
Evaluation Plan:	

Figure 6.3
Program Planning Checklist

Program Title:
Scheduling Checklist:
☐   Registration form at reference desk ☐   Registration begins: ☐   Registration ends:
☐   Meeting room reserved
☐   Recorded on library staff master calendar ☐   Recorded on library Web site calendar ☐   Recorded on library newsletter events calendar ☐   Recorded on department calendar ☐   Recorded on personal calendar
☐   Staff scheduled for program: ☐   Staff scheduled for desk coverage:
Marketing Checklist:
☐   Press release written ☐   Press release faxed to newspaper ☐   Press release faxed to high schools for announcements ☐   Press release faxed to junior high schools for announcements ☐   Press release provided to Friends newsletter ☐   Press release mailed to homeschooling association ☐   Press release e-mailed to young adult list ☐   Modified press release submitted to cable network bulletin board / crawl
☐   Poster created (Total # ____) ☐   Poster posted on library events board ☐   Poster posted at grocery stores ☐   Poster posted at bookstores
☐   Flier / Handbill created (Total # ____) ☐   Fliers at circulation desk (# ____) ☐   Fliers delivered to churches for bulletins (# ____) ☐   Fliers delivered to schools (# ____)

(continued)

**Figure 6.3
(Continued)**

☐ Fliers mailed to Boys and Girls Clubs (# ____)   ☐ Fliers mailed to YMCAs (# ____)   ☐ Fliers mailed to other organizations or agencies:
☐ Invitations created (Total # ____)   ☐ Invitations mailed to youth advisory board
☐ Newspapers contacted to cover the event
☐ Display set up (Date: _____)   ☐ Display to be taken down (Date: _____)
Performer Checklist:
☐ Payment arranged with treasurer   ☐ Payment made / mailed (date):   ☐ Confirmation made (date / details):   ☐ Map / directions to library sent (date):
Gratitude Checklist:
☐ Thank-you notes to volunteers   ☐ Thank-you notes to staff   ☐ Thank-you notes to performers
Evaluation:
Total registration:
Total attendance:
Total # survey responses:
Summary of responses:
Total cost: ▪ Staff Hours: ▪ Volunteer Hours: ▪ Supplies:
Notes on how to improve program if repeated:

have them in your collection or borrow from your colleagues), library Web sites, homeschooler Web sites, and library listservs. Many traditional young adult programs will translate well to your homeschooling teen participants.

Better yet, try to create opportunities to ask the teens themselves what kinds of programs they would like to attend, and when. This doesn't have to be a formal process. Try chatting with your homeschoolers in the stacks or ask the circulation staff to chat with homeschoolers when they are checking out materials. Ideas that might sound fun to you may be the last thing a homeschooling teen would like to attend. Don't forget to ask the homeschoolers' parents. They can probably offer several ideas on the spot.

The young adult librarian's best idea generator will always be a teen advisory group. If you plan on sharing your homeschool programming ideas with your teen board, though, you should have a representative number of homeschoolers on your board. Non-homeschooling teens will not likely be able to predict successful homeschooling programs as well as the homeschoolers themselves.

Remember Your Mission

Although some of the more flashy and popular library programs (crafts, murder mysteries, after-hours parties) tend to bring in the most teens, remember that programs should not only serve the purpose of attracting new users to the library; they should also promote the library's mission. These programs can leave a lasting positive impression with your patrons, but do they promote your collection and services? Be wary of creating a programming vicious cycle. Some patrons only come to the library to attend programs and are not seen or heard from until the next program. Your library's mission may be to provide social events for the public, so this might be right in line with the mission. But if your mission is to promote reading, then try to work collection promotion into your programs.

Collection Connections

Programs that promote library materials have great value. Remove all of the programs and services from your library, and as long as you have materials, you still have a library. Our collections are our foundation, and without our collections we would need to consider ourselves activity directors instead of librarians.

Some programs are better suited to promoting our materials than others. For example, book discussion groups and reading incentive programs obviously have the collection connection built in. Other programs like craft and hobby programs, contests, and passive programs may require an additional display of related materials or a book list handout to remind our participants that our programs support the library collection.

Evaluation

How do you know you have accomplished what you set out to do? The first step is to articulate exactly what you set out to accomplish; then, create a tool for measuring success. Evaluation is more than simple statistics. Statistics are useful measures that often help us justify our programs, but do they truly measure the success of our programs or indicate how we can improve them in the future?

Some Notes on Statistics

Before embarking on any new program, find out what statistics need to be reported:

- Number of programs each year
- Number of sessions in a series of programs
- Number of library tours or visits
- Number of participants
- Ages of participants
- Total costs of programs (This can be broken down in many different ways, so find out how to keep track of these numbers.)
- Circulation of materials

Find out how and where these statistics will be reported:

- For your own departmental annual report
- For the library's annual report
- For state or federal statistical reports (Again, statistics can be generated for these documents in a number of ways. Knowing how these numbers are to be reported will help you record the appropriate statistics.)

Check out this valuable resource:

- Walter, Virginia A. *Output Measures and More: Planning and Evaluating Public Library Services for Young Adults*. Chicago: American Library Association, 1995.

There are many ways to evaluate your programs, and some evaluation tools are more formal than others. The most informal way to evaluate your program is to simply jot down your impressions after the program is finished. This type of evaluation may suffice for your own needs, but chances are you will need to provide evaluative information to your library administration. Therefore you might consider a more formal approach to program evaluation.

Formal evaluations can result in both quantitative (statistical) and qualitative data. We often use the more quantitative evaluations because these are usually fairly easy to collect and analyze and are often requested for our statistical reports. The quantitative evaluations include collecting data at the programs (attendance, ages, costs) as well as statistics collected after the programs (circulation numbers, percentage of the target population reached by the program). Although it may be fairly time consuming to develop more qualitative tools for evaluation, these tools usually result in more revealing data. Qualitative tools include surveying program participants, suggestion boxes, observations, interviews, and focus groups. See chapter 7 for more information on how these tools can offer helpful evaluations of your programs and services.

Regardless of what tools you use for evaluation, at the end of a program you should be able to answer the following questions:

- How did the actual attendance compare to the anticipated attendance?
- What factors may have affected attendance for this program? (Poor/superb marketing, weather, conflicting events, etc.)
- How has the mission of the library been served by this program? (You may have had unanticipated results at your program that may or may not be in support of your library's mission.)
- Did you have adequate supplies/prizes for all of the participants?
- How could this program be improved if repeated?
- Would you recommend repeating the program in the future?

PROGRAMMING WITH HOMESCHOOLING TEENS AND THEIR PARENTS IN MIND

After considering the basics of young adult programming, consider the ways to approach programming for the homeschooling teen audience. When considering programming targeted to homeschoolers, you may want to consider offering special benefits to your participants that would make the experience even more valuable to them.

First, consider offering certificates of completion for single programs or after a series of programs. Many homeschoolers compile extensive portfolios of their independent work. These portfolios include examples of their work and proof of accomplishments that can then be used when applying for scholarships and admission into college. Certificates are inexpensive, can be personalized for your participants, and would make a nice addition to any homeschooler's portfolio.

Second, consider throwing out that tried-and-true rule of inviting only teens to participate in your program. Opening the audience to include the homeschooling teen's entire family may make it easier for some teens to attend, especially if they can bring their siblings along. (Although like other teens, many would welcome an opportunity to be independent from the rest of the family!) Some of the program ideas are more suited for the entire family than others. Just keep in mind that when starting to reach out to the homeschooling community, family programming opportunities may attract a larger group.

Finally, consider offering programs at times when only homeschoolers are likely to attend. Many homeschoolers seek programs during weekdays instead of waiting for their school-attending peers to hear the last bell of the day. Additionally, some parents of homeschoolers may prefer that their teens attend programs with other homeschooling teens. You might get more support from the homeschooling parents if you plan the program at a time and day that will likely only include other homeschoolers.

SPECIFIC PROGRAM IDEAS

If you are unable to get enough input from homeschooling teens or their parents, there are programs that have been successful at other libraries. The following program ideas have been compiled from successful library programs as well as suggestions from homeschooling families (via an e-mail survey). Many of the programs are perfectly suited for all of your teen patrons, not just homeschoolers. In fact, many of the program ideas make frequent appearances on young adult programming calendars. These programs are presented with the homeschooling teen and their parents in mind.

Open House/Library Orientations

This program is an excellent "coming out" for your newly created project to target homeschooling teens. Depending on the preferences of your patrons, this program works equally well as a morning, afternoon, or evening program. Weekends may not be as ideal, since the library may be more crowded, staffing may be limited, and there may be many other activities competing for your patrons' attention. This program may also be an inexpensive way to reach many patrons early in your project. The extent of your expenses will include your time, the time of assisting staff, and any marketing costs.

The ideal audience for this program would include homeschooling teens attending with their parents, although some of your patrons may wish to attend independently. Some homeschooling families may wish to attend together, including younger siblings. The best approach to your first open house would be to leave your audience fairly open and see who shows up. If you find that your attendance is made up primarily of teens, then you may have a better idea of who to invite to future programs.

The content of your program can include any of the following activities:

- A tour of the reference collection, highlighting reference works and services that would be helpful to a homeschooling teen's curriculum
- A presentation of other special services to homeschoolers
- A demonstration of online databases available at the library
- A demonstration of safe and effective Internet searching techniques
- A demonstration of homeschooling Internet sites
- Booktalks from the young adult or adult nonfiction book collections: biographies, science books, career books, inspirational stories, etc.
- Booktalks from the parent/teacher/homeschooling collection
- As with any teen program: Refreshments

Try not to pack too much into your first homeschooling open house. As with many programs, the general rule of "less is more" can apply here. Each listed segment could easily be molded into a single event. Try doing a few activities/presentations and prepare handouts for your participants to take home and look over at their leisure. Your first homeschooler open house could simply include a tour, a demonstration of a single database, an outline of upcoming homeschooler-targeted programs, and refreshments. Allow plenty of time for hands-on experience, questions, and social interaction. If your open house is the only homeschooling program you have planned, you can take the refreshment time period to question or survey your participants for future program ideas.

This is also an ideal time to compile information for a mailing list, so set out a sign-up sheet. Be sure to make it clear to your participants that any mailing list you compile would be kept confidential and would be completely voluntary. Some homeschoolers may be put off by any obtrusive attempts to gather personal information, and you would likely not see those participants again.

Finally, you may want to consider taking the open house program idea to the next level by offering a modular approach to library orientation. You could create a series of programs offered on a weekly or monthly basis to highlight specific resources. The first session may concentrate on print resources, the next could cover subscription databases, and a third could focus on Internet searching. These modules could then be repeated as new resources become available or at a time when you want to attract new homeschooling teen patrons.

As you can see, traditional library orientation could easily be adapted to focus on homeschooling teens. If you have tried library orientations in the past with little or moderate success, try an open house specifically for homeschoolers and you should be pleased with the results.

Library Bingo

A library orientation program with a slight competitive variation may attract teens who are looking to interact with other homeschooling teens. The goal of Library Bingo is to highlight various programs and services (tour stops) while the participants record the stops on their individual blank bingo cards. After the tour, you will then play Bingo with the completed cards and award a small prize. To get started, ask the participants to record each stop of the tour on a blank bingo card. Participants should be encouraged to record their tour stops in different places than their friends so that they will not all get a Bingo at the same time. (Remember that bingo cards have a free space in the middle.) Be sure to have enough stops on the tour so that all blank spaces on a bingo card can be filled. Write all the tour stops on slips of paper and at the end of the tour simply pull the slips out of a hat. Have the participants cross off each tour stop as it is read. The first person to cross off stops on their card in the traditional bingo formations (across, down, diagonal, four corners, etc.) wins. Be sure to have enough prizes for multiple bingos.

The stops on the tour can be entire departments (reference, children's, young adult) as well as specific collections or services (homeschooling collection, homeschooling news bulletin board, pay phone, photocopier, meeting room). A library bingo card can be easily made using a word processing program. (See Figure 6.4.)

Figure 6.4
Sample Bingo Card

B	I	N	G	O
		Free Space!		

Library Instruction Programs

Much like the library orientation programs, programs that teach library and research skills are highly desirable to teen homeschoolers. These program ideas can be tied into the library orientation or integrated into a modular library orientation/instruction approach.

Reference Source Scavenger Hunt

Teaching teenagers how to use basic print and electronic resources can be an unexciting endeavor. Instead of approaching these necessary skills with the usual demonstration, try mixing in some physical activity and even prizes. Remember that homeschoolers are used to learning independently, so it is not always effective to stand in front of a group and teach them how to use resources. Instead, give them the challenge of learning how to use the resources independently or in groups.

You can start by having a library catalog scavenger hunt. Allow your participants to work independently or in groups and have them discover the many ways of searching the online catalog. Be sure to announce at the beginning of the program that their performance will not be timed. Participants should take their time working on their clues since all participants will receive a prize for completing the scavenger hunt. Provide each participant or group with clues for four different items in your library's collection. Each clue will prompt the participants to search in four different ways: by title, author, subject, and keyword. Sample questions may include:

- Perform a title search using the online catalog. Locate the call number for the book titled *The Power of Positive Thinking for Teens.* Locate the book on the shelf and retrieve the green flag.
- Perform an author search using the online catalog. Remember that authors are listed by their last name followed by their first name. Locate the call number for a book by the author Linda Menzies. Locate the book on the shelf and retrieve the yellow flag.
- Perform a subject search using the online catalog. The official subject heading for materials on applying for colleges is "College Applications." Locate the call number for the first title listed under this subject heading, then locate the book on the shelf. Retrieve the red flag.
- Perform a keyword search using the online catalog. There is a book that has the following three words in the title: seven, effective, and teens. Locate the call number of the book, then locate the book on the shelf and retrieve the blue flag.

Once the participants locate the pertinent information in the online catalog they should take the location and call number information and locate the materials on the shelf. Each item on the shelf could have a colored flag inserted inside that can be retrieved and presented to the librarian. (Be sure to check each item immediately prior to the program to make sure it is indeed on the shelf!) Once the participants or groups have retrieved all four flags, they receive their prize. It is important in a program like this to make sure each group or participant has different clues resulting in completely different library items on the shelves. Although some programs are more fun with a little competition, this program is designed to teach how to locate items using the library catalog, not how to do it in the shortest time possible. Possible prizes for this kind of scavenger hunt include bookmarks, candy, or other small trinkets. One variation of this program is to do it in conjunction with other library materials instruction, and hold out for a prize at the very end. Let your participants collect their flags along the way and turn them in at the end for a single small prize or certificate of completion.

Other sections of the reference scavenger hunt can include:

- Searching a phone book (white pages, yellow pages, government agencies)
- Searching a periodical index (online and/or print)
- Searching encyclopedias (general and subject-specific; using alphabetic entries/using the index)

Regardless of the kinds of reference tools you want to include in your scavenger hunt, be sure to include appropriate hints or tips in the clues provided to your participants. You can announce at the beginning of the program that the library staff is there to assist but not to offer answers. You can also make the program interesting by only answering questions with "yes/no" or "hot/cold."

Reference books of interest specifically to homeschooling teens can also be highlighted. For example, using clues to highlight the *College Blue Book*, *Peterson's 2 Year Colleges*, or *Peterson's 4 Year Colleges* would be especially interesting to older teens.

Online Database Instruction

Many homeschooling library patrons learn basic database searching through regular reference interactions, but do they really understand how to search them? Are they familiar with the more advanced features that would allow them more independence in their research? Compared to your non-homeschooling teen patrons who usually only want to know how to find the information they need at that particular moment, you might find that your homeschooling teens are willing to learn how to use the resource so that they can use it properly whenever the need arises.

A series of programs demonstrating individual online research tools (electronic reference books, online periodical indexes, etc.) will attract not only homeschooling teens, but also adults who wish to be more independent in their online searching. Be sure to allow plenty of time for participants to try out the demonstrated searches on their own (allow them to choose their own topics, but have some topics in mind for those who cannot think of one) and be available to answer questions as they try searching on their own. This type of program works best in a computer lab setting with an overhead projector with a live, interactive search demonstration. If this is not a possibility in your library, consider taking the program on the road, perhaps to the high school or community center (although you might not have live access to your databases if you do this).

One way to demonstrate online databases without a live connection is to create a Powerpoint presentation with sample searches, and demonstrate the sample searches in a community room with a projector. Then move your group to the reference area where they can try out the databases as you circulate and offer guidance. It is helpful to have more than one librarian during the hands-on session, especially when trying to come up with ideas for searching or troubleshooting those less effective searches.

At the beginning of any online database instruction program, it is useful to go over some basics of online searching before even turning to the computer:

- Explain the difference between subscription databases and resources freely available on the Internet. I like to explain subscription databases by comparing cable television to regular local stations. There are lots of great shows on regular television, but by subscribing to cable, you expect to get more content and agree to pay for it.
- Explain the basics of online searching: natural language searching vs. Boolean searching, truncation and wild cards, and field-specific searches. Explaining these concepts before using the database is reinforced in your sample searches.

Information Literacy Course

If you're looking for a way to offer a series of library instruction programs that cover the entire research process, consider offering an information literacy course that spans several weeks.

The concept of information literacy (also referred to as information competence) has become a high priority not only at colleges and universities, but also at high schools and middle schools. At a time when standardized tests force schools to spend more time teaching the basics, they have discovered that an emphasis needs to be placed on how students discover an information need, and the steps involved in satisfying that information need. By offering a series of programs that walk teens through the entire research process, you would not only be preparing them for college research, but also preparing them to be lifelong, independent learners.

To prepare for an information literacy course, you should start out by choosing a set of information literacy standards. For example, the Association of College and Research Libraries has approved Information Literacy Competency Standards for Higher Education (http://www.ala.org/acrl/acrlstandards/standards.pdf) that could serve as an outline for the skills to be covered in the course. Some of the specific information literacy outcomes are geared more for upper-division and graduate study at college, so it may be appropriate to cover only those skills that are appropriate for teen library users.

Probably more commonly known is the concept of the Big6™ skills, developed by Mike Eisenberg and Bob Berkowitz (http://www.big6. com/).[1] Alternatively, you might consider using the standards set forth by the American Association of School Librarians (AASL) and the Association for Educational Communications and Technology (AECT). Marjorie Pappas and Ann Tepe explore this set of standards and present the Pathways to Knowledge® approach to information literacy and lifelong learning in the recent title *Pathways to Knowledge® and Inquiry Learning*.

Whichever information literacy standards you wish to embrace for your program, you can create a series of programs that give your homeschooling teens experience along the entire spectrum of library research from start to finish. One effective approach to the course would be to provide each of your participants a research journal at the beginning of the program. They would define their own information need based on an individual interest or topic. Throughout the following weeks and at subsequent programs, the participants would record their progress and research in the journal. At the end of the course they could present their findings to the group in one of several ways: a research paper, a speech, or a multimedia presentation.

It is vital that at the end of a program of this magnitude, each participant be given a certificate of completion. As previously noted, the certificate, along with the research journal and final project, can be added to the homeschooler's portfolio.

Literature-Based Programming

Once you have tried hosting one or more open house events and have a better idea of your homeschooling teen patronage, a natural transition would be to offer literature-based programming. These programs would likely fit into any library's mission and goals and would not be a hard-sell to homeschoolers who already use the library. You may have a hard time attracting very conservative homeschoolers to a book discussion group or reading circle, but a more passive reading program or incentive program may be the way to attract these homeschooling teens to your programs.

Book Discussion Groups

When we surveyed families with homeschooling teens, we found that many said they would be interested in teen book discussion groups. Keep in mind that some families may hesitate to allow their teens to attend such programs if they think the books being discussed might contain objectionable content or that objectionable topics might be discussed. Some parents may prefer that the discussion group be limited to homeschooling teens. These concerns may be addressed by allowing the participants to choose the materials to be discussed or by planning discussion groups to meet during weekdays and restricting participants to homeschooling teens. Consider having discussion questions prepared ahead of time so that parents can decide if the topics would be appropriate for their teens. You may also want to consider inviting interested participants to attend a planning meeting for the book discussion program and allow the participants to voice any concerns, or even offer suggestions, for book choices. You may not be able to reach total consensus in the planning meeting, but you might be able to address concerns and plan a discussion group that many of the parents would be comfortable allowing their teens to attend.

Keep in mind that book discussion groups tend to include an enormous amount of work. Choosing an appropriate and interesting title to discuss can be mind-boggling. Once a title is chosen, reading and rereading the book and compiling discussion questions can take hours. Book discussion planning also usually falls under "work that is accomplished at home" since many librarians are not comfortable sitting at their desks reading. Many young adult librarians would also say that the amount of work is not worth the limited interest that these programs generate with their teen audience.

Fortunately, the upside to book discussion groups is that they are usually well-received by homeschoolers. Most homeschooling teens aren't required to read textbooks and take tests (although some homeschoolers do follow standardized curriculums). You will probably find that if you allow your participants to have some say in the titles that are discussed, they will be very enthusiastic participants.

Listed in the third edition of *Excellence in Library Services to Young Adults*[2] is one of the nation's top young adult programs—the King County (North Bend, Washington) Library System's Lunch 'n' Lit program. This program is open to all teens between twelve and eighteen who are available on Mondays from noon to 1 P.M. This successful program has all of the elements you need to apply to your homeschooling book discussion group: the participants choose the books, direct the discussions, and set the pace.

Another popular and lively book discussion group meets at the Skokie (Illinois) Public Library. Started in October 2001, the "Bridging Generations: Adults Discuss Children's Books" meets on a weekday evening and is limited to adults. This concept can be adapted to include an intergenerational audience or for homeschooling teens. The participants can revisit classic children's literature or discover stories for the first time along with younger brothers and sisters. Popular titles discussed by the Skokie Public Library participants have included Richard Peck's *A Long Way from Chicago*, Mildred Taylor's *Roll of Thunder, Hear My Cry*, and Avi's *Nothing but the Truth*.

Some suggestions for books to share with homeschooling teens include:

- *Little Women* by Louisa May Alcott
- *Sounder* by William Armstrong
- *The Secret Garden* by Frances Hodgson Burnett
- *A Wrinkle in Time* by Madeleine L'Engle
- *The Hobbit* by J.R.R. Tolkien
- *Pride and Prejudice* by Jane Austen
- *Shoeless Joe* by W. P. Kinsella
- *The Princess Bride* by William Golding
- *The Time Machine* by H. G. Wells
- *Cheaper by the Dozen* by Frank Gilbreth

Resources on Book Discussion Groups:

Dodson, Shireen. *The Mother-Daughter Book Club: How Ten Busy Mothers and Daughters Came Together to Talk, Laugh and Learn Through Their Love of Reading.* New York: HarperPerennial, 1997.

Ellington, Elizabeth. *A Year of Reading: A Month-By-Month Guide to Classics and Crowd-Pleasers for You and Your Book Group.* Naperville, IL: Sourcebooks, 2002.

Jacobsohn, Rachel W. *The Reading Group Handbook: Everything You Need to Know to Start Your Own Book Club.* New York: Hyperion, 1998.

Knowles, Elizabeth. *More Reading Connections: Bringing Parents, Teachers, and Librarians Together.* Englewood, CO: Libraries Unlimited, 1999.

Knowles, Elizabeth. *The Reading Connection: Bringing Parents, Teachers, and Librarians Together.* Englewood, CO: Libraries Unlimited, 1997.

Laskin, David. *The Reading Group Book: The Complete Guide to Starting and Sustaining a Reading Group, with Annotated Lists of 250 Titles for Provocative Discussion.* New York: Plume, 1995.

Simic, Marjorie R. *Family Book Sharing Groups: Start One in Your Neighborhood.* Bloomington, IN: Family Literacy Center: EDINFO Press, 1995.

Slezak, Ellen. *The Book Group Book: A Thoughtful Guide to Forming and Enjoying a Stimulating Book Discussion Group.* Chicago: Chicago Review Press, 2000.

(continued)

(Continued)

Resources on Title Selection:

Cooper-Mullin, Alison. *Once upon a Heroine: 400 Books for Girls to Love.* Lincolnwood, IL: Contemporary Books, 1998.

Dodson, Shireen. *100 Books for Girls to Grow On: Lively Descriptions of the Most Inspiring Books for Girls, Terrific Discussion Questions to Spark Conversation, Great Ideas for Book-Inspired Activities, Crafts, and Field Trips.* New York: HarperCollins Publishers, 1998.

Odean, Kathleen. *Great Books about Things Kids Love: More Than 750 Recommended Books for Children 3 to 14.* New York: Ballantine Books, 2001.

Odean, Kathleen. *Great Books for Boys: More Than 600 Books for Boys 2 to 14.* New York: Ballantine Books, 1998.

Odean, Kathleen. *Great Books for Girls: More Than 600 Recommended Books for Girls Ages 3 to 14.* New York: Ballantine Books, 2002.

Junior Great Books Club

The Great Books Foundation offers a program of book discussions designed specifically for students in grades K-12. (http://www.great books.org/programs/junior/index.shtml). Many homeschoolers are already familiar with the Junior Great Books discussion groups and may be more likely to join a discussion group if it is officially associated with the Junior Great Books Foundation. There is a higher cost for participating in the Junior Great Books program, including training of leaders and materials. It may be worth the cost and time involved if the result is more confidence from your homeschoolers' parents, as well as the materials that the Foundation provides. Perhaps the cost of this program could be supported by a Friends group or shared with another agency or association, and may be a perfect opportunity for cooperation.

Literature Circles

A variation of the book discussion group that is especially appropriate for homeschooling teens is the literature circle. Literature circles (also referred to as reading circles or cooperative book discussions) are formed when members choose to read the same book and embrace specific roles in the discussion. The groups are temporary and change when new books are chosen, changing the group dynamics with each new book. Some of the roles the group members may choose include any of the following:

- The Discussion Director: The member in this essential role facilitates the discussion and directs the flow of activities. Eventually one of the group members can embrace this role. For the first meeting the librarian can direct the discussion to model what is expected at future discussions. Once the members get an idea of what is expected, the librarian can remain in the background, offering direction or assistance only when needed.
- The Passage Picker: This member's role is to choose representative passages from the text to share with the rest of the group to spark discussion. The passage picker can simply use "sticky notes" to mark the passages. The passages can be read aloud by this member or other members can volunteer to read passages.
- The Connector: The connector's role is to connect the book to the personal lives of the group members. The connector can speak from personal experience or generalize if that is more comfortable. Events in the books can also be connected to world events or events from other books.
- Vocabulary Enricher: This role requires the member to keep track of words or concepts that may be unfamiliar or that might need further explanation or discussion.
- The Artist: The artist is in charge of representing his or her thoughts about the book in any artistic fashion. The artistic expression is then shared with the group to enhance the discussion.

Literature circles are ideal programs for supporting adolescent development, especially for homeschooling teens who seek opportunities to interact socially, embrace meaningful tasks, and who love to discuss books. What sets literature circles above traditional book discussion groups for homeschooling teens is the opportunity to exercise choice: choice in the books to discuss and choice in what role to play in the discussion. A literature circle is ideal for the librarian because you only need to plan the program; the teens themselves run the actual discussion.

Once you have a number of homeschooling teens who have expressed interest in a book discussion group, plan an organizational meeting. At this meeting, plan to booktalk several books that your participants will choose for their individual discussions. Do not worry about reading level or content, just try to include a variety of genres. The true beauty of literature circles is that the participants take full responsibility for their book choices. The number of literature circles that will evolve out of this meeting will depend on how many participants are present. Ideally you would have at least four participants sign up for each book, but not more than you have designated roles. Once your participants decide which book they will read (this creates the individual literature circle groups), then they will need to decide which roles they will embrace. They might be able to decide this with a brief discussion or they may want to choose roles out of a hat. Again, for the first meeting of the literature circles the librarian should act as the discussion director, just to get the ball rolling.

Resources on Literature Circles

Books:

Daniels, Harvey. *Literature Circles: Voice and Choice in Book Clubs and Reading Groups.* Portland, ME: Stenhouse Publishers, 2002.

Hill, Bonnie Campbell, Nancy J. Johnson, and Katherine L. Schlick Noe, eds. *Literature Circles and Response.* Norwood, MA: Christopher-Gordon Publishers, 1995.

Hill, Bonnie Campbell, Katherine L. Schlick Noe, and Nancy J. Johnson. *Literature Circles Resource Guide: Teaching Suggestions, Forms, Sample Book Lists, and Database.* Norwood, MA: Christopher-Gordon Publishers, 2001.

Knowles, Elizabeth. *Reading Rules: Motivating Teens to Read.* Englewood, CO: Libraries Unlimited, 2001.

Neamen, Mimi. *Literature Circles: Cooperative Learning for Grades 3–8.* Englewood, CO: Teacher Ideas Press, 1992.

Neamen, Mimi. *More Literature Circles: Cooperative Learning for Grades 3–8.* Englewood, CO: Libraries Unlimited, 2001.

Noe, Katherine L. Schlick, and Nancy J. Johnson. *Getting Started with Literature Circles.* Norwood, MA: Christopher-Gordon Publishers, 1999.

Internet:

Literature Circles Resource Center (Seattle University School of Education): http://fac-staff.seattleu.edu/kschlnoe/LitCircles/

Booktalks

One program that can be easily planned and implemented is a booktalk program. Chances are that you are already booktalking titles at the local schools, especially in preparation for summer reading programs. Why not take these booktalks that you have already prepared and present them to a homeschooling crowd? You can create a brownbag lunch program by inviting your homeschooling teens to bring in their lunch (the library can provide beverages or dessert) and simply perform your booktalks while the teens eat lunch. Leave plenty of time at the end for the teens to circulate, share information about some of the books they have been reading, and to look at the titles presented.

Passive Reading Programs
(With or Without Incentives)

If you offer a summer reading club, you already offer passive reading opportunities. A passive reading program allows your participants to join in when they want to, not at any specific time or place. You can expand the existing programs to include teens if your library has only offered summer reading for children, or you can have a year-round program for home-schoolers who sometimes do not take summers off. Perhaps you have the year-round reading program culminate during Teen Read Week. Although these types of programs usually involve the awarding of prizes, they can also be offered exclusively to homeschoolers who read a certain number of books to receive a certificate of completion. Try creating a checklist of books to act as a guide for your participants. For some ideas of reading lists to use, explore the Web sites in the box below. Keep in mind that any of these suggested reading lists may contain materials that your homeschoolers or their parents might find objectionable, so use your best judgment to guide you in choosing the items to add to any suggested reading list or checklist.

Web sites for Award Winners and Lists

Alex Awards

http://www.ala.org/yalsa/booklistawards/alexawards/

Best Books for Young Adults

http://www.ala.org/yalsa/booklists/bbya/

The Coretta Scott King Award

http://www.ala.org/ala/srrt/corettascottking/corettascott.htm

Michael L. Printz Award

http://www.ala.org/yalsa/printz

Newbery Medal Home Page

http://www.ala.org/ala/alsc/awardsscholarships/literaryawds/
newberymedal/newberymedal.htm

(continued)

(Continued)

Outstanding Books for the College Bound

http://www.ala.org/yalsa/booklists/obcb/

Popular Paperbacks

http://www.ala.org/yalsa/booklists/poppaper/

Quick Picks for Reluctant Young Adult Readers

http://www.ala.org/yalsa/booklists/quickpicks/

Selected Audio Books

http://www.ala.org/yalsa/booklistawards/selectedaudio/

Selected DVDs and Videos

http://www.ala.org/yalsa/booklistawards/selecteddvds/

Poetry Club

Yet another variation on the book discussion group is the poetry club. A poetry club can meet on a regular basis to share their writing or to discuss the works of favorite poets. You might find that a poetry club may evolve out of a book discussion.

Creative Writing Workshop

A creative writing workshop is one of those programs that require someone with some special skills to present. If you have taken courses in creative writing you may feel confident enough to present this program yourself. Others may be more comfortable contacting the nearest community college to see if there is someone who could present the program voluntarily or for a small fee.

Keep in mind that any time creative writing is shared, there is the chance that someone might be offended. This may be a program that would be best limited to homeschoolers, although this might not be possible if the cost for the speaker is high.

Art and Hobby Programs

Hobby and Craft Programs

Any traditional hobby or craft program can be targeted to homeschoolers by changing the time it is offered. Some program ideas that may be of particular interest to homeschoolers include: genealogy, heraldry, astronomy, wearable art (jewelry, tie-dye, knitting, etc.), bookmaking, journaling, origami, cartooning, calligraphy, juggling, kites, or storytelling. Some hobby or craft programs that may not be a hit with conservative homeschoolers might include mendhi (henna tattoo body art), anime (Japanese animation), or astrology.

Art Exhibits

If your library has space to display artwork, offering a homeschoolers' art exhibit would give them the opportunity to show off their work and get that sense of pride many of us remember in our school days, having our treasured works of art on display in the hallways for all to see and admire. The exhibit might be the end result of an art contest. (See section on Contests.)

Pen Pals

In this e-mail crazy world many teens do not know the experience of having a true pen pal. With the quick return of e-mail correspondence, today's teens do not have to wait for the mailman to arrive with their response. A pen pal program that connects homeschooling teens at one library to the homeschooling teens at another library would allow them to experience the lost art of letter writing.

In *Teen Library Events: A Month-by-Month Guide*, Kirsten Edwards describes a very successful pen pal program that coordinates pen pal applications from libraries across the country.[3] Kirsten describes how to join the already successful pen pal program, although you may want to set up your own. For more information on the national pen pal program, see Kirsten's book.

If you happen to have contact with another young adult librarian from a different state, perhaps the two libraries can begin by simply exchanging pen pal applications. Such a program is described in the New York Library Association's *The Basic Young Adult Services Handbook*.[4] This program involves the exchange of pen pal applications between libraries in two states as part of a "Summer Pen Pal Letter Exchange." Having two libraries participate in the program is less complicated, but it does not offer as much variety as the national program Kirsten Edwards describes. This might just be a great way to get started with a pen pal program to test the interest level before expanding the program in the future.

Regardless of how you start your pen pal exchange, there are concerns about sharing personal information with strangers, even if it is through a library-sponsored pen pal program. It would be wise to offer all participants a handout discussing appropriate/desirable pen pal behaviors (for example, how quickly you need to respond to be a good pen pal!) and tips on how to get the ball rolling. You may also want to include a parental permission slip attached to the application so that the participant's parents are aware of the program and know who to contact if they have any concerns.

Career and College Preparation Programs

ACT/SAT Programs

Homeschooling teens who wish to go on to earn a college degree will be interested in taking either the ACT or SAT examinations. The thought of taking standardized tests after being homeschooled may be an intimidating proposition. A program that provides test-taking tips and explains what to expect may help alleviate some of the tension for your homeschoolers. A program on ACT/SAT preparation would be of interest to both homeschoolers and non-homeschoolers. Again, be sure to have materials in your collection for your participants to check out after your program.

Career Fair

One way to get a homeschooling teen's parents involved in the library programming is to recruit them to present their careers in a homeschooler's career fair. Teens who attend traditional school have many opportunities to explore various careers through assignments and school-sponsored career events. You may also be able to gather participants by contacting the local homeschoolers' association. By all means don't forget to have the many library field opportunities represented at your fair!

Job Fair

When summer is right around the corner, many teens begin to think about revenue-generating opportunities. A job fair at your library will attract many teens, not only homeschoolers. When you are recruiting local businesses to be represented at your fair, let them know you are expecting homeschoolers to be present and that these participants may be interested in working after summer is over. This proposition might be especially attractive to businesses that would be interested in hiring a teen who can work during normal school hours. If you have any potential library page positions opening up, you might consider having the library represented as well.

Interview Skills

If you plan on offering a job fair program, you might want to first offer a program that presents desired interviewing skills. This is another program that would be appropriate for both homeschoolers and non-homeschoolers. The program could cover traditional interview questions, appropriate answers, and tips on dressing for an interview. This program would be ideal for your teen board to assist with role-playing and might add some humor for a "do's and don'ts" demonstration.

Searching for Colleges Online

Many colleges now have their complete catalogs available online and some even offer virtual tours of their campuses. A program that combines traditional print resources (using the *College Blue Book* to determine which colleges offer the desired degrees) with Internet searching can help home-schoolers decide which colleges are potential matches. Be sure to highlight how to find admission requirements and locate pertinent contact information for the college Web sites. This program could be combined with the next two program ideas to create a college preparation series.

Financial Aid Night

Contact your local community college to see if a financial aid counselor is available to speak at the library. Along with your financial aid expert, you can cover your print and online resources for scholarships, loans, and grants and offer advice on how to fill out the FAFSA (Free Application for Federal Student Aid) online.

The College Application Process

Again, see if there are counselors available from a local college to speak about the college application process. Be sure to ask the speaker to address the concerns of homeschoolers. You can also contact several colleges and universities that are popular with your teen population and request information about the application materials required from prospective students.

Speech and Drama Programs
Debate Night

A couple of our survey respondents suggested that libraries offer debate programs for homeschoolers. Outside of school, teens have few opportunities for public speaking. Although many teens would prefer to avoid public speaking, others may welcome the opportunity.

First, make sure there is a genuine interest in a debate program with several interested participants. You may consider contacting your local high school to see if there is an existing debate club. The coach may offer tips for getting a club started as well as offer advice on moderating debates.

To connect your program to your collection, feature items from the *Opposing Viewpoints, At Issue,* or *Current Controversies* series. If your library subscribes to *CQ Researcher,* this is an excellent source for generating debate topics. Any nonfiction titles on social issues would be appropriate for a debate program, although you may consider featuring less controversial topics if your homeschooling population tends to be more conservative.

Drama Programs

If you have several homeschoolers interested in drama, perhaps they would like to put together a play or puppet show for your children's story hour. Your collection most likely includes collections of one-act plays for holidays or special events, or your homeschoolers could probably write a play based on the stories being featured for the story hour. Because homeschoolers are available during the daytime hours when their peers are in school, they can attend weekday story hours and add a wonderful feature to the story hour schedule. When a particular play or puppet show is especially successful, consider presenting a special performance for the entire community. Have an evening story hour and invite your patrons to arrive in their pajamas and feature your homeschooler's best plays for the whole community to enjoy.

A less expensive and less time-consuming alternative to a full-blown stage play would be to have your homeschoolers perform readers' theatre. There are many helpful guides to creating reader's theatre programs, as well as script collections. Check out the resources listed below:

Resources for Readers' Theatre

Barchers, Suzanne I. *From Atalanta to Zeus: Readers Theatre from Greek Mythology*. Englewood, CO: Teacher Ideas Press, 2001.

Dixon, Neill, Ann Davies, and Colleen Politano. *Learning with Readers Theatre*. Winnipeg, MB: Peguis Publishers, 1996.

Frederick, Anthony D. *Frantic Frogs and Other Frankly Fractured Folktales for Readers Theatre*. Englewood, CO: Teacher Ideas Press, 1993.

Frederick, Anthony D. *Readers Theatre for American History*. Englewood, CO: Teacher Ideas Press, 2001.

Frederick, Anthony D. *Science Fiction Readers Theatre*. Englewood, CO: Teacher Ideas Press, 2002.

Frederick, Anthony D. *Silly Salamanders and Other Slightly Stupid Stuff for Readers Theatre*. Englewood, CO: Teacher Ideas Press, 2000.

Frederick, Anthony D. *Tadpole Tales and Other Totally Terrific Treats for Readers Theatre*. Englewood, CO: Teacher Ideas Press, 1997.

Kaye, Marvin, ed. *Readers Theatre: What It Is and How to Stage It, and Four Award-Winning Scripts*. Newark, NJ: Wildside Press, 1995.

Lance, Janice. *First Literature Experiences: Readers Theatre Scripts and Activities for Henny Penny, Three Little Pigs, Gingerbread Boy, Little Red Hen, The House That Jack Built*. O'Fallon, MO: Book Lures, 1991.

Latrobe, Kathy Howard. *Readers Theatre for Young Adults: Scripts and Script Development*. Englewood, CO: Teacher Ideas Press, 1989.

Latrobe, Kathy Howard. *Social Studies Readers Theatre for Young Adults: Scripts and Script Development*. Englewood, CO: Teacher Ideas Press, 1991.

Laughlin, Mildred. *Social Studies Readers Theatre for Children: Scripts and Script Development*. Englewood, CO: Teacher Idea Press, 1991.

McBride-Smith, Barbara. *Tell It Together: Foolproof Scripts for Story Theatre*. Little Rock, AR: August House Publishers, 2001.

Porter, Steven, ed. *New Monologues for Reader's Theatre*. Studio City, CA: Phantom Publications, 1995.

Porter, Steven, ed. *New Works for Reader's Theatre*. Studio City, CA: Phantom Publications, 1994.

Powell, Matthew. *Performing Parables: Religious Folk Tales, Legends, and Fables for Readers Theater*. San Jose, CA: Resource Publishers, 2000.

Ratliff, Gerald Lee. *Introduction to Readers Theatre: A Guide to Classroom Performance*. Colorado Springs, CO: Meriwether Publishers, 1999.

Reid, Rob. *Something Funny Happened at the Library: How to Create Humorous Programs for Children and Young Adults*. Chicago: American Library Association, 2003.

Shepard, Aaron, ed. *Stories on Stage: Scripts for Reader's Theater*. New York: H. W. Wilson, 1993.

Sierra, Judy. *Multicultural Folktales for the Feltboard and Readers' Theater*. Phoenix, AZ: Oryx Press, 1996.

Sloyer, Shirlee. *From the Page to the Stage: The Educator's Complete Guide to Readers' Theatre*. Westport, CT: Teacher Ideas Press, 2003.

(continued)

(Continued)

Tanner, Fran Averett. *Readers Theatre Fundamentals: A Cumulative Approach to Theory and Activities.* Topeka, KS: Clark Publishers, 1993.

White, Melvin R. *Mel White's Readers Theatre Anthology: Twenty-Eight All-Occasion Readings for Storytellers.* Colorado Springs, CO: Meriwether Publishers, 1993.

Mystery Programs

Many young adult departments have sponsored library murder mystery programs, although when you are targeting a program to a more conservative audience consider removing any violent content. When planning a mystery program that will be promoted to homeschooling teens, consider a more lighthearted crime like stolen library books or a kidnapped library pet. However, this does not always have to be the case. For example, at a planned Buffy the Vampire Slayer murder mystery program one of the most enthusiastic and creative participants was, in fact, a homeschooled teen. Not all are brought up in ultraconservative homes, and you might be surprised by their interests and hobbies. There are many commercially available kits for hosting a mystery party, but it may be an especially memorable program if participants plan and create the event themselves. This is a great project for a teen advisory board and can be performed as part of a fundraising activity.

Science and Math Programs

Family Math Night

Programs designed for participation by the entire family are especially attractive to homeschooling families. Take a look at your collection and see what kinds of materials you might be able to promote with a family math night. From counting picture books all the way up to adult math logic books and titles that teach everyday practical math, you have a wealth of ideas for activities for a fun and educational evening. This is a great program to get several library departments involved. Consider setting up stations throughout the library with math games for different ages and skill levels. Cap off the evening with a session of "Family Math Feud" where families can compete as teams answering questions that increase in difficulty. This program will leave participants with many happy memories of being in the library and playing games as a family. This is a fantastic program for promoting library services during a levy campaign! Be sure to take lots of pictures and invite your local press.

Science Fair

It seems as though schools are now requiring students to participate in science fairs in more grades than ever. Offering a science fair program to your homeschoolers is a valuable service that they will certainly want to take advantage of. Try to plan your homeschooling science fair at a time during the year when the rest of your students are not preparing their science fair projects. If your summer schedule is not too jammed with activities for summer reading programs (not a very likely scenario!), then this would be an ideal time to offer a homeschooling science fair. So many wonderful science fair projects could revolve around growing plants, sunlight, and rain, which tend to be more plentiful during the summer months. A summer science fair has more opportunities for interesting projects that just can't be performed during the winter months (unless you're in one of those lovely sunny states!).

There are many helpful resources for science fairs, so this is a program that can be pulled off with some good planning and the helpful hands of volunteers. Offer planning meetings or programs to go over the rules and the timeline and to review expectations. Consider offering a preparatory program to explain the scientific method as well as various display options. Ask local science teachers to participate in the judging. Perhaps winning participants can also submit their projects to other fairs on a more competitive level. Regardless of their success with their projects, each participant should receive a certificate to be included in their portfolio.

Entertainment Programs

Movie Night

By far one of the most requested programs on our homeschooler survey was for movie nights at the library. Movie presentations, complete with traditional movie refreshments, create an opportunity for homeschoolers and non-homeschoolers to socialize in a relaxed atmosphere.

Your choice of movies to be shown will be affected by several factors. First, you will be limited to movies that are currently in your collection, unless you plan to lease a movie from an authorized vendor that provides public performance rights. This factor brings us to our next consideration: you must obtain public performance rights for any movie you show, even if you do not charge an admission fee. You can obtain rights for public performance through the Motion Picture Licensing Corporation (http://www.mplc.com), but be sure to include these costs for licensing in your program or collection budget. Third, you will need to choose a film that will be appropriate for your audience. When in doubt, choose classics (*Gone with the Wind, Indiana Jones, The Princess Bride*) and sure-fire hits (*Lord of the Rings, Tuck Everlasting*), and distribute detailed information ahead of time. One way to serve a diverse market and avoid possible complaints is to announce the chosen movie well in advance and advertise an opportunity to preview the movie to homeschooling and other parents. Distributing promotional material that lists the title of the movie, the MPAA rating, and a short synopsis would be one way to announce the movie and give parents an opportunity to voice any concerns.

The ideal setup for a teen movie night would be in a large meeting room (or in your young adult department if the area is large enough) with a projector. A large television with a VCR or DVD player would suffice, but the image may be difficult to see and the program's ambiance may be affected. Arrange chairs in movie fashion with an aisle down the center. Place the chairs far enough away from the screen to allow your participants to sit or lay on the floor if they wish. You may want to obtain some beanbag chairs or oversized pillows to encourage your teens to lounge while viewing the movie.

For refreshments, purchase bags of popcorn, or for a more authentic feel, borrow or rent a small popcorn machine. To save money on refreshments you can purchase larger packages of candy and place them in bowls instead of passing out individual boxes of candy. Candy is one of those program costs than can be reduced by asking for donations. Contact your local supermarkets, movie theaters, or video rental establishments to try to obtain donations. If they don't want to donate candy, perhaps free passes or movie rental coupons would suffice. You can use these as door prizes at the end of the night as your participants fill out program evaluations.

The teen movie night program can be repeated on a regular basis or added to other programs (for example, having a movie viewing as part of a teen lock-in program, as described below). The movie night can also be promoted as the grand prize for your summer (or winter) reading club participants. Social programs can be powerful incentives for teens when other, more expensive, prizes are not an option for your library.

To add more charm to your teen movie night, consider planning a themed party, for example, a costume party or Oscar night. Invite your participants to dress up as their favorite movie star, to wear clothing that reflects the period of the movie (e.g., '50s, Victorian), or to dress in completely black and white to create extra atmosphere for your program. These themes can then translate into your decorations as well.

To connect this program to your collection, consider a display of TV-movie tie-in novels or books about movies and movie star biographies. For decorations, see if there are any old 35mm films that you can use (just place the movie cans on tables or if the films can be withdrawn, run long strips of the film down the center of your snack and display tables).

Coffeehouse

Second in popularity on our homeschooler survey was the suggestion for a teen coffeehouse night at the library. Like the movie night program, this program allows homeschooling teens social interaction in a relaxed environment.

The role of the librarian at the coffeehouse program is to host the program and let the teens drink warm, frothy beverages, listen to music, and possibly play some board games. The coffeehouse can be combined with a poetry jam, booktalks, art show, talent show, or other artistic programs. By itself, it is rather low-maintenance. Simply provide a variety of beverages (make sure you offer non-caffeinated and sugar-free drinks as alternatives) and other refreshments, set the mood with some soft classical music and soft lighting, and provide some board games. If you cannot control the intensity of overhead lighting, see if the lights can be left off altogether and borrow some lamps to place in the program area. Lighting can really set the mood for your coffeehouse, so try not to have excessively bright lights if at all possible.

Once you decide the kinds of beverages you would like to serve your teens, consider how they will be distributed. Will the teens help themselves or will there be servers making the beverages for them? When considering your approach, keep the following in mind: Teens left to make their own beverages will sometimes create strange, unpalatable concoctions with the refreshments you worked very hard to provide. This sometimes results in lots of discarded beverages before they create something they actually want to drink. If you plan to allow your participants to create their own drinks, offer them guidance (perhaps decorative signs describing different combinations to try) or inform them upon arrival that they are limited to a single beverage.

To add to the coffeehouse atmosphere, consider borrowing a variety of real coffee mugs instead of disposable cups. This adds to your cleanup time at the end of the program (and the possibility of breaking a mug you borrowed), but it certainly adds to the authenticity of the program. Along with the beverages, consider offering a variety of toppings like whipped cream, flavored creamers, cinnamon sticks, chocolate sprinkles, and so forth. For easier cleanup, try lining your tables with disposable plastic so the spills and crumbs can simply be rolled up and thrown out. (Lay down your plastic table covering and cover with large, colorful paper napkins. The napkins will absorb small spills and the plastic will keep spills from soaking the table.) Be sure to have plenty of places for your participants to place their drinks while they are talking, viewing artwork, browsing the collections, or playing games. Try to borrow small stacking tables or cover stepping stools with pieces of plastic tablecloth. At the onset of your program, be sure to inform your participants of acceptable places to place their beverages (designated tables vs. library shelving) and where they are not allowed to go while carrying their drinks.

The length of this program depends on your goal. If you plan to offer this program as an opportunity for teens to "drop in" and socialize, then you might want to leave the program open for a couple of hours and let your participants come at any point in the program. If you plan to offer a specific event with the coffeehouse, then you will want to indicate a specific start time that you would prefer your teens to arrive.

To connect this program with your library's collection, consider displaying coffee table books throughout the program area. Often our oversized book collections are overlooked, so this is the perfect opportunity to promote them. Of course, books about coffee, tea, and chocolate are always fun display items for a program of this nature, as are dessert cookbooks.

Family Board Game Night

Another program that will attract homeschooling families is the family board game event. By offering the program in the evening you will attract all kinds of families, but if you want the program to be exclusive to homeschoolers, then offer the program during the day when kids are in school. This is a rather low-hassle program; just consider featuring games of various levels of skill and try to bring the whole group together at the end of the program with a family participation game in the fashion of *Family Feud*, *Jeopardy*, or *Who Wants to be a Millionaire?*

Interest Clubs

Depending on what your patrons happen to be interested in, you can offer the space and guidance for a club. If you have a group of homeschoolers who are interested in learning and playing chess, provide the guidance and materials to start a chess club. Other games that might generate interest include dominos, bridge, or mah jongg. Once these clubs form, most of your work is complete. You can offer a space for them to meet, assist with promoting upcoming meetings or events, but allow the members of the club to set the pace and perform the work. Many young adult departments have decided to provide chess sets and decks of cards for their teens to check out for use in the library, and these materials can be purchased fairly inexpensively. Your participants may prefer to bring their own games or materials.

Library Lock-ins

Few other programs attract as much interest as library lock-ins. Lock-ins, especially those planned as overnight events, are not for the faint of heart. Having chaperoned many overnight teen lock-ins imparts the knowledge that the planning and coordination of a lock-in requires many volunteers and more than a little caffeine.

The time and costs involved with library lock-ins, whether for a few hours or as an overnight program, usually mean that they cannot be offered as often as other programs. Lock-ins are especially effective as reward programs, either for participation in a reading program or after a year of service as teen advisory board members or homeschooling volunteers.

Lock-ins require the highest level of permission of all programs: permission from parents, permission from library administration and legal council, as well as permission from appropriate community agencies. Be sure to contact your local police department to inform them that there will be people in the library after hours and that these minors have received permission from their parents to be out past community curfews.

When considering when to offer the lock-in, be sure to consider the library's standard hours of operation. For example, if you are planning an overnight party with participants leaving at 8:00 the following morning, will the library be opening for service that morning? Will you have enough time to clean up after the program before the library is open for business?

Another consideration for any lock-in is which areas of the library are accessible and which areas are off-limits. Clearly mark these areas so there is no confusion for your participants. Having clearly defined space limits will also make the rest of the staff more comfortable with your program if they are assured that teens will not be allowed in their office spaces. Confining your program to smaller areas of the library will make the program somewhat less interesting to your participants, but you might be able to get by with fewer volunteer chaperons if you have fewer areas to cover.

Recruiting volunteer helpers can be a tricky endeavor. Who do you ask? Probably not any parents of participants unless you want those participants not to come or not to enjoy themselves. Look to your staff and see if there are any young, energetic staff members who might want to make a few extra dollars (if your administration will pay them for their time). You may want to ask librarians at other local libraries and see if they will offer their chaperoning services in exchange for your services at a future date. You should plan to have at least one chaperon for every five teens. Regardless of who helps out as chaperons, be sure to thank them time and time again, and maybe they will consider helping out again in the future!

Filling your lock-in program with activities is essential to keep the momentum up and your participants interested and not bored. Start your program with plenty of ice-breakers and plan for additional ice-breakers throughout the evening. You can plan a craft at some point in the program, perhaps decorating the young adult department for a holiday or event, or even helping cut out shapes for an upcoming children's program (if your participants are already volunteers or teen board members. If this is a reward program, you probably don't want to put your participants to "work.") You may plan to show a movie or allow computer time, but both of these activities will require an additional permission slip from parents.

Games and food are traditional lock-in favorites, so you may want to plan for specific times to play games and eat food. Serving ice cream sundaes at midnight is a fun way to gather the participants and to mark the "middle" of the event. Variations of hide-and-seek are perennial favorites at library lock-ins; just be sure to be very clear about off-limits areas.

If you have a particularly close-knit group of teens, consider scheduling a talent show. With all of the high-activity events in an evening, you may want to schedule "quiet times" for resting (this is a good time to show a movie), or even require a "lights out" session so that some of your participants can get rest at some point during the evening.

A lock-in that includes homeschoolers may have additional considerations. You might have to spend extra time discussing the program with parents to assure them that there will be plenty of activities throughout the lock-in and that there will be plenty of adult chaperons monitoring the activities. If you have many homeschooling teen volunteers, you may even be able to have a lock-in that is exclusive to them, which might reassure those parents who are uncomfortable having their children socializing with other teens they do not know.

Regardless of how long your lock-in will last or the activities you have planned, be sure to secure permission, have a schedule of events, reliable chaperons, a set of lock-in rules that are read at the beginning of the program and posted in all areas, and lots of coffee!

Language Programs

Language Clubs

Our survey of homeschoolers revealed that several homeschooling teens would welcome the opportunity to join a language club. If the homeschoolers are not taking private language lessons, they may be relying on audio- and video-tapes to learn a foreign language. A language club gives these teens an opportunity to practice speaking in their foreign language among others who are studying the same language. Talk to the language teachers at your local schools (high schools and colleges) to see if anyone would be interested in volunteering their time for monthly meetings. You also might be able to find native speakers in your own community. Post signs throughout the library to generate interest and to find out if there might be people who could share their language abilities with your homeschooling teens.

Connecting your collections to language club programs is fairly easy—simply promote those books that are related to the club theme, and try to regularly purchase materials in those areas to keep the club members coming back for more.

International Night

When you poll your homeschoolers, you might find that many of them are studying several languages and cultures. If this is the case, you can allow them to share what they are learning by sponsoring an international night. Usually these programs revolve around food, but you can also showcase books about the various cultures and if your teens are up for it, they can even create traditional costumes (although this might seem a bit too much like schoolwork!).

Sign Language Workshop

A single program or series of programs on sign language will be popular with homeschooling and non-homeschooling teens alike. You might be able to locate an instructor at a community college or community center. A series of programs starting with learning the alphabet, followed by common words and phrases, and a discussion of deaf culture would be sure to please many of your teen patrons. This is another instance where it would be ideal to offer a certificate of completion. Be sure to have plenty of sign language materials in your collections for those participants who want to continue to learn more.

Teen Participation Programs

Overwhelmingly, the best way to offer the most to your homeschooling teens is to provide them opportunities for participation. There are many ways your teens already participate at your library; the most common way is by attending programs and events. But true participation means taking a more active role in the planning and decision-making process of your library's services. You can think of youth participation as being on a continuum with program attendance on one end and a teen advisory board on the other. Along this continuum you will find many opportunities for your teens to actively participate in library services. Whether a homeschooling teen participates as a member of a single focus group, contributes as a member of a volunteer program, or serves as a member of a youth advisory board, there are many opportunities to include homeschooling teens in your participation programs. If you include homeschooling teens in these capacities, you will likely find that they are more flexible than traditionally schooled teens with the hours they can contribute, and the homeschoolers will benefit by having opportunities that support their developmental needs.

Volunteer Opportunities

Because homeschooling teens do not have to report to school every day, they are usually much more flexible with the hours they can come to the library. Any teen volunteers can be helpful assistants but they are often at school when the library needs assistance. Here are some ideas for offering volunteer opportunities to your homeschooling teens:

- *Assisting with the children's story hours.* They can help with the preparation, cutting out of materials, and actual story telling/puppetry in the program. A group of homeschooling teens might be interested in volunteering their time and talents to write skits and perform readers' theater as part of a children's program.

- *Assisting with activities associated with a Friends organization.* When there are fundraising activities, homeschooling teens can contribute their time in preparing mailings or even making phone calls (with the proper training!).

- *Assisting with general fundraising activities.* Homeschooling teens could help out with book sales, bake sales, car washes, or other fundraising activities. Non-homeschooling teens would also be able to volunteer in these capacities, but homeschoolers might be able to play a more active role in the planning and implementation if they are available at times when their peers are not.

- *If you have homeschooling volunteers who are especially helpful, consider hiring them as members of your staff.* Not all homeschoolers are looking for employment, but those who are would find working at the library a perfect fit.

Teen Advisory Boards/Councils

Getting started with a youth participation program or teen board can be a time-consuming matter. Without proper planning it may end up that much of your time has been spent with little to show for it. Fortunately there is a very well-laid-out plan and timeline available in *Young Adults and Public Libraries: A Handbook of Materials and Services.*[5] Lynn Cockett's two-year plan is excellent advice for a young adult librarian new to a library without existing young adult services. This plan can also be transformed to expand young adult services in an existing program that has little or no teen participation. Although this plan does not address homeschoolers, you can use the plan with an additional effort to target the homeschooling population. When you begin targeting the local schools to drum up interest, just be sure to send information to local homeschooling organizations as well. Keep plenty of applications in the young adult area of your library and bring them to your programs. It has been our experience that homeschoolers are already frequenting the library on a regular basis, so try to approach them individually to see if they would be interested in serving on your teen board.

Here are some special considerations to keep in mind for including homeschooling teens in your participation programs/library boards:

- If you limit membership on the teen board or have quotas to ensure a representative population from local schools, be sure to include a representative number of homeschooling teens.

- Consider electing officers and establishing an advisory board constitution and bylaws. Traditional students have opportunities to serve as elected officers in a variety of clubs, but homeschoolers may not have the same opportunities. Being able to document a leadership position on an advisory board might make a difference on a homeschooler's college application or resume.

- Consider having a homeschooler subcommittee or task force. If you have a number of homeschoolers on your board, they could meet to work on common goals at a time when the other members are unable to meet. Your homeschooling task force could possibly meet on a Tuesday morning, when the meeting room is available, to work on a homeschooling newsletter or to add content for homeschoolers to your Web site.

Once you have homeschooling teens on your teen advisory board, or even have them on a special task force, here are some project ideas to consider for them:

- Book reviews: Like other young adult patrons, homeschoolers often request recommendations for good books to read. Who better to recommend good books to homeschoolers than the homeschoolers themselves? If you already have a system set up for your young adult patrons to turn in book reviews (see Figure 6.5), you can run off the forms in a special color to indicate that a homeschooler has written the review. Post the reviews on a bulletin board or publish them in a newsletter. When you are asked by a homeschooling teen or parent for a recommendation, point out which reviews were written by other homeschooling teens.
- Newsletters: Have homeschooling members of your teen advisory board write a column in your newsletter to homeschoolers. They can highlight items from the collection, incorporate book reviews, comment on past programs or highlight upcoming programs.
- Web site production: If you have any homeschooling teens who are technologically oriented, perhaps they would be interested in helping with the design and upkeep of your library's young adult Web site. They might be interested in overall Web design or perhaps just interested in contributing to a section geared for homeschoolers. Either way, work with your Webmaster to ensure that teen input is alive and well on your Web site.

Skills Programs

Homeschooling teens are often seeking opportunities to improve their skills in an interesting, hands-on way. The library can offer programs that help teens build skills that will undoubtedly offer many practical applications. Skills programs that are popular with teens, regardless of how they are educated, include the following:

Figure 6.5
Sample Book Review Form

Author:					
Title:					
Genre:					
Rating:	*	**	***	****	*****
Review:					
Reviewer's Initials:					

Babysitting Programs

You can contact the American Red Cross to offer their program in your library (there are usually fees associated with their programs) or plan your own babysitting program. There are many books on establishing a babysitting business that can be used as an outline, and this program could easily be turned into a series of programs due to the amount of information that would need to be covered.

First Aid

First aid programs are best left to the professionals. You can contact the American Red Cross to see what is involved in offering their certified program to your teens.

Driver Safety

Work with a local driving school or car dealership to put together a program on driver safety. For a more extensive program, you can include basic car care and maintenance.

Nutrition

Contact your local high school, community college, or hospital to see if there is someone available to present a program on basic nutrition. As part of the program, you can offer nutritious snack ideas as your refreshments.

Money/Budget/Economics

Offer a program on basic money management for teenagers. Again, you can contact your local high school or community college to see if there is someone who can present the program, or you might be able to compile enough information by turning to your collection. There may be someone through a local bank or consumer organization that can provide you with materials or a speaker.

Contests

Many homeschoolers do not have many contest opportunities, since contests often tend to be sponsored through the schools. When libraries sponsor contests, whether the contest is a talent contest, lip sync contest, art contest, photography contest, creative writing or poetry contest, special effort should be made to invite homeschooling contestants. Not only do contests support adolescent development, they also offer homeschooling teens avenues for creative expression and experiences that will support their portfolios and college applications.

When planning a contest for teens at your library, here are some general considerations:

- *Eligibility:* Who is eligible for the contest and what categories will be used? Many libraries split the young adult contestants into age categories because skills vary greatly between ages twelve and eighteen. Libraries may also want to exclude library employees if library employees will be judging the contest. When winning categories are awarded by schools, the library should be sure to include a category for homeschoolers in the middle school and high school age groups.

- *Entries:* How are the entries to be submitted? If there is an official entry or registration form, it is advisable to keep the contestant's name off of the main entry, either on a separate page or on the back side of the entry, in order to ensure fair judging. You may also want to limit the number of entries per contestant so you don't overwhelm your judges. Contestants should be provided with specific instructions on how entries are to be submitted, for example: Are art or photography entries to be framed or matted? What sizes will be allowed? This may affect how the entries are to be displayed.

- *Prizes:* What kinds of prizes will be awarded and how many prizes will be needed? Where will the prizes or funds come from?

Having multiple categories in a single contest (e.g., black-and-white photos/color photos or age/school categories) will require more prizes. Fortunately, contests are such visible programs that libraries will undoubtedly find some sponsors in the community. Many libraries look to their Friends organization for prizes for contests.

- *Judges:* Who will do the judging? The easiest set of judges would be library staff, but to add to the prestige of your contest, consider asking your mayor or other public official to serve on your panel of judges. If you decide to include officials from the local schools, try to make an effort to invite a representative from the home-schooling community to serve as a judge. In addition, consider enlisting an expert in the field, for example, a photography teacher or an editor from your local newspaper. You may want to consider having peer judges for your contest, but be especially sure that contestant identities are kept confidential to avoid biased judging by their friends. Finally, you may want to add the element of a "people's choice" award by allowing your patrons to vote for their favorite entries. Regardless of who you ask to judge your contest, be sure to provide them with specific criteria to aid them in their judging.

- *Display:* Which entries will be displayed and how? Due to space constraints some libraries only display visual art contest winners along with honorable mentions. Creative writing entries can be compiled into a booklet and awarded to all contestants and made available for free or a small charge to other patrons.

- *Ceremony:* An awards ceremony should be planned to recognize winners and all contestants. Be sure to provide certificates of participation to all contestants. The ceremony would be an excellent public relations opportunity, so be sure to invite all of your judges as well as the press.

FURTHER READING

Braun, Linda W. *Hooking Teens with the 'Net.'* New York: Neal-Schuman Publishers, 2003.

An excellent resource for teaching information literacy skills, Braun offers ideas on how to connect popular Web sites to teaching critical Internet research skills. Each section includes an overview, lesson plans, and activities.

———. *Teens.library: Developing Internet Services for Young Adults.* Chicago: American Library Association, 2002.

Includes information on what teens are doing on the Internet, what they want from the Internet, and how to create a library Web site with teens in mind. Appendices include a teen Web site development checklist, a checklist for teen participation in Web site development, programming opportunities for teens who wish to be involved with Web site development, an evaluation checklist, and usability tips.

Caywood, Caroline A., ed. *Youth Participation in School and Public Libraries: It Works.* Chicago: American Library Association, 1995.

Offers guidelines for implementing youth participation, training ideas, a list of libraries with youth participation programs, and national guidelines.

Champelli, Lisa. *The Youth Cybrarian's Guide to Developing Instructional, Curriculum-related, Summer Reading, and Recreational Programs.* New York: Neal-Schuman Publishers, 2002.

Includes sample programs from around the nation in the areas of instructional, curriculum-based, summer reading, and recreational programs. Each program is listed with a general overview, target audience, required equipment, program description, contact information, and section on "insights and improvements."

Chelton, Mary K., ed. *Excellence in Library Services to Young Adults.* 1st ed. Chicago: American Library Association, 1994.

————. *Excellence in Library Services to Young Adults.* 2nd ed. Chicago: American Library Association, 1997.

————. *Excellence in Library Services to Young Adults.* 3rd ed. Chicago: American Library Association, 2000.

Each edition includes the nation's top programs in areas including collaborative efforts, reading promotion, intergenerational programs, special needs, staff development, and youth participation. Each program includes a description of the setting/community, a program description, how programs were funded, and contact information.

Edwards, Kirsten. *Teen Library Events: A Month-by-Month Guide.* Westport, Connecticut: Greenwood Press, 2002.

Includes a wealth of detailed program ideas designed around a twelve-month calendar. As each month is presented, information is provided on how to begin preparing and laying groundwork for future programs throughout the year.

Honnold, RoseMary. *101+ Teen Programs that Work.* New York: Neal-Schuman Publishers, 2002.

This practical guide to young adult programming offers ideas that can be easily adapted to homeschooling programs. Honnold includes feedback from participants, as well as guidance for starting young adult programs and services. Additionally, collection connection ideas are offered for the program ideas.

Kan, Katherine. *Sizzling Summer Reading Programs.* Chicago: American Library Association, 1998.

Broken down by kinds of reading programs (incentive, themed, participation, etc.); Kan offers many practical ideas for summer programs to work with a variety of young adults. Suggestions for funding programs and sample promotional materials make this an accessible and useful book for planning a variety of reading programs.

Pappas, Marjorie L., and Ann E. Tepe. *Pathways to Knowledge® and Inquiry Learning.* Greenwood Village, Colorado: Libraries Unlimited, 2002.

An excellent guide for planning information literacy skills programs for grades K-12; Pappas and Tepe explore the information literacy standards set forth by the AASL (American Association of School Librarians) and the AECT (Association for Educational Communications and Technology).

Reid, Rob. *Something Funny Happened at the Library: How to Create Humorous Programs for Children and Young Adults.* Chicago: American Library Association, 2003.

Humorous programs are broken down into age categories, including a section on programs for middle school and high school patrons. Reid includes a special section on readers' theater, ways to work humorous rap songs into booktalks, and a bibliography of humorous titles.

Simpson, Martha Seif. *Reading Programs for Young Adults: Complete Plans for 50 Theme-Related Units for Public, Middle School and High School Libraries.* Jefferson, North Carolina: McFarland & Company, 1997.

Includes fifty themed reading program ideas for young adults. Simpson offers ideas for program promotion, activities, and collection and curriculum connections.

NOTES

1. The "Big6™" is copyright © (1987) Michael B. Eisenberg and Robert E. Berkowitz. For more information, visit: http://www.big6.com.

2. Mary K. Chelton, ed., *Excellence in Library Services to Young Adults,* 3rd ed. (Chicago: American Library Association, 2000), 59–60.

3. Kirsten Edward, *Teen Library Events: A Month-by-Month Guide* (Westport, CT: Greenwood Press, 2002), 89–98.

4. Lisa C. Wemett, ed., *The Basic Young Adult Services Handbook: A Programming and Training Manual.* (Albany, NY: New York Library Association, 1997), 49–50.

5. Lynn Cockett, "Youth Participation: Involving Young Adults in Library Services," in *Young Adults and Public Libraries: A Handbook of Materials and Services* (Westport, CT: Greenwood Press, 1998), 165–180.

7

◇ ◇ ◇

THE MARKETING MAMBO: YES, WE CAN TEACH YOU TO DANCE

A recent call from a telemarketer went like this:

> "Hello. I'm calling from Joe's Glass Shop. Do you have a cracked windshield you'd like an estimate on?"

Pretty straightforward, except that it's a terribly inefficient (and expensive) way to reach potential customers—start at the beginning of the telephone book and call every number until you happen to reach someone whose need fits your service. Granted, most telemarketing works just that way, but the odds seem particularly long in this case. Take a quick look around the mall parking lot. Most cars don't have a cracked windshield.

What is the point of this example? To demonstrate that marketing—promoting your goods and services to potential customers—needs a studied approach, one that will maximize your message and your money. Rather than randomly taking aim at anything that moves, the careful marketer researches and knows his market, knows who and where his potential customers are, has determined what their needs are, and then directs his message to them in ways that are most likely to reach them. With better marketing, Joe's Glass Shop might realize that its true customers are independent auto repair shops, new and used auto dealers, or body shops. Personal sales calls to these businesses—rather than telemarketing—will increase the volume of Joe's business. He may choose to develop a brochure to place in the waiting rooms at dealerships and repair shops. An ad in the Yellow Pages helps direct individual customers to his store. Maybe Joe can volunteer his time to instruct vocational students in auto glass installation. He can encourage customers to make referrals by offering discount incentives. Finally, he might have all his employees carry brochures or business cards to place under the windshield wiper of cars that need new glass. In so doing, Joe hasn't placed all his marketing eggs in one basket. He's using different methods to reach different customers. He's tailoring the message and its delivery to those different customers.

But, you say, we aren't selling auto glass. Libraries are service institutions. We "loan," we don't "sell." We have patrons, not customers. Our patrons include everyone in the community; we don't have specific "target markets." Everybody needs the library sometime—all we have to do is sit back and wait for them to line up at the desk. We have no competition, we're the information specialists, the only game in town. Guess again.

"Erase from your thinking any idea that marketing is unnecessary for your library because you are somehow protected. Whether you have recognized it or not, competition is out there. Customers looking for more current information than their public library provides can be lost to commercial suppliers of information....The result of ignoring the needs of your customers will be that they become someone else's customers."[1]

Libraries face more competition today than do many businesses, because that competition comes from every activity that in some way demands the time and attention of our potential customers. Think of some possible competitors:

- Bookstores
- Video stores
- Other libraries
- Television
- Electronic "toys" (VCRs; DVD players; CD players; video games, computers)
- The Internet
- Sports
- Hobbies
- Career
- Volunteering
- Family obligations

If you only thought of bookstores and video rental centers, perhaps you can now see that there are many more things vying for your teen customer's attention. Anything that impacts on available time to spend in the library is direct competition. Your customers aren't captives; they will go to another provider who meets their needs if they're unhappy with your service. What can you do? How can you market your services so that the library becomes a first choice for people trying to squeeze too much day into too few hours?

MARKETING VS. PUBLIC RELATIONS

At the outset, we need to define our terms because marketing and public relations aren't the same thing—although many outside the profession have a tendency to substitute one term for the other. Public relations focuses on selling or promoting the product; marketing focuses on the customer—who he is, what he needs, what benefits he expects from the library. Public relations encompasses all aspects of the promotion or "selling" part of a library's marketing effort. It includes every contact between library staff and customers.[2] It is about making the library's resources known to the community, so it may include not only press releases, but also speakers' bureaus; broadcast e-mail announcements; radio and cable television public service announcements (PSAs); and paid advertising like billboards, newspaper ads, newspaper inserts, posters, and fliers. All of these elements fall under public relations and are actually the tools by which you can market your program or service.

Marketing is about responding to customer needs. A marketing approach to library management changes how librarians define what they do, moving from an emphasis on the product (collections and services) to an emphasis on the customer. Market-oriented management identifies markets (specific segments of the community), researches their needs, taking into account the library's resources and ability to implement new services.[3] It is not solely for the purpose of providing new services, but must also reinforce and improve existing ones. Librarians must understand and identify with the users they serve. Every staff member must "buy into" the marketing concept and be full participants.[4]

Right now, we invite you to consciously shift your thinking and make a change in your vocabulary. We'll substitute the word "customer" for "patron" when referring to library users. It's the first step toward embracing a marketing model for promoting your library's services. Libraries serve customers. We are a customer-focused institution.

Take a walk through a shopping mall and make some comparisons. Christie Koontz did that for her article in *Marketing Library Services* and makes these observations:

> Successful retailers assess the strengths and weaknesses of competitors and look for that advantage that will keep more customers coming through their doors than their competitors'. Libraries have only recently recognized an ever-growing competitive environment in which people can and do choose from myriad information sources. And it is this element of competition that is turning library users into customers...by constantly assessing actual and potential customer wants and needs, prioritizing customer markets, and identifying the competition, libraries can (and must) enter the fray of a world that is customer-driven.[5]

By applying modern marketing techniques to how we deliver service, we can also substitute research-based planning for intuition and guesswork. Marketing always requires choices of what services to provide. The reality is that no one library can do everything.[6] Budget and staffing constraints mean that every effort must count. Whatever program or service is planned, good marketing means we'll realize the most bang for our buck.

MARKETING PLANS

A change in public attitude about the value of libraries, coupled with competition from the Internet, have made it increasingly important that libraries take a more proactive approach to strategic planning and marketing to keep libraries from becoming discounted even more.[7] A growing awareness on the part of library directors and trustees of the importance of marketing library services has caused them to adopt business models that include the creation of marketing plans.

But what if you're not the public relations or marketing specialist in your library or you don't have one available on staff or under contract? Assuming that you, the reader, are a professional or paraprofessional librarian working with teens, we know that you already wear many hats. How can you possibly be expected to design a marketing plan? The samples you've seen are probably designed for businesses that spend millions on marketing research. How can you make this work for your library?

The truth is, at its most basic level, a marketing plan is simply that: a plan. Even a down-and-dirty, quickly sketched marketing plan for how you want to approach your customers and what you want to accomplish is worth the effort. Any time you sit down and put thoughts on paper and organize a plan of attack, you are less likely to miss something important.

STEP-BY-STEP GUIDE TO BUILDING A MARKETING PLAN

Don't think that you have to hire a consultant or invest in expensive plan writing software in order to complete a useful marketing document. What follows are the very basic elements that should be included in your plan:

Your Library's Mission Statement

It is vital that a library mission statement be in place before developing a marketing plan. The mission and role of the library in the community must be defined, and that mission must be known and understood by staff, funding sources, and customers. Without a clear understanding of the library's mission, the ability to communicate the library's message and promote its services is impeded.[8]

The mission statement should answer questions about the library's purpose. In just two or three sentences, set out the overall focus of your library. Are you the community's primary information resource? Do you want the community to use the library as a gathering place? Is your primary focus on self-education? Pleasure reading and listening? Reference and research? Run a Web search to read samples of library mission statements. Good ones are succinct and capture the essence of the library in language that is free of ambiguity.

Identifying Your Target or Niche Market

That's easy…you want to serve the homeschooled teens in your community. But wait. What do you really know about them? How many teens are in your target market? Do you know the kinds of services and programs they want or need from you? How will you find out? Later in this chapter we'll review the various survey methods you can use to learn more about your homeschooled teens.

Describe Your Services

What programs and services do you already offer that can be modified for and promoted to homeschooled teens? In answer to your survey, what additional services have your customers requested? As you list these items, determine what it will cost in terms of staff and supplies to implement them.

Promotion Strategies

If you develop a wide assortment of programs and services for homeschoolers and they don't know that you offer them, your efforts are wasted. In what ways will you promote these activities so that teens know about them? Some methods to consider:

- Posters in libraries and at area churches
- Handouts and bookmarks
- Presentations to local homeschool organizations; participation in workshops and conventions
- E-mail announcements to homeschooled teens and parents
- Articles in homeschool newsletters, church bulletins, and on your library's Web site

Don't forget that one of your most critical promotion strategies is conversation at the library's circulation desk. No matter what you are promoting, be certain that all frontline staff is knowledgeable about the details of your program or services and that they are prepared to answer customer questions. One way to ensure that everyone is on the same page is to create an update sheet that can be filled out with the details of a specific program or new service and posted near the circulation desk phone. Dates, times, location, intent, and the name of the program are the basics. Be sure to remind staff that if they are asked a question that they do not know the answer to, they should take the customer's name and phone number so that you can respond.

Identify Your Competitive Edge

Who is your competition? It may be the Internet, the college library in the next town, or simply the many activities in which your homeschooled teens are already involved. What gives you the competitive edge? Sell your library as the place where a real human being helps find the answers on the Web, where there's a collection of books set aside for homeschoolers trying to identify an independent study project, where information about colleges that embrace homeschoolers is maintained and made available. Incorporate these messages into the promotional items you design. Remind your target market of the unique benefits they'll get by using your library.

Set Measurable Goals

Librarians are typically great gatherers of numbers. What numbers have value for you? Will it be the percentage of your target market that you reach with a specific service or program? An increase in the circulation of your homeschool resources? Determine what you feel defines success and set a specific number as your goal.

Evaluation

Your marketing plan should outline methods for evaluating what's working and what's not. Some suggestions include asking homeschoolers who attend a program how they heard about it. Use their responses to gauge the effectiveness of your advertising and promotion. If most of them read about it in their homeschool newsletter, but no one saw the press release in the local paper, you might consider saving press releases for big events and the day-to-day program schedule for inclusion in their organizational newsletter. Ask them what other ways they use for finding out information and then include those with your promotional strategies.

A formal way of evaluating your marketing plan is to conduct a marketing "audit." The audit assesses customer needs, explores community patterns, and analyzes the internal environment—the library itself, and its mission, goals, resources, organizational structure, strengths, and weaknesses.[9] With this information in hand, the marketing system is analyzed. Are we using the right combination of promotional strategies to reach our target market (in this case, our homeschooled teens)? What organizational changes or shifts in resource allocation can be made to strengthen our promotional work and our marketing plan?

Ultimately, the goal of evaluation is to help you make necessary adjustments in programs, services, and, ultimately, in your marketing plan. Be prepared to revise your plan as needed and don't be afraid of failure. Not surprisingly, it can take many repetitions or varied formatting of your message before it is heard by your homeschooled teens and their parents. Feel free to tweak your promotional strategies until you hit on a combination that works.

Marketing Plan Checklist

☑ Review your library's mission/vision statement

☑ Identify your target or niche market

☑ Describe your services

☑ Choose and develop promotional activities

☑ Identify and articulate your competitive edge

☑ Set measurable goals

☑ Marketing audit/evaluation (what worked, what didn't)

SURVEYS: WHAT CAN I DO FOR YOU?

As we said earlier, market-based planning begins with the identification of the target or "niche" market to be served. In our case, the market is already identified as the homeschoolers who are or could be using our library, but the same marketing principles can be applied no matter who you've identified as potential customers: seniors, the homebound, the underserved, teachers, local businessmen, etc.

Homeschoolers, however, may not be as easily identifiable as those populations in the previous list. To gain some understanding about how many homeschoolers are in your market, you may have to locate data maintained by the school districts in your service area. This is easily done in places where homeschooling families are required to report to the school superintendent. There are states in the United States, however, that don't require any form of reporting. This may make your data collection somewhat more difficult, but not impossible. Contact local churches to identify those homeschool groups that may be affiliated with a particular church. Pay attention to families with children, obviously school-age, who are in your library during regular school hours. Casual conversation with these families may help you network with other homeschoolers in your service area. Be aware when asking questions of homeschooling families that some are sensitive to anything that they perceive as being intrusive. As we said earlier, some homeschooling parents have had a difficult time with public school authorities and are wary of anyone asking questions. Reassure all with whom you speak that your interest is purely to determine how the library can better assist them and their children in the learning process. At this early point in your research, all you're trying to determine is the size of your customer base. Obviously, the number and kinds of services and programs you will be offering may differ depending upon the number of potential participants. In this way, your marketing research greatly enhances program and service planning.

Now that we know the "who," let's move on to the "what." Having identified your customer base or market niche, you next want to find out what your customers need. The best way to find out? Ask them! Only by surveying your customers can you be certain that the programs or services you want to provide are what they really need and want. Surveys can be of several types; we'll describe each one and suggest which might work best with your homeschooling teens.

Telephone Surveys

Phone surveys feature simple questions utilizing multiple choice or fill-in-the-blank responses. These surveys are more about breadth than depth. You'll reach a large number of people and you'll be able to identify a broad range of information, but you're not likely to reach your homeschooled teens this way. One possible exception to this would be if you had already developed a call list for contacting your homeschooling customers for some other purpose (announcements of new services or upcoming programs, for example). These homeschoolers might be happy to answer a quick phone survey; otherwise, save the phone surveys for things like judging public perception of library service and as a warm-up to a levy campaign.

Written Surveys

You'll gain more information from a written survey than from a phone survey, because you'll be able to ask open-ended questions and allow your customers the time for thought-out responses. A written survey would work with your homeschoolers, provided that the questions are clear and unambiguous.

Sample Surveys

The first sample survey was designed by the authors in 2001 to solicit information from homeschooled teens and parents for this book. Volunteer participants were sought by posting to homeschooling e-lists, with questions and responses handled via e-mail. The questionnaire was in three parts, with the first part seeking an overview of the respondents' homeschool experience, followed by two sections specific to library services. The survey was worded as though the parent or guardian would be responding, but some were completed by the teens themselves. A total of seventeen surveys were returned.

Survey of Homeschoolers

Part 1 Your Homeschooling Experience

1. Please provide your first name, city, and state (or province)
2. Please list the current ages of all the children being homeschooled
3. Please list the ages of the children when they began homeschooling
4. Do you plan to homeschool your children through high school?
5. What kinds of standardized tests has your teen taken, or is planning to take? (e.g., GED, SAT, ACT, etc.)
6. What, if any, homeschooling organizations or associations do you belong to?
7. What online listservs or newsletters do you subscribe to?
8. What homeschooling magazines/newsletters/journals do you subscribe to?
9. What, if any, prepared curricula/correspondence schools do you use with your homeschooled teen?
10. Please list any books that have greatly influenced or assisted in the homeschooling of your teen.
11. Please describe any specialized lessons or classes (e.g., art, music, subject-specific tutoring) used to supplement your teen's homeschooling
12. Please describe any extracurricular activities (e.g., band, sports, special interest clubs) in which your teen participates.
13. Does your homeschooled teen have a job? If so, please briefly describe the position and average weekly schedule.
14. Does your homeschooled teen volunteer? If so, please describe various duties and the average hours volunteered each week.

Part 2 Your Library Experience

1. Please describe the various types of libraries you use (e.g., public, bookmobile, church, college, homeschooling group, etc.)
2. Do you have a personal homeschooling library at home? Please describe the types of materials you collect for your home library.
3. How often does your teen visit the public library?
4. How often does your teen attend public library programs? (Please answer either "never" or "number of times per week, month, year.")
5. What kinds of library programs does your teen participate in? (e.g., summer reading, book discussions, crafts, volunteering, teen advisory board or council)

(continued)

(Continued)

6. What library materials or services has your teen found helpful for homeschooling? (e.g., fiction, nonfiction, videos, computer programs, Internet access)

7. How often do you ask for assistance from the librarian? Please share any experience, positive or negative.

8. Does your library have a special collection of homeschooling materials? If so, please describe the types of materials included.

9. Does your library offer any special lending periods or privileges to homeschoolers (e.g., teacher cards, extended loans)

10. Do you use any library meeting rooms? For what purpose?

11. Does your library have a homeschooling resources manual? If so, please describe its contents.

12. Describe any programs or services designed specifically for homeschooled teens at your library.

13. Does your library provide any reading or resource lists for homeschoolers? If so, please describe.

14. How does your library promote services to homeschoolers? (e.g., bulletin boards, newsletters, e-mail lists)

15. Please share any library experiences when you felt that the library went above and beyond in its service to your family.

16. Please describe any instances when you felt you were unfairly denied library services or treated unfairly because of your child's homeschooling status.

Part 3 Your Ideal Library

1. What kinds of print resources do you wish your library offered? (e.g., specific kinds of books, magazines, newspapers)

2. What kinds of nonprint resources do you wish your library offered? (e.g., videos, audio materials, kits, computers, software, online materials)

3. What kinds of programs do you wish your library offered? (e.g., reading incentives, crafts, discussion groups)

4. What kind of materials would you like to see in a homeschooling collection?

5. What kinds of services do you wish your library offered? (e.g., meeting rooms, special homeschooling library cards, homeschooling manuals, curriculum exchanges)

6. How would you prefer to find out about library programs, services, and materials? (e.g., newsletters, bulletin boards, e-mail lists)

7. Finally, feel free to add any of your personal experiences that were not covered by any of the survey questions.

If our survey had been intended for measuring general library customer satisfaction, it's highly unlikely that anyone would take the time to complete it because of its length. Homeschoolers, however, tend to be highly motivated. By explaining in our initial request the purpose of the survey—to provide us information about how homeschoolers use their libraries and what they need to make the experience more satisfying—we invited respondents to "buy in" to our project. They were more than willing to take the time, since they could see the benefit of helping to reach many librarians at once through this book.

The survey example in Figure 7.1 is a customer satisfaction survey conducted by the Wadsworth (OH) Public Library in 1998. Volunteers were posted near the front entrance of the library during varying hours throughout a one-week period. The volunteer approached every third person entering the library and invited them to participate. In addition to the survey instrument shown, individual surveys were designed for completion by students and teachers served by the library's Outreach Department and for homebound customers using the library's books-by-mail program. The survey exercise yielded several hundred responses; information from the survey was used to form the basis for long-range planning and for planning the eventual construction of a building addition.

DESIGNING THE SURVEY INSTRUMENT

Writing survey questions and designing the survey instrument can seem daunting. Rest assured that should it appear to be more than you or your library director are willing to undertake on your own, consultants are available to help with the entire process from researching your target market, through conducting the survey, to analysis and proposals for action. However, the authors believe that for the purpose of determining the needs of a narrow group like homeschooled teens, a simple, self-designed survey will gather the information you want.

Writing Survey Questions

The temptation when writing and compiling survey questions is to ask anything and everything out of intellectual curiosity. Resist the urge. A survey instrument that asks every question under the sun is going to provide a mountain of data, much more than you need to determine what homeschoolers want from your library. Unless you want to sift through the minutiae, take care to ask only those questions that will provide useful

Figure 7.1
Sample Customer Satisfaction Survey

Wadsworth Public Library
Customer Satisfaction Survey   *Fall 1998*

What was the purpose of your visit to the Library today? (Mark all that apply.)
- ☐ Return Library items
- ☐ Use photocopier
- ☐ Get an answer to a specific question
- ☐ Study or read
- ☐ Check out books
- ☐ Check out audio-visual materials
  (Videos, audiocassettes, CDs, CD-ROMs)
- ☐ Browse
- ☐ Place an item request/pick up reserved items
- ☐ Use the Internet
- ☐ Other _____

Did you find what you needed? ☐ Yes ☐ No

Did you ask for help? ☐ Yes ☐ No
If not, was there a reason for not asking?
- ☐ Help was offered before I could ask
- ☐ I found the item myself
- ☐ I didn't know I could ask
- ☐ I didn't know **who** to ask
- ☐ Everyone was busy
- ☐ Other _____

If an item you were looking for was unavailable, did you ask to have it reserved (held for you when it becomes available)?
☐ Yes   ☐ No   ☐ Didn't know I could reserve

What could the Wadsworth Library do to better help you locate the items you need? (Mark all that apply.)
- ☐ Provide more/better staff assistance
- ☐ Provide better signs
- ☐ Provide guided tours
- ☐ Provide illustrated, instructional brochures
- ☐ Re-arrange the materials (different shelving
  & displays)
- ☐ Other
_____

Did you need assistance in using the Library's computerized catalog today? ☐ Yes ☐ No
Were you able to get help if you needed it? ☐ Yes ☐ No
What could the Library do to make using the computerized catalog easier for you?
- ☐ Provide written instructions
- ☐ Provide one-on-one instruction classes
- ☐ Provide small group instruction classes

Please rate your satisfaction with the following items, putting a checkmark in the appropriate box.

ITEM	Satisfied	Neutral	Dissatisfied
The books or materials you found today	☐	☐	☐
The help you received from Library staff	☐	☐	☐
The physical appearance of the Library	☐	☐	☐
The ease of using the computer catalog	☐	☐	☐
The ease of finding what you need on the shelves	☐	☐	☐
The hours during which the Library is open	☐	☐	☐
Library programs for children	☐	☐	☐
Library programs for teens	☐	☐	☐
Library programs for adults	☐	☐	☐
Parking at the Library	☐	☐	☐
Amount of space in the building	☐	☐	☐
The Internet computers	☐	☐	☐
Your overall library experience	☐	☐	☐

Which of the following would **increase your satisfaction** with Wadsworth Public Library? (Mark all that apply.)
- ☐ No change necessary
- ☐ More books for adults
- ☐ More books for children
- ☐ More books for teens
- ☐ More magazines
- ☐ More videos
- ☐ More audiocassettes
- ☐ More CDs
- ☐ More CD-ROMs
- ☐ More staff available to provide customer service
- ☐ More computer terminals
- ☐ More programs for adults
- ☐ More programs for children
- ☐ More programs for teens
- ☐ More specialized services for aging, handicapped, and
  homebound
- ☐ More copies of popular items
- ☐ Something else? (Please list) _____
_____
_____

Did you have any physical difficulty using the computerized catalog? ☐ Yes   ☐ No
If yes, describe nature of difficulty:
- ☐ Using the mouse or keyboard because of arthritis or
  other physical problem
- ☐ Seeing items on the computer screen because of a
  vision problem
- ☐ Other (please describe)_____
_____

Continued...

feedback. Remember the KISS method and "Keep It Simple, Suzie." Survey questions should be focused, brief, simple, and in plain language. The most popular type of survey question utilizes the Likert Scale, a continuous scale usually having an odd number of possible replies.[10] An example of a question using the Likert Scale follows on page 145.

Figure 7.1
(Continued)

In what ways could the Library improve its facilities?
(Mark all that apply.)
☐ More tables and chairs
☐ Better physical access to materials
☐ More computer terminals
☐ More quiet places
☐ Coffee bar
☐ Special area for young adults
☐ Better traffic flow at check-out desk
☐ Other_____

What do you like **best** about Wadsworth Public Library? _____

_____
_____
_____

What do you like **least** about Wadsworth Public Library?_____

_____
_____
_____

How do you **most often** hear about what's new at Wadsworth Public Library?
☐ Word-of-mouth
☐ The Ellagram - the Library newsletter
☐ Library Calendar
☐ Business newsletter
☐ Article in the newspaper
☐ Signs or brochures in the Library
☐ A staff person
☐ Wadsworth Cable TV announcements
☐ Other _____

Please tell us about yourself...
☐ Age 13-18
☐ Age 19-24   ☐ Male   Postal zip code
☐ Age 25-44   ☐ Female
☐ Age 45-64   _____
☐ Age 65+

Please add anything else you would like to share with us _____

_____
_____
_____
_____
_____
_____
_____
_____

Thank you for your time!

Reprinted with permission of the Wadsworth Ella M. Everhard Public Library, Wadsworth,
Ohio. http://www.wadsworth.lib.oh.us.

Likert Scale Example Question

1. Overall, I am satisfied with the services my library provides to home-schoolers

☐ Very satisfied ☐ Somewhat satisfied ☐ Neutral ☐ Somewhat dissatisfied ☐ Not at all satisfied

---

Questions such as the above example are useful for measuring satisfaction, importance, and agreement. For our purpose, we also want to gain input from homeschoolers to determine how we might meet their needs. In a written survey, we might design questions that offer a series of possible services or programs and ask the respondents to indicate the ones they would be most likely to use. Alternately, we might ask them to rank suggested services or programs by the order of personal importance or likelihood that the service or program would be used.

Sample Survey Questions

Examples:

1. From the following list of items, select those that would be of most use to you as a homeschooler:

    ☐ Teacher loan cards
    ☐ Extended loan periods
    ☐ Curriculum exchanges

2. Please rank the following items by order of importance to you as a homeschooler. Use "1" for the most important and so on:

    ☐ Library has collection of items specifically for homeschoolers
    ☐ Library has collection of samples of commercial curricula
    ☐ Free use of library meeting rooms
    ☐ Special programs or events designed just for homeschoolers

---

Ideally, surveys should include questions that are both qualitative and quantitative, that is, they should measure both hard numbers and the perceptions or attitudes behind those numbers. An example of a quantitative question might be "How often do you visit the library? Once a week? Once a month? Never?" A qualitative question seeks the respondent's perception: "True or false: The library never has the things I need when I ask."

Organizing the Survey Instrument

There seem to be several schools of thought regarding how to organize your carefully crafted questions into a finished survey tool. You may opt to place your demographic questions—age, gender, zip code—at the beginning to serve as a warm-up and to get your respondents comfortable with the survey. These questions may also be placed at the end; perhaps those you are surveying don't want to answer personal questions until they get to "know" you a bit better. Other considerations include mixing the types of questions. A long series of true/false or yes/no (discreet) questions may lull the respondent into simply zipping down the list and not paying real attention to the question being asked. An interruption, in the form of a question using the Likert Scale, or one that asks for a detailed response may wake your homeschooler up again. The best way to determine how your survey will work in the "real" world is through field testing. Gather a few homeschoolers when they visit your library. Tell them that you want to test your survey before inviting a larger group to complete it. Keep track of how long it takes your test group to finish the survey, and note any questions for which they need further clarification before answering. If you've promised that the survey will only take a few minutes, make sure it's true by timing the test takers. If a question is not clear to them, discuss how it might be reworded to make it clearer.

INTERVIEWS

In the course of a typical workday, you constantly interview your customers. Any reference request can become the opening question for an informal interview. "Did you find what you needed? Are there other kinds of materials that would work better? Are there any programs that we might offer to help you with that assignment?" More formal interviews can be set up to try out ideas for programs and services or to determine specific needs. When homeschooled teens visit your building, ask them if they'd participate in a short, one-on-one survey. Or ask your local homeschooling association for the opportunity to meet with teens during a parents' meeting.

FOCUS GROUPS

Focus groups can address not only your desire to survey your homeschooled customers, but also provide them with a chance to interact and consider together ways to improve or add library services especially for them. Make certain that your moderator has the skill to elicit responses and to maintain an atmosphere of give-and-take. Your group can help determine the direction for further development of programs and services. Again, recruit your participants from among those already using your library or by contacting a local homeschooling organization.[11] Focus groups can also be a good way to begin preparation for a written survey. Through discussion with focus group members, questions that can be used with the larger group can evolve, plus you realize the added benefit of "field testing" the questions with the focus group before including them in your written survey.

The following article on setting up and running a focus group gives tips on question development, session planning, and facilitation:

Basics of Conducting Focus Groups

Focus groups are a powerful means to evaluate services or test new ideas. Basically, focus groups are interviews, but of 6–10 people at the same time in the same group. One can get a great deal of information during a focus group session.

Preparing for Session

1. *Identify the major objective of the meeting.*
2. *Carefully develop five to six questions (see below).*
3. *Plan your session (see below).*
4. *Call potential members to invite them to the meeting.* Send them a follow-up invitation with a proposed agenda, session time and list of questions the group will discuss. Plan to provide a copy of the report from the session to each member and let them know you will do this.
5. *About three days before the session, call each member to remind them to attend.*

Developing Questions

1. *Develop five to six questions*—Session should last one to 1.5 hours—in this time, one can ask at most five or six questions.
2. *Always first ask yourself what problem or need will be addressed by the information* gathered during the session, e.g., examine if a new service or idea will work, further understand how a program is failing, etc.
3. *Focus groups are basically multiple interviews.* Therefore, many of the same guidelines for conducting focus groups are similar to conducting interviews.

Planning the Session

1. *Scheduling*—Plan meetings to be one to 1.5 hours long. Over lunch seems to be a very good time for others to find time to attend.
2. *Setting and Refreshments*—Hold sessions in a conference room or other setting with adequate air flow and lighting. Configure chairs so that all

(continued)

(Continued)

members can see each other. Provide name tags for members, as well. Provide refreshments, especially box lunches if the session is held over lunch.

3. *Ground Rules*—It's critical that all members participate as much as possible, yet the session should move along while generating useful information. Because the session is often a one-time occurrence, it's useful to have a few, short ground rules that sustain participation, yet do so with focus. Consider the following three ground rules: a) keep focused, b) maintain momentum and c) get closure on questions.

4. *Agenda*—Consider the following agenda: welcome, review of agenda, review of goal of the meeting, review of ground rules, introductions, questions and answers, wrap-up.

5. *Membership*—Focus groups are usually conducted with 6–10 members who have some similar nature, e.g., similar age group, status in a program, etc. Select members who are likely to be participative and reflective. Attempt to select members who don't know each other.

6. **Plan to record the session with either an audio or audio-video recorder.** Don't count on your memory. If this isn't practical, involve a co-facilitator who is there to take notes.

Facilitating the Session

1. *Major goal of facilitation is collecting useful information to meet goal of meeting.*

2. *Introduce yourself and the co-facilitator, if used.*

3. *Explain the means to record the session.*

4. *Carry out the agenda*—(See "agenda" above).

5. *Carefully word each question* before that question is addressed by the group. Allow the group a few minutes for each member to carefully record their answers. Then, facilitate discussion around the answers to each question, one at a time.

6. *After each question is answered, carefully reflect back a summary of what you heard (the note taker may do this).*

7. *Ensure even participation.* If one or two people are dominating the meeting, then call on others. Consider using a round-table approach, including going in one direction around the table, giving each person a minute to answer the question. If the domination persists, note it to the group and ask for ideas about how the participation can be increased.

8. *Closing the session*—Tell members that they will receive a copy of the report generated from their answers, thank them for coming, and adjourn the meeting.

(continued)

> *(Continued)*
>
> ### Immediately After Session
>
> 1. *Verify if the tape recorder, if used, worked throughout the session.*
> 2. *Make any notes on your written notes,* e.g., to clarify any scratching, ensure pages are numbered, fill out any notes that don't make sense, etc.
> 3. *Write down any observations made during the session.* For example, where did the session occur and when, what was the nature of participation in the group? Were there any surprises during the session? Did the tape recorder break?
>
> Used by The Management Assistance Program for Nonprofits, 2233 University Avenue West, Suite 360, St. Paul, Minnesota 55114 (651) 647-1216. With permission from Carter McNamara, PhD. Copyright 1999

SELLING IT

This is when the promotional strategies of your marketing plan come into play. You've identified your customers. You've taken the time to ask them what they need. Using the results of your research, you've developed a "product." Now you have to get your customers to come into your library and "buy" what you're selling. How do you reach those for whom you've carefully crafted a particular program or service? And what can you do to make sure they'll come back again and again? This is where the promotion strategies and evaluation portions of your marketing plan come into play.

Think about how you get information about sales, programs, concerts, and events of any kind. Usually it's through some form of promotional material: an ad in the paper, on radio, or on television; a direct mail flier; an e-mail message; a telemarketing call; a handbill stuck in your front door, a poster on the grocery store bulletin board. In truth, we are being marketed to so relentlessly that we suffer from information overload. Soon we don't pay any attention because we can't decide what to pay attention to. It takes something downright remarkable to even break through all the marketing "noise."

Therefore, don't be surprised that the promotional tools you need to reach homeschooling teens have to be very carefully crafted and delivered. Teens gather information in different ways and from different sources than do adults. True children of the computer age, teens are much more likely to embrace and use electronic communication than are their parents. They want and expect their information in the ubiquitous "sound bite" preferably delivered right into their e-mail inboxes. A newspaper notice buried in the entertainment section or a radio spot on a station that plays oldies just isn't going to reach them.

And the painful truth is, your homeschooled teens may not be readers of your library's newsletter, either. The only way to reach them is by manner and means that are specifically tailored for them.

Those who responded to our survey, when asked about the ways in which they would most like to receive notice of library services and events listed e-mail most often. As part of your marketing research, consider a brief survey of your homeschooling customers to determine if e-mail is indeed their first choice. Depending on the complexion of your community, you may find that some other means is preferred. While some homeschooled parents fully embrace the treasure trove of information available on the Internet, others won't even have a computer in their homes. Be prepared to be flexible, even if e-mail is really the easiest and most efficient communication method for you. Just don't become locked into a single means of communication; let your public tell you how and where they expect to find out about the library.

In addition to e-mail, try setting up a moderated e-list and invite your homeschooled teens to participate. Use the e-list to promote what's new at the library, announce program schedules, or request feedback about needs. An e-list, especially a moderated one, can require a good deal of time and attention. An excellent explanation about what's involved in setting up and running an e-list is available at http://www.emoderators.com/papers/how2sdg.html.

Another possible promotion tool is a teen newsletter. This can be produced by library staff or a combination of staff and teen volunteers. Make the newsletter available as a handout at the library, send copies to your local homeschooling groups, and put up a display at your community's recreation center, hobby shops, bowling alleys, and other places where teens gather. The newsletter doesn't have to be elaborate; a single page, front and back, using graphics and fonts that grab the attention, is sufficient. Field-test a draft of your newsletter with teens who visit your library. If they think it's dull and boring, ask for suggestions to boost its appeal, then head back to the drawing board. If producing a teen newsletter seems too time-consuming, ask if you can submit articles to newsletters produced by your local homeschool support groups. Include book lists, program announcements, and highlight special homeschooling resources within your collection.

Your library's Web site can be a very powerful promotional tool, assuming you or whoever is designing it keeps some principles in mind. The design itself should be clean, uncluttered, and logical in terms of where on the page you place key information or navigational links. Think of the Web site as a virtual visit to the library. Is the front door clearly marked and easy to find, that is, is the link to your online catalog front-and-center? Is your directional signage understandable to a new visitor? Do you succumb to the use of library-ese or do your signs convey the purpose of the service provided? Rather than a link to "Reference Databases and Resources" suppose the link button reads "Questions Answered Here"?

Don't forget your homeschooled teens when designing or upgrading your library's Web site. A page set aside for homeschooled teens can be the perfect place to announce programs, list services, provide links for everything from teen entrepreneurial projects to college entrance exams, or start an online book/movie discussion group. Be sure to include links to local, regional, and state homeschooling organizations, as well as another to your state's homeschooling regulations. Again, field-test whatever you design, asking for suggestions for improvement as necessary. Chapter 4 gives three examples, including web addresses, of libraries with terrific Web pages for homeschoolers.

Word-of-mouth is, was, and shall be one of the best marketing tools you can use. No amount of advertising can match the power of someone sharing their experience with others. Teens are particularly apt to listen to what their peers are saying and make decisions based on the experiences of others. The best word-of-mouth comes from satisfied teen customers responding positively to the way they are treated at the library. They have a low tolerance for being patronized and they can spot phonies. Teens may not be dazzled by your expertise and reference skills; they are much more likely to remember that they were treated respectfully and with a genuine desire to meet their information needs. While you may find that the behavior of homeschooled teens is different than that of traditional school students, they are still human adolescents with all the sensitivities, worries, and "angst" of their peers. Be honest and open with them and you will be rewarded with the kind of positive PR for which there is no price.

Selling It Checklist

- ☑ Press releases
- ☑ Public service announcements
- ☑ Paid advertising
- ☑ E-mail alerts to subscribed customers
- ☑ Articles in homeschool newsletters
- ☑ Library newsletter specifically for homeschoolers
- ☑ Posters, fliers, bookmarks, bulletin board displays
- ☑ Homeschool link on library Web site
- ☑ Talk it up! Word-of-mouth is the best promotion tool
- ☑ Brainstorm other ideas with homeschooling customers

PRESS RELEASES, PSAS, ADVERTISING, AND WORKING WITH REPORTERS

Press releases and PSAs (Public Service Announcements) are the basic means by which you can promote your program or service. The writing required for either is simple and direct and follows an established format, which, once learned, can be easily produced. Take a look at the press release example in Figure 7.2.

Press releases should be printed on your library letterhead and should be double-spaced. Under most circumstances, a press release should not exceed one page, although feature stories about new services or a special event may run longer. Spelling, grammar, and factual accuracy all count.

Figure 7.2
Sample Press Release

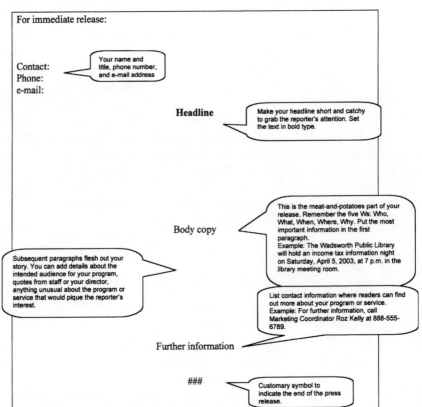

Public Service Announcements

The Federal Communications Commission requires that radio and television stations donate a portion of their airtime to serve the public and the community. Public Service Announcements (PSAs)—usually about community events sponsored by nonprofit groups—are read or aired in fulfillment of this federal requirement.

Writing a PSA is much like writing a press release: the key information is still who, what, when, where, and why. Most PSAs run from 10 seconds to 60 seconds. The best way to judge the length of your PSA is to read it aloud at a moderate pace, and time your reading.

A printed PSA might look like this:

Figure 7.3
Sample Public Service Announcement

```
                    PUBLIC SERVICE ANNOUNCEMENT
                                        For use: March 1–31, 2003
                                            Contact: Roz Kelly
                                            Phone:888-555-6789
                                        e-mail: rkelly@library.org


          Wadsworth Library holds tax info night April 5

                    The Wadsworth Public Library

                    will hold a tax information night

                    on Saturday, April 5, 2003, at 7 p.m.



              Volunteer tax preparers will be on hand.

                    To schedule an appointment

                        call 888-555-6789.
```

As with a press release, your PSA should be printed on library letterhead.

When and Where to Send Press Releases/PSAs

Making decisions about when to send press releases can depend upon the publication frequency of the newspaper or magazine you wish to use. The very best way to determine a newspaper or magazine's "lead time" (how far ahead of your event they must receive your information for publication) is by calling and asking. Lead time can vary: if your information is for a community calendar that only prints on certain days in your daily newspaper, a different lead time may be required than for an article that will appear in the regular news sections. Monthly magazines can have lead times many months in advance of publication.

When you call your local paper, ask to speak to the reporter who covers your community or who handles the community calendar. Having a name to put on the envelope with your press release helps make sure that it doesn't get misdirected in the newsroom. The reporter is in the best position to tell you how much lead time is required. Of course, that phone call can also open up dialogue about the library, its services, upcoming events, and new materials. Make the most of any time spent in conversation with a newspaper reporter!

Lead time for PSAs can also be determined by calling the television or radio station. Ask for the name of the person who handles the community calendar. You can also address PSAs to the public service director at each station.

Your library's marketing plan should address which media outlets will be used for promoting library events and services. Obvious choices would include your community's daily and/or weekly newspapers; radio stations with reception within your service area; and television stations (commercial and local cable) that broadcast into your service area. If there is a community or regional magazine that has readership in your area, include that as well.

A good place to start in identifying the media outlets that serve your area is by consulting a news media directory. Check with your reference librarian to see whether your library has such a directory. Several are available, including:

- News Media Directories, Mt. Dora, FL (800) 749-6399
- Gebbie Press, New Paltz, NY (845) 255-7560 or http://www.gebbieinc.com

- http://www.newsdirectory.com/
- http://www.mediapost.com/

Scheduling the mailing of your press releases and PSAs should be part of the planning process for your event or the launch of a new service. Make note of the varying lead times for each media outlet and adhere to them; there are few things as embarrassing in the library marketing person's life as a press release that's published after an event has taken place!

While radio and television stations have a legal obligation to provide promotional support to nonprofit organizations free of charge, newspapers are under no such requirement to print your press releases. Once a newspaper receives your release, they are completely in control of the placement of your news in the paper and the timing of its publication. You may have dreams of front page, above-the-fold coverage and find your release relegated to Page 10, Section B. Two things will give you some control over your message: you can buy advertising or you can "sell" your story to the reporter. We'll cover paid advertising first.

Buying Paid Advertising

There are two basic types of newspaper ads: classified ads and display ads. Classified ads are the small ones, typically at the back of the paper, used to advertise everything from hot tubs to Labrador puppies. Classified ads are usually priced by the number of words or lines in the ad. Newspapers frequently offer package pricing, allowing the advertiser to run their ad for a certain number of days or on certain days of the week.

Display ads are the larger, boxed ads that appear toward the front of the newspaper, among the news stories. Display ads are placed on the page beginning at the bottom, with the news stories stacked above. Unless you buy a full-page ad, you may not have control over the actual placement of your ad on a page; you may, however, be able to designate a specific section of the paper where you would like your ad to appear.

Display ads are usually sold by the column inch, although they may also be sold as a fractional portion of a full page. Column inches are measured by counting the number of columns the ad takes up in width and multiplying that number by the number of inches the ad is in height. So an ad that is four column inches in size may be: two columns wide and two inches high; one column wide and four inches high; or four columns wide and one inch high.

Pricing for display advertising depends on an array of factors. Cost obviously is impacted by the size of the ad, whether the ad uses a color other than black, and the number of times the ad will run. Newspapers may offer unique pricing for special advertising opportunities, for instance, a tabloid insert highlighting your community's United Way kickoff. They may offer special deals on color, perhaps giving buyers a discount to use orange during a particular week in October. Newspapers may also offer special pricing for nonprofit or government agencies. It is always worth asking whether the library qualifies for special price considerations.

Since pricing is specific to each media outlet, there is little merit in discussing advertising costs in this book. The best way to determine a newspaper's ad pricing and offers is to call the advertising department and ask for a display ad rate sheet. Newspapers employ advertising sales representatives who will work with you to determine the size of your ad, layout and graphics, placement, and frequency.

A quick word about magazine advertising. Again, pricing is dependent upon the size of your ad, the use of color, and frequency. Buying ads in magazines is generally a more expensive proposition than buying newspaper ads. Magazine ads run for as little as $100, but the prices quickly reach the high three figures, and the covers (inside front, inside back, and back) can easily cost thousands.

"Pitching" Your Story to a Reporter

There are some stories about your library that are too exciting or important to be conveyed in a press release. There are those rare stories or special events that deserve a personal phone call to a reporter. Be very judicious in making these kinds of calls; save your story "pitches" for things like grand openings, nationally known guest speakers, groundbreaking for a new building, or placing a library issue on the ballot. Program announcements, the winners of the bookmark coloring contest, and the annual arrival of income tax forms can usually be handled in a press release.

Before you make your "sales" call, be sure that you have all of the information about your program or event written out in front of you. You can actually write a press release to organize your thoughts; even though you've made the personal contact, the reporter may still ask you to send a release. Remember that deadlines are a key motivating factor for reporters. Find out what day your weekly paper goes to print and avoid calling that reporter until the next morning. The reporter at the daily paper may not arrive at the office bright and early, but may work into the evening. A call during the early afternoon might work best. In either case, when you get your reporter on the telephone, be sure to ask them if they are on deadline and whether they have time to allow you to pitch a story to them. Respect their need to make deadline and offer to call at another time of their choosing if necessary. On occasion you may need to field a media inquiry regarding a program, new service, or to flesh out a press release you sent. Calls from reporters should be handled with some urgency, but don't feel pressed to respond to questions if you are uncertain of the correct answers. If you need time to research an answer, tell the reporter that you will get the information she is requesting and will call back. Again, ask whether the reporter is on deadline and how quickly an answer from you is required. Respect the fact that the reporter is simply doing a job; despite the occasional portrayal of media encounters as adversarial, there is much you can do to promote a workable relationship by being open and honest. If you are not the best person to respond to a reporter's question, say so and put the reporter in touch with the person who can respond.

If television coverage of an event is your goal, many of the same rules for pitching your story apply. Television news directors are looking for stories that can be told in ten- to twenty-second sound bites accompanied by exciting or dramatic visuals. Be sure to emphasize those elements of your event that promise the most visual impact. Remember when talking to television news directors that they, too, have deadlines to meet, so always ask whether you are calling at a convenient time.

Several excellent resources for learning how to pitch news stories are available on the Internet. See the section titled "Library Marketing— Online Resources" at the end of this chapter.

YOUR INTERNAL CUSTOMER

Remember your internal customer—your coworkers at the library. All of your careful planning of services and programs will be wasted effort if you have not fully engaged the imagination and enthusiasm of your library staff. These are the frontline people who work with your external customers every day. They are the ones in the best position to make connections between those customers and everything that the library has to offer. If your staff is caught unaware of a new service or suddenly find themselves expected to perform some new duty that you have devised without their input, don't expect them to climb happily on your bandwagon. Particularly where service to teens is concerned, you may be working against negative and strongly held personal impressions. Explore and honestly address those concerns as you gather staff input. Remind staff of the important role they play in "selling" library services. Model the behavior that you know will work with teens and consider role playing and other training for staff as necessary.

SUMMARY

The need to market is an inescapable reality for today's libraries—indeed, your library's survival may depend on it. No longer can we assume that everyone looks to their library as the preferred provider of information. Our users may not discern the differences in the quality of the information they receive from other sources; they're in a hurry, they want the answer quickly, and thoroughness doesn't impress them much. Like it or not, today's library user is a customer, as well as a patron. As a customer, those visiting your library weigh the value of what they've received against convenience, personal service, friendliness, timeliness, and a whole host of other intangibles. If your library is found wanting, your customer will go elsewhere. Marketing—finding out what people need and want and then providing those things to the best of your ability—can make the difference. Homeschooled teens represent one select portion of our customer base; what we learn by addressing and meeting their specific needs can become a model for marketing other services and programs in our libraries.

FURTHER READING

Block, Maryline. "The Secret of Library Marketing: Make Yourself Indispensable." *American Libraries* 32, no. 8 (Sept. 2001): 48–50.

de Saez, Eileen Elliott. *Marketing Concepts for Libraries and Information Services.* 2nd ed. London: Facet Publishing, 2002.
    This introduction to a wide range of basic marketing concepts and techniques includes an extensive discussion of marketing in the digital age. It explores the potential of e-marketing for librarians and information managers; data mining and customer relationship management; as well as basic marketing techniques.

Dworkin, Kristine D. "Library Marketing: Eight Ways to Get Unconventionally Creative." *Online* 25, no. 1 (Jan./Feb. 2001): 52–4.

Jain, Abhinandan, et al., eds. *Marketing Information Products and Services: A Primer for Librarians and Information Professionals.* N.p.: International Development Research Center, 2000.
    Recognizing that libraries face competition from a wide array of sources and that a proactive approach is the only way to compete, the editors set out to provide a practical guide to the fundamentals of marketing in the context of libraries. Chapters include "How to Conceive, Design and Introduce New Information Products and Services," "How to Promote Information Products and Services," and "Preparing the Organization for Marketing of Information Products and Services."

Karp, Rashelle S. *Powerful Public Relations: A How-To Guide for Libraries.* Chicago: American Library Association, 2002.

This title was originally published as *Part-Time Public Relations with Full-Time Results,* but has been expanded in this new edition that promises to be a one-stop resource. Essays by practicing library public relations professionals aim to help librarians make their institutions as user-friendly and as user-oriented as possible. The book includes many sample press releases, brochures, and flyers.

Kies, Cosette N. *Marketing and Public Relations for Libraries.* Metuchen, NJ: Scarecrow Press, 1989.

Written by a professor of library science, this title explains marketing practice as it applies to libraries and as it can be applied. The book includes the definition of marketing and public relations; library marketing and PR promotion techniques; analysis and evaluation; marketing/PR plans for specific libraries; national library marketing and PR; and trends in library marketing/PR. All types of libraries are covered: academic, public, school, and special.

Marketing and Libraries Do Mix: A Handbook for Libraries & Information Centers. Columbus: State Library of Ohio, 1993.

This is an accessible handbook on marketing for the library professional. It begins with an overview of what marketing is and isn't; addresses the special concerns of different types of libraries (public, academic, corporate, government, institution, law, medical, school); and, as part of extensive appendices, shows examples of surveys, interview forms, and marketing assessment worksheets.

Marketing Library Services, published six times a year by Information Today, Inc., Medford, NJ.

This newsletter is valuable not only for marketing professionals working in libraries but for any library staff member who has been given marketing responsibilities. On occasion the articles are a bit heavy in theory and too light on practicalities, but features such as the book review; a marketing ideas column based on Chase's Calendar of Events, and general library-related news briefs are worthwhile.

Taney, Kimberly Bolan. *Teen Spaces: The Step-by-Step Library Makeover.* Chicago: American Library Association, 2003.

Packed with ideas for creating spaces for teens in libraries, this title also includes tips on merchandising, space planning, and budgeting that can be applied to plans for marketing to homeschooling teens.

Walters, Suzanne. *Marketing: A How-To-Do-It Manual for Librarians.* New York: Neal-Schuman Publishers, Inc., 1992.

Here is another basic guide for librarians attempting to incorporate marketing practices into the management of their libraries. Walters covers the principles of marketing including the concepts of product, pricing, placement, and promotion, and also discusses marketing research, merchandising, and the role of marketing in fundraising and politics.

Weingand, Darlene E., *Marketing/Planning Library and Information Services,* 2nd ed. Englewood, CO: Libraries Unlimited, 2000.

This is an update of the 1987 edition, written when librarians were first becoming aware of the need to shift to a customer-driven mind-set. The new edition covers how to create a marketing team, conduct a marketing audit, set goals, set budgets, promote services, and evaluate the marketing effort.

Library Marketing—Online Resources

http://www.owls.lib.wi.us/info/desks/bc/imarket/about/about.htm
> Authored by Beth Carpenter, the Web services manager for the Outagamie Waupaca Library System in Appleton, WI. Carpenter has written and been a conference speaker on library marketing. The site focuses on public library marketing.

http://www.librarysupportstaff.com/marketinglibs.html
> One-stop "shopping" for all things related to marketing library services both on and off the Internet. Includes information on writing a marketing plan; library signage; creating surveys and polls; strategic planning; and fundraising.

http://www.galegroup.com/free_resources/marketing/index.htm
> Gale offers free marketing resources including graphics and simple-to-use templates.

http://www.sla.org/chapter/cwcn/wwest/v1n3/cavilb13.htm
> Special Library Association; Western Canada Chapter. Online worksheet for developing a library marketing plan.

http://www.infotoday.com/mls/jun99/how-to.htm
> Follow this link to a June 1999 article on writing a marketing plan.

http://www.winslo.state.oh.us/services/LPD/tk_market.html
> Bibliographic resources list of articles, books, and Web sites relating to marketing library services

http://www.ssdesign.com/librarypr/
> Strategies, tools, tips, and resources for library communicators. Includes the Little Black Book of essential contacts including ALA PIO; Booksale Finder; Library PR Council; and information on library PR contests.

http://www.chrisolson.com/marketingtreasures/
> Marketing Treasures offers tips, ideas, and insights to librarians and others on how to promote and apply marketing tools to their information services and products.

http://www.alia.org.au/~jcram/MARKETMA.PDF
> Article in PDF format. "Marketing for Non-School Libraries: A guide to an essential management activity." Department of Education, Queensland, Australia.

http://mediarelations.ifas.ufl.edu/index.html
> An online media relations training program produced by the University of Florida. The section titled "Getting Out The News" explains the basics about how news-gathering organizations function and how best to reach them.

http://www.101publicrelations.com/index.html
> Sells a series of publications on public relations including how to pitch stories over the phone and handling crisis communications.

http://www.prmadeeasy.com/
> Sells a series of downloadable public relations guides on topics including writing press releases and pitching stories.

NOTES

1. State Library of Ohio, *Marketing and Libraries Do Mix: A Handbook for Libraries and Information Centers* (Columbus: State Library of Ohio, 1993), 8.

2. Ibid., 3.

3. Barbara Dimick, "Marketing Youth Services," *Library Trends* 43, no. 3 (Winter 1995).

4. State Library of Ohio, 3–4.

5. Christie Koontz, "Customer-Based Marketing: Stores and Libraries: Both Serve Customers!," *Marketing Library Services* 16, no. 1 (January–February 2002).

6. Amelia Kassel, "How to Write a Marketing Plan," *Marketing Library Services* 13, no. 5 (June 1999).

7. State Library of Ohio, 3.

8. Dimick.

9. Darlene E. Weingand, *Marketing/Planning Library and Information Services* (Littleton, CO: Libraries Unlimited, 1987), 38–45 (cited in Dimick).

10. Author's notes from workshop: "*Finding and Keeping Library Users through Survey Methods*" (Cleveland Area Metropolitan Library System, November 2002).

11. State Library of Ohio, 18–20.

8

◇ ◇ ◇

FROM SOUP TO NUTS: RESOURCES FOR LIBRARIANS, HOMESCHOOLED TEENS, AND THEIR PARENTS

There is considerably more information available for today's home-schooler than there was just a decade ago. In addition to books on every-thing from making the homeschool choice to choosing a college for a homeschooled teen, the Internet is being used to excellent advantage by homeschoolers who can now complete all coursework for a high school diploma without even leaving home.

This chapter identifies books, articles, and Web sites that the authors deem most useful for homeschoolers and the librarians working with them. The first section includes those books the authors have identified as important inclusions for a core collection on homeschooling. That list is followed by titles of general interest and titles specifically geared toward homeschooled teens. Magazine and journal articles come next, and the chapter concludes with lists of homeschooling organizations and contact information for boards of education, arranged in alphabetical order by state.

A CORE COLLECTION FOR LIBRARIES SERVING HOMESCHOOLERS

Barfield, Rhonda. *Real-Life Homeschooling: The Stories of 21 Families Who Teach Their Children at Home.* New York: Fireside, 2002.

Twenty-one chapters explore various homeschooling families' experiences. Each chapter introduces the makeup of the family, offers the best and worst advice given to them, a favorite quote, and favorite resources used by that family. Testimonials include a single mother, a Jewish homeschooling experience, homeschooling children with special needs, and many stories that homeschooling families can relate to and learn from.

Brostrom, David C. *A Guide to Homeschooling for Librarians.* Fort Atkinson, WI: Highsmith Press, 1995.

Offers valuable insight into homeschooling for librarians. Chapters include an overview of the homeschooling movement, how to determine the needs of the homeschooling community and determine policies and programs, specific challenges that may arise, and ideas for cooperation. The appendices include homeschooling organizations, periodicals, correspondence schools, curriculum and audiovisual suppliers, software suppliers, Web sites, and a homeschooling bibliography.

Cohen, Cafi. *And What about College?: How Homeschooling Can Lead to Admissions to the Best Colleges and Universities.* Cambridge, MA: Holt Associates, 2000.

This title is a "must-have" for homeschooled teens. Topics covered include choosing a homeschool learning approach for high school, guidelines for college preparatory work, the admissions process, testing, choosing a college, writing the college entrance essay, and attending college from home (distance education).

Cohen, Cafi. *Homeschoolers' College Admissions Handbook: Preparing Your 12- to 18-Year-Old for a Smooth Transition.* Roseville, CA: Prima Publishing, 2000.

This companion to *And What about College* covers much of the same ground with information about researching for the right college "fit," writing the entrance essay, preparing portfolios, and writing transcripts. A section on campus visits and interviews is also included.

Cohen, Cafi. *Homeschooling the Teen Years.* Roseville, CA: Prima Publishing, 2000.

A practical handbook for parents preparing to or currently homeschooling their teenaged child. Beginning with a chapter on how to get started, Cohen proceeds to cover many of the special concerns of working with teens—teaching advanced topics; driver's education; socialization—and offers ideas and examples of how to approach them. Each chapter ends with a "Resources" section including book titles, Web sites, and support organizations.

Colfax, David and Micki. *Homeschooling for Excellence.* New York: Warner Books, 1988.

The Colfax family is frequently cited as the prime example of homeschooling success, since, at the time this book was written, one son had graduated from Harvard and two others were students there. Micki Colfax says that they didn't intend to be pioneers, but certainly they are viewed that way today. In *Homeschooling for Excellence,* the Colfaxes tell the story of their homeschooling experience, beginning with a review of the problems they find inherent in formal education and the ways in which homeschooling may provide an alternative for families. Resources listed for teaching the basics and beyond are likely outdated or surpassed by more recently produced materials, but the Colfaxes' book is still a valuable read as a story from the early days of modern homeschooling.

Dobson, Linda. *Homeschoolers' Success Stories: 15 Adults and 12 Young People Share the Impact That Homeschooling Has Made on Their Lives.* Roseville, CA: Prima Publishing, 2000.

An ideal addition to any homeschooling collection, this title will satisfy requests for more homeschooling testimonials. Includes stories of home-schooled adults and young adults who have led successful, meaningful lives. Additionally, a chapter includes "the homeschooling legacy" pointing out famous homeschoolers past and present including presidents, scientists, businesspeople, artists, and more.

Downs, Laurajean. *You're Going to do What? Helping You Understand the Homeschool Decision.* Elkton, MD: Holly Hall Publications, Inc., 1997.

This title is unique, written as a response to grandparents concerned about their children's decision to homeschool. The author addresses the issue of socialization—always a concern raised early by well-meaning family and friends—the various reasons for choosing homeschooling, and suggests ways that grandparents can be both emotionally and materially supportive.

Heuer, Loretta. *The Homeschooler's Guide to Portfolios and Transcripts.* Foster City, CA: IDG Books, 2000.

Record keeping is of extreme importance for college-bound homeschoolers, since they don't have the traditional course transcripts that colleges are more accustomed to seeing. This guide to preparing portfolios and transcripts includes chapters on evaluating, documenting, and communicating the homeschooler's experience, the basics of assessment, the basics of portfolios, how to create a portfolio, how to present the portfolio, using technology, the basics of transcripts, creating transcripts, preparing for college admissions, the college application, and appendices with samples and resources.

Leppert, Mary, and Michael Leppert. *Homeschooling Almanac 2002–2003.* Roseville, CA: Prima Publishing, 2001.

Divided into four sections, this comprehensive guidebook can serve as both launching pad and catalog. Part 1, "The Nuts and Bolts of Homeschooling" is precisely that, with chapters covering learning styles, homeschooling approaches, and how to get started. Parts 2 and 3 cover products and resources; the product pages include photos of items and contact information for purchasing them. Part 4 is a state-by-state compilation of homeschooling laws and organizations. Finally, bound in at the back of the book are coupons good toward the purchase of items listed in the catalog section. While the coupons for this edition expire on December 31, 2003, the book is certainly valuable even without them.

Llewellyn, Grace, ed. *Real Lives: Eleven Teens Who Don't Go to School.* Eugene, OR: Lowry House Publishers, 1993.

Here, homeschooled teens speak directly from their own experiences about how they educate themselves outside the traditional school setting. *Real*

Lives is the perfect companion to Llewellyn's "liberation" handbook, illustrating as it does her theory that teens are perfectly capable of learning when permitted the freedom to follow their interests. Chapter titles reveal a lot—"My Favorite Teacher is a Horse", "What Radio and Bicycles (and Everything Else) Have to do with My Education", "Homeschooling is Another Word for Living." The reader can't help but admire these bright, articulate teens.

Reed, Jean, and Donn Reed. *The Home School Source Book.* 3rd ed. Bridgewater, ME: Brook Farm Books, 2000.

Contains a combination of essays and commentaries with a catalog of resources useful to any home school. Helpful reviews of products will be of use to homeschoolers and librarians alike.

Rupp, Rebecca. *The Complete Home Learning Source Book: The Essential Resource Guide for Homeschoolers, Parents, and Educators Covering Every Subject from Arithmetic to Zoology.* New York: Three Rivers Press, 1998.

Encyclopedic in scope, this book lives up to its title. All manner of resources are listed and reviewed including books, Web sites, board games, CD-ROMs, videos, magazines, and catalogs. Just about any interest a homeschooler could want to explore is covered in this exhaustive compilation.

Saba, Laura, and Julie Gattis. *The McGraw-Hill Homeschooling Companion.* New York: McGraw-Hill Trade, 2002.

Another comprehensive guide for homeschool beginners. The whys and hows are covered first of all. The authors then move on to specific topic areas such as literature, math, and science, and discuss how each of these topics might be addressed at different grade levels. Preparation for career and college are also covered.

Scheps, Susan G. *The Librarian's Guide to Homeschooling Resources.* Chicago: American Library Association, 1998.

This is a terrific resource directory—although perhaps in need of updating—which lists state, regional, and provincial support organizations; correspondence schools; publishers of homeschooling materials; periodicals; and an extensive bibliography that also includes Web sites.

Wade, Theodore E. *The Home School Manual: Plans, Pointers, Reasons, and Resources.* 7th ed. Berrien Springs, MI: Gazelle Publications, 1998.

This practical guide starts with a section on the principles of home education, then looks at teaching various subject areas and age groups, and offers advice ranging from self-discipline, organization, the role of dads, and teaching several children—all of concern to homeschooling families. The appendices include many valuable resources including high school distance education programs, a typical K-12 curriculum, and contacts for many homeschooling resources.

ADDITIONAL BOOKS ON HOMESCHOOLING

Allee, Judith Waite, and Melissa L. Morgan. *Educational Travel on a Shoestring: Frugal Family Fun and Learning Away from Home.* Colorado Springs: WaterBrook Press, 2002.

Offers many inexpensive ideas for travel or field trips for homeschooling and non-homeschooling families alike. Along with specific travel ideas, this title includes researching tips and ideas for funding. Travel ideas include family volunteering opportunities, day trips, working vacations, and more.

Bailey, Guy. *The Ultimate Homeschool Physical Education Game Book.* Camas, WA: Educators Press, 2003.

Offers ideas for physical education programs for the entire family and for all ages. Expensive equipment is not required, and children can learn the basics of movement, fitness, and sports-specific skills in the homeschool environment.

Berquist, Laura M. *Designing Your Own Classical Curriculum: A Guide to Catholic Home Education.* San Francisco: Ignatius Press, 1998.

This valuable resource for Catholic homeschoolers offers guidance in developing a curriculum. Starting with kindergarten and going through the twelfth grade, each grade level includes a curriculum plan, sample weekly schedule, and resource list. Suppliers for the resources are included.

Callihan, David, and Laurie Callihan. *The Guidance Manual for the Christian Home School: A Parent's Guide for Preparing Home School Students for College or Career.* Franklin Lakes, NJ: Career Press, 2000.

Designed to fill in the gaps of information that might be provided to traditional students by their guidance counselors, this guide for Christian homeschoolers offers insight through short, focused chapters. Many portions of this guide will also be of assistance to non-Christian homeschoolers, including the chapter titled "Basic Training" which covers basic life skills like managing money, as well as chapters on testing, working during the high school years, and keeping records. A chapter on military opportunities makes this title a well-rounded guide for preparing homeschoolers for life after the high school years.

Caruana, Vicki. *The Organized Home Schooler.* Wheaton, IL: Crossway Books, 2001.

Offers practical advice on organizing time, space, supplies, and paperwork, as well as how to create a filing system. Written from a Christian homeschooling perspective, the advice in this title can apply to other homeschooling families as well.

Clark, Mary Kay. *Catholic Home Schooling: A Handbook for Parents.* Rockford, IL: Tam Books, 1993.

From the director of the Seton Home Study School, this title offers advice for the Catholic homeschooling family. It touches on issues such as the father's role in homeschooling, discipline, the single-parent family, teaching children with learning disabilities, and socialization. Resources include Catholic publishers and periodicals of interest to Catholic homeschoolers.

Farenga, Patrick. *The Beginner's Guide to Homeschooling.* Cambridge, MA: Holt Associates, 2000.

Written by the publisher of *Growing Without Schooling Magazine,* this is a short, concise introduction to the basics of homeschooling, with nearly half of the book taken up by listings of materials, resources, and homeschooling organizations.

Field, Christine M. *Help for the Harried Homeschooler: A Practical Guide to Balancing Your Child's Education with the Rest of Your Life.* Colorado Springs: Walter-Brook Press, 2002.

A title with a decidedly Christian viewpoint, it is, however, one with a different approach than most homeschooling books in that it addresses the issues of time management and balance. Chapters like "When Your World Falls Apart: Homeschooling through Crises" and "New Life in the Valley of Dry Bones: Learning from Burnout" share coping skills for dealing with the very real stresses that homeschooling can involve.

Gold, LauraMaery, and Joan M. Zielinski. *Homeschool Your Child for Free: More Than 1,200 Smart, Effective, and Practical Resources for Home Education on the Internet and Beyond.* Roseville, CA: Prima Publishing, 2000.

This invaluable guide to all the best in free educational material—from reading-readiness activities for preschoolers to science projects for teens—categorizes, reviews, and rates more than 1,200 of the most useful educational resources on the Internet and beyond.

Gralla, Preston. *The Complete Idiot's Guide to Volunteering for Teens.* Indianapolis: Alpha Books, 2001.

Although not written with homeschooling teens in mind, this helpful guide offers insights into volunteering, how to prepare for a volunteer experience, how to choose an appropriate volunteer experience, and specific ideas. Experiences include hospitals and health care, working with the elderly and needy, zoos and animal shelters, environmental projects, building better neighborhoods, museums, politics and government, literacy and educational programs, and public safety. Resources include organizational contacts with address, phone, and Web site.

Griffith, Mary. *The Homeschooling Handbook,* rev. 2nd ed. Rocklin, CA: Prima Publishing, 1999.

Another excellent first read for those considering the homeschooling decision. Griffith reviews the history of modern homeschooling and provides families with information to combat the naysayers among family and friends. Her style is light and witty, as witnessed by chapter titles like "Structure or Can We Wear Our Pajamas to School?" Unlike a lot of homeschooling primers that ignore older children, Griffith includes a chapter on the teen years, and one on college and other postsecondary alternatives. Further, Griffith recognizes that even the best-intentioned parent wears out under the demands of homeschooling and so includes the chapter "Coping with the Rough Spots."

Griffith, Mary. *The Unschooling Handbook: How to Use the Whole World as Your Child's Classroom.* Roseville, CA: Prima Publishing, 1998.

For those who have followed a more traditional approach to homeschooling, unschooling may sound like anarchy—the "education" is student-led and based on his or her interests and curiosity. But unschooling may be an excellent choice for teens, giving them control over what they want to learn and when. Griffith invites unschoolers to share their own stories and advice, including along the way Web resources, mailing lists, and catalogs that these autodidacts may find of interest.

Holt, John. *How Children Fail,* rev. ed. New York: Addison-Wesley Publishing Company, 1982.

Holt, John. *How Children Learn.* New York: Addison-Wesley Publishing Company, 1983.

How Children Fail and *How Children Learn* provide the foundation for the later writings of Holt in which he advocates for homeschooling. Through his own observation of students in his classroom as well as children of family members and friends, Holt concluded that the way in which children learn and the ways in which they are forced to learn in the institutional settings makes failure a foregone conclusion. *How Children Learn* further reveals Holt's true affection for and understanding of children and how they learn. Observing that young children use their minds well and do their best learning before they get to school, Holt concludes that school teaches children to think badly and in ways contrary to their innate and natural learning style.

Jones, Steve. *Internet for Educators and Homeschoolers.* Friendly, WV: Etc Publications, 2000.

Here's a basic beginner's guide to using the Internet for learning. It begins by defining the Internet, gives guidelines for keeping down costs and maintaining security. Several chapters specifically address the needs of homeschoolers, including one on distance learning.

Kochenderfer, Rebecca, and Elizabeth Kanna. *Homeschooling for Success: How Parents Can Create a Superior Education for Their Child.* New York: Warner Books, 2002.

From the creators of the popular Web site Homeschool.com, this guide includes answers to the traditional questions posed by parents interested in homeschooling. Chapters offer advice to parents on getting started, homeschooling through the high school years, as well as college and "uncollege" alternatives. Information on discovering a child's multiple intelligences and approaches to homeschooling with working parents makes this guide stand out among other general question-and-answer books. Like other how-to guides, this one includes ample resource ideas for a family considering homeschooling.

Lande, Nancy. *Homeschool Open House.* Bozeman, MT: WindyCreek Press, 2000.

Following up on many families featured in the book *Homeschooling: A Patchwork of Days,* this title includes interviews with fifty-five homeschooling families. Charming black-and-white cutout photographs of many of the families are scattered throughout the text. The variety of families, in number, geography, and experience, will offer homeschooling patrons a wealth of ideas and experiences to learn from.

Leistico, Agnes. *I Learn Better by Teaching Myself* and *Still Teaching Ourselves.* Cambridge, MA: Holt Associates, 1997.

A combined printing of two related books. *I Learn Better by Teaching Myself* includes chapters on: Getting started, Choosing our learning materials, Scheduling our learning opportunities, Trusting our children to lead the way, Keeping future educational opportunities open, Coping with parent-teacher wear and tear. *Still Teaching Ourselves* includes chapters on the author's family situation, her family's goals and course of study, activities and resources, support groups and friends, achieving balance, and chapters on each homeschooled family member.

Llewellyn, Grace. *Freedom Challenge: African American Homeschoolers.* Eugene, OR: Lowry House Publishers, 1996.

In the style that marks her classic contributions to homeschool literature, Llewellyn allows African-American homeschooling parents and students to tell their stories in their own words. Llewellyn explains the ways in which African-American families fit and don't fit into the rest of the homeschooling movement, but also why they view homeschooling as a positive continuation of the civil rights movement.

Llewellyn, Grace, and Amy Silver. *Guerrilla Learning: How to Give Your Kids a Real Education With or Without School.* New York: Wiley, 2001.

Not written specifically for homeschoolers, this helpful guide offers advice for parents of homeschoolers and traditional schoolers alike to help students become excited about learning, wherever they are learning. The authors propose that the five keys to guerrilla learning are opportunity, timing, interest, freedom, and support. Much practical advice is to be had in this guide to learning beyond the school's walls.

McKee, Alison. *Homeschooling Our Children, Unschooling Ourselves.* Madison, WI: Bittersweet House, 2002.

This is an insightful book written by a trained teacher, in which she shares her transition from traditional classroom instructor to unschooling parent. Even parents who are convinced that homeschooling is the best option for their children have difficulty letting go of the traditional school model by which they themselves were educated. A fear that their child might not be learning what they are "supposed" to learn can drive some parents to simply duplicate the classroom at home. McKee invites such parents to relax and trust in their child's innate ability to learn.

Chapters in McKee's book include "Will We Ever Conquer Math?" and "Learning to Trust in Our Children's Ways," both demonstrating key issues in child-led learning. Appendices include information of special interest for teens including how to document "good student" qualifications for auto insurance discounts and managing college admissions.

Morgan, Melissa L., and Judith Waite Allee. *Homeschooling on a Shoestring.* Wheaton, IL: Harold Shaw Publishers, 1999.

Economics are a concern for homeschoolers, especially when the decision to homeschool might mean the loss of one parent's income. This title walks would-be homeschoolers through the economic decision-making, helping readers weigh the realities of a two-paycheck family and identifying the reasons for considering homeschooling. The book then goes on to share many ways to make the homeschool experience happen through frugality, budgeting, and making the most of free and inexpensive resources.

Penn-Nabrit, Paula. *Morning by Morning: How We Home-schooled our African-American Sons to the Ivy League.* New York: Villard, 2003.

An inspiring memoir from an African-American family who homeschooled three sons, this title explores the family's experiences with the homeschool transition, provides information on developing an appropriate curriculum, and offers much advice to other homeschooling families.

Perry, John, and Kathy Perry. *The Complete Guide to Homeschooling.* Los Angeles: Lowell House, 2000.

Chapters include a wealth of practical advice including many of the usual questions posed by parents considering and just starting the homeschooling process. It discusses curriculum options, specific age concerns for the elementary, middle school, and high school years, and even discusses the possibilities of homeschooling part-time or reentering the school system. Success stories of homeschoolers are included throughout the text.

Ransom, Marsha. *The Complete Idiot's Guide to Homeschooling.* Indianapolis: Alpha Books, 2001.

Information is provided in the familiar format of *The Complete Idiot's* series. This title covers the usual territory of how to get started, choosing a curriculum, advice for homeschooling various age groups, keeping records and testing, and how to avoid burnout. Appendices include a glossary, curriculum resources, homeschooling organizations, independent study programs, vendors, and a bibliography.

Ray, Brian D. *Strengths of Their Own: Home Schoolers Across America: Academic Achievement, Family Characteristics, and Longitudinal Traits.* Salem, OR: NHERI Publications, 1997.

Based on the findings from a nationwide study of homeschooling families in the United States, Ray describes family characteristics, students' academic achievement, and overall longitudinal research. An excellent overview filled with facts that might be used when justifying specialized services or when preparing grant applications.

Rivero, Lisa. *Creative Home Schooling for Gifted Children: A Resource Guide.* Scottsdale, AZ: Great Potential Press, 2002.

Geared specifically to families homeschooling gifted children, this title also offers advice most homeschooling families could use. Offers insight and research on traits of "giftedness," including social and emotional needs, intellectual needs, and learning styles. Includes advice on socialization, curriculum resources, record keeping, college planning, and costs.

Rupp, Rebecca. *Getting Started on Home Learning: How and Why to Teach Your Kids at Home.* New York: Three Rivers Press, 1999.

Includes advice for parents considering homeschooling and practical tips about socialization, the costs of homeschooling, and advice for homeschooling teens with college in their future. Helpful resource lists are included throughout the text.

Rupp, Rebecca. *Home Learning Year by Year: How to Design a Homeschool Curriculum from Preschool Through High School.* New York: Three Rivers Press, 2000.

A comprehensive guide that details the subjects to be covered for each school year, sets a standard of knowledge for each subject, and suggests books to use as texts.

Stevens, Mitchell L. *Kingdom of Children: Culture and Controversy in the Homeschooling Movement.* Princeton: Princeton University Press, 2001.

Examines the homeschooling phenomenon as a social movement by looking at the world of homeschooling, examining homeschooling literature and curricula, looking at the role of the homeschooling mother, and studying how homeschoolers have organized and created their political convictions.

Waring, Diana. *Beyond Survival: A Guide to Abundant Life Homeschooling.* Lynn-wood, WA: Emerald Books, 1996.

The abundant life referenced in the title quotes biblical promise, the jumping-off point for this author's highly practical guide to homeschooling. Weaving journal entries and recommended book lists into each chapter, Waring covers a lot of ground. Particularly interesting are her chapters on learning styles and teaching styles—topics not always addressed in homeschool literature.

Waring, Bill, and Diana Waring, eds. *Things We Wish We'd Known.* Lynn-wood, WA: Emerald Books, 1999.

Fifty veteran homeschoolers—some well known as authors and homeschool conference presenters and others simply pursuing the education of their children—share their "aha!" revelations about homeschooling. Each chapter begins with a biographical introduction of the author and a photograph. The subsequent text is like reading a long, newsy letter from a friend.

Workman, Katrina. *Homeschooling: Untangling the Web of Confusion.* Mesa, AZ: Blue Bird Publishing, 1999.

This guide offers short chapters of advice on getting started, choosing a curriculum, record keeping, grading, how and what to teach, curriculum enhancers, and testing. The appendix includes reproducible forms to be used in planning, grading, and keeping track of assignments.

Wise, Jessie, and Susan Wise Bauer. *The Well-Trained Mind: A Guide to Classical Education at Home.* New York: W.W. Norton and Company, 1999.

This mother-daughter team explore both aspects of providing a classical education at home—that of teacher and student. Utilizing the "trivium" style of classical teaching (grammar, logic, and rhetoric), Wise sought to homeschool her children in a way that would stimulate and challenge. The book is divided into three sections with suggested lessons and resources for each. The section titled "Rhetoric Stage" covers grades 9–12.

HOMESCHOOLING TEENS

Bear, Mariah P., and John B. Bear. *Bears' Guide to Earning Degrees by Distance Learning,* 15th ed. Berkeley, CA: Ten Speed Press, 2003.

Called by some reviewers "the best book on nontraditional education," this latest edition includes a list of over 3,000 schools offering distance-learning programs. A subject list makes it easy to find schools offering specific degree programs; programs are also rated for their "acceptability."

Dennis, Jeanne Gowen. *Homeschooling High School: Planning Ahead for College Admission.* Lynnwood, WA: Emerald Books, 2000.

Information reflecting a national survey of over 250 college admissions departments is provided in an easy-to-follow format. Offers advice on keeping records, preparing transcripts, and searching for a college and includes many reproducible forms.

Duffy, Cathy. *Christian Home Educators' Curriculum Manual: Junior/Senior High.* Westminster, CA: Grove Publishing, 2000.

A very comprehensive handbook for Christian parents setting out to homeschool their teens. High school can be the time when even the most dedicated homeschooling parent may feel overwhelmed. Duffy's thoroughness should give even the most apprehensive parent the courage to undertake high school. Early chapters cover logistics, shared responsibility, and how to outline a course of study. Later chapters address each field of study, review curriculum from homeschool publishers, and include information on purchasing support materials.

Grand, Gail L. *Free (and Almost Free) Adventures for Teenagers*. New York: Wiley, 1995.

Although the information contained in this title is somewhat outdated, homeschooling teens may still gather ideas for ways to supplement their studies. Most of the adventures fall into the summer adventure category, but the guide also offers ideas for adventures during the traditional school year as well. Each adventure includes basic information including any host school, location, duration, qualifications, housing, costs, credits available, and contact information.

Greene, Rebecca. *The Teenagers' Guide to School Outside the Box*. Minneapolis: Free Spirit Publishing, 2001.

A valuable resource for both homeschooling and non-homeschooling teens, this title includes ideas for volunteer opportunities, internships, mentorships, job shadowing, apprenticeships, and studying abroad. When specific resources are given, address, phone, and Web information are provided.

Kohl, Herbert. *The Question is College: On Finding and Doing Work You Love*. Portsmouth, NH: Boynton/Cook Publishers, 1998.

Despite what guidance counselors may say, college may not be right for everyone. Kohl talks to teens about finding work they love and helps parents relax about their child's decisions for life after high school.

Mason, Renee. *Homeschooling All the Way Through High School*. Wheaton, IL: Tyndale House Publishers, Inc., 1999.

In this first-person account, Mason tells how she and her husband undertook to homeschool their eight children. Interspersed with her narrative are sections authored by several of Mason's young adult daughters, Mason's mother, and her husband. The publisher categorizes this title under Christian Life and, indeed, there is continual reference to scripture throughout.

McKee, Alison. *From Homeschool to College and Work: Turning Your Homeschooled Experiences into College and Job Portfolios*. Madison, WI: Bittersweet House, 1998.

Using her own experience as the parent of two unschooled children, McKee outlines the process through which her family devised successful college portfolios. Topics she covers are: how to get started, documenting the learning process, compiling data for a portfolio, and putting a final document together to create a college admissions portfolio or job resume.

Orr, Tamra B. *After Homeschool: Fifteen Homeschoolers Out in the Real World*. Los Angeles: Mars Publishing, 2003.

This personal look at the lives of fifteen homeschoolers between the ages of seventeen and twenty-two examines life after homeschool and offers insights into the effects of homeschooling as these students reenter the mainstream.

ARTICLES

Apple, Michael W. "The Cultural Politics of Home Schooling." *Peabody Journal of Education* 75, no. 1/2 (2000): 256–71.

Blum, Debra E. "Home-schooled Athletes." *The Chronicle of Higher Education* 42, no. 39 (June 7, 1996): A33–A35.

Brockett, Diane. "Home-school Kids in Public-School Activities." *Education Digest* 61, no. 3 (November 1995): 67–70.

Brostrom, David C. "Assessing Homeschooler Needs." *Public Libraries* 34 (July/August 1995): 201–2.

———. "No Place Like the Library." *School Library Journal* 43, no. 3 (March 1997): 106–109.

Butler, Shery. "The 'H' Word: Home Schooling." *Gifted Child Today* 23, no. 5 (September/October 2000): 44–50.

Caruana, Vicki. "Partnering with Homeschoolers." *Educational Leadership* 57, no. 1 (September 1999): 58–60.

Cohen, Cafi. "The Satisfied Learner: How Families Homeschool Their Teens." *Mothering* (March/April 2000): 74.

Dembeck, David A. "A Homeschooler's Perspective." *Public Libraries* 34 (July/August 1995): 202–3.

Farenga, Patrick. "Homeschoolers & College." *Mothering* (fall 1989): 76–81.

———. "Homeschooling in the '90s: A Beginner's Guide to Learning at Home." *Mothering* (fall 1996): 56–63.

Farris, Michael P., and Scott A. Woodruff. "The Future of Home Schooling." *Peabody Journal of Education* 75, no. 1/2 (2000): 233–55.

Furger, Roberta. "Home Room (Home Schooling Online Information Services)." *FamilyPC* 7, no. 10 (October 2000): 51.

Gatten, Susan B. "The Development of Home Schooling Services in the Public Library: A Case Study." Master's thesis, Kent State University, 1994.

Geist, Paula, Peter Dubaugh Smith, and Kathleen de la Pena McCook. "Florida Librarians Respond to Home Education." ERIC document (September 1994).

Gibbs, Nancy. "Home Sweet School: Seeking Excellence, Isolation or Just Extra 'Family Time,' More and More Parents are Doing the Teaching Themselves." *Time* 144, no. 18 (October 21, 1994): 62–64.

Hancock, LynNell. "The Dawn of Online Home Schooling." *Newsweek* 124, no. 15 (October 10, 1994): 67.

Holt, John. "How Schools Can Cooperate with Home Schoolers." *Education Digest* 49 (October 1983): 2–6.

"It's All Homework" (Homeschooling Statistics). *American Demographics,* (November 1, 2001): 25.

Kennedy, John W. "Home Schooling Keeps Growing." *Christianity Today* 41, no. 8 (July 14, 1997): 68.

Kleiner, Carolyn. "Home School Comes of Age." *U.S. News & World Report* 129, no. 15 (October 16, 2000): 52.

Kleist-Tesch, Jane M. "Homeschoolers and the Public Library." *Journal of Youth Services in Libraries* 11, no. 3 (Spring 1998): 231–41.

Klipsch, Pamela R. "An Educated Collection for Homeschoolers." *Library Journal* 120, no. 2 (February 1, 1995): 47–50.

Lange, Cheryl M., and Kristin Kline Liu. "Homeschooling: Parents' Reasons for Transfer and the Implications for Educational Policy." ERIC document (June 1999).

LaRue, James, and Suzanne LaRue. "Is Anybody Home? Home Schooling and the Library." *Wilson Library Bulletin* 66, no. 1 (September 1991): 32–39.

Leake, Janet. "Homeschooling through High School." *Backwoods Home Magazine* (September 2000): 32.

Lines, Patricia M. "Homeschooling Comes of Age." *The Public Interest* (Summer 2000): 74.

———. "When Home Schoolers Go to School: A Partnership between Families and Schools." *Peabody Journal of Education* 75, no. 1/2 (2000): 159–86.

Lord, Mary. "Home-Schoolers Away from Home." *U.S. News & World Report* 129, no. 15 (October 16, 2000): 54.

Lubienski, Chris. "Whither the Common Good? A Critique of Home Schooling." *Peabody Journal of Education* 75, no. 1/2 (2000): 207–32.

Lyman, Isabel. "What's Behind the Growth in Homeschooling." *USA Today* 127, no. 2640 (September 1998): 64–66.

Masters, Denise G. "Public Library Services for Home Schooling." ERIC Digest (December 1996).

McDowell, Susan A. "The Home Schooling Mother-Teacher: Toward a Theory of Social Integration." *Peabody Journal of Education* 75, no. 1/2 (2000): 187–206.

McKethan, Robert N., Brett W. Everhart, and Jamie Herman. "Starting a Home-School Physical Education Clinical Program on Your Campus." *Journal of Physical Education, Recreation & Dance* 71, no. 8 (October 2000): 38–44.

Medlin, Richard G. "Home Schooling and the Question of Socialization." *Peabody Journal of Education* 75, no. 1/2 (2000): 107–23.

Moore, Raymond, "Homegrown and Homeschooled" *Mothering* (Summer 1990): 78.

Moran, Rosemary. "Planning Homeschooler Services." *Public Libraries* 34 (July/August 1995): 203–4.

O'Mara, Peggy. "Mortarboards from Home." *Mothering* (March 1999): 33.

Pfleger, Katherine. "School's Out." *The New Republic* 218, no. 14 (April 6, 1998): 11–12.

Ray, Brian D. "Home Schooling for Individuals' Gain and Society's Common Good." *Peabody Journal of Education* 75, no. 1/2 (2000): 272–93.

———. "Home Schooling: The Ameliorator of Negative Influences on Learning?" *Peabody Journal of Education* 75, no. 1/2 (2000): 71–106.

Rich, Dorothy. "Good News about Family Learning." *Instructor* 104, no. 3 (October1994): 23.

Robertson, Brian. "Is Home Schooling in a Class of its Own?" *Insight on the News* 10, no. 42 (October 17, 1994): 6–9.

Rockney, Randal. "The Home Schooling Debate: Why Some Parents Choose It, Others Oppose It" *The Brown University Child and Adolescent Behavior Letter* 18, no. 2 (February 2002): 1.

Rutkowski, Kathleen. "Homeschool Pioneers on the Web." *Multimedia Schools* 5, no. 3 (May/June 1998): 76–80.

Sager, Donald J. "Public Library Service to Homeschoolers." *Public Libraries* 34 (July/Aug. 1995): 201.

Scheps, Susan G. "Homeschoolers in the Library." *School Library Journal* 45, no. 2 (February 1999): 38.

Schwartz, Robin L. "Ohio Home-Schooled Children and Their Use of Public Library Resources." Master's thesis, Kent State University, 1991.

Stahnke, Linda. "Homeschooling the High School Student" (video recording), Pikes Peak Library District, Colorado Springs, CO, 1995.

Stewart, Mark. "Homebodies (The Stories of Two Homeschooled Students)."
Insight on the News 16, no. 35 (September 18, 2000): 32.

WEB RESOURCES
General Homeschooling

http://www.nhen.org

The Web site of the National Home Education Network (NHEN). Created by members with all sorts of homeschooling backgrounds, this Web site is packed with helpful and accurate information, up-to-date networking possibilities, and support for those interested in homeschooling.

http://www.hslda.org

The Home School Legal Defense Association is a nonprofit advocacy organization established to defend and advance the constitutional right of parents to direct the education of their children and to protect family freedom. HSLDA publishes a bimonthly magazine, *The Home School Court Report*, providing news and commentary on current issues affecting homeschoolers.

http://www.nheri.org/
National Home Education Research Institute

Produces research on home-based education; serves as a clearinghouse of research for homeschoolers, researchers, and policy makers; and educates the public concerning the findings of all research on home education.

http://www.homeschooltoday.com/

Online site for *Homeschooling Today* magazine. Describes itself as one of the most comprehensive home education magazines available. Publishes six times a year. Place subscription order online.

http://www.homeschoolfoundation.org/

The Foundation's stated mission is to preserve parental freedoms, promote home schooling, provide assistance to needy homeschooling families, and support like-minded organizations.

http://www.midnightbeach.com/hs/

Jon's Homeschool Resource Page, one of the largest, most popular homeschooling sources on the Web. Neutral and noncommercial, it includes resources selected "on the basis of clarity and breadth, not politics or religion."

http://www.homeschool.com/

Very comprehensive Web site with lots to explore. Has message boards organized by curriculum subject; religious or ethnic; support including teen boards. "Homeschool.com's founding principal is to consistently provide resources, information, and support to all homeschooling families."

http://www.nathhan.com/
National Challenged Homeschoolers Associated Network

Christian families homeschooling special needs children

http://www.arabesq.com

Web site for Islamic homeschooling and Arabic resources.

http://www.pacinfo.com/~handley/index.html

Homeschooling deaf and hard-of-hearing children.

http://www.americanhomeschoolassociation.org/

A service organization sponsored in part by the publishers of *Home Education Magazine.* It was created to network homeschoolers on a national level. Services include an online news and discussion list with news, information, and resources for homeschoolers, media contacts, and education officials.

http://www.chsna.org/

Web site for the Catholic Home School Network of America. Lists Catholic curriculum publishers and state organizations for Catholic homeschoolers.

http://www.snj.com/jhen/

Subscription information for JHEN (Jewish Home Educator's Network) newsletter.

http://www.muslimhomeschool.com/index.html

Muslim Homeschool Network and Resources online. For both Muslim and non-Muslim homeschoolers.

http://www.eho.org/default.asp

An excellent site with many, many resources that could take days to explore. Promotes creative homeschooling through unique resources, teaching methods, and online help. *The Eclectic Homeschool Online* is published from a Christian worldview, but articles and resources are not limited to purely Christian material.

http://www.gomilpitas.com/homeschooling/

A to Z Home's Cool Homeschooling Web Site. Huge and full of links for kids and adults. Articles and links organized by topic. Plan to spend a long time exploring all the resources gathered here.

http://www.homeschoolportal.com/directory/

The directory is a comprehensive listing of educational resources, Web sites, and businesses that provide support to the homeschooling community, parents, teachers, educators, and students.

http://www.hsadvisor.com/index.shtml

Answers to many commonly asked questions about home education. Topics include legal issues, teaching the difficult subjects, preparing for college, and suggested topics to teach each grade level.

http://www.quaqua.org/

The Quaqua Society, Incorporated offers scholarships and grants to the homeschooled, as well as providing recruitment and placement support for companies and schools wishing to hire, recruit, or mentor homeschooled graduates. Web site includes lists of financial aid or honors programs targeted at homeschoolers.

http://www.homeschoolingcorner.com/

General resource Web site for homeschoolers.

http://www.home-ed-magazine.com/wlcm_HEM.html

Home Education Magazine is one of the oldest, most respected, and most informative magazines on the subject of homeschooling. Check the Web site for subscription information.

http://www.learninfreedom.org/

As the name suggests, this site is about learning independently, with or without schools and teachers. Includes link to list of colleges that accept homeschooled students.

http://www.home-school.com/

The official site of *Practical Homeschooling* magazine and *The Big Book of Home Learning.*

http://www.unschooling.org/

Web site for the Family Unschoolers Network. Contains newsletter articles, reviews, resources, Web sites, books, and lots of other information related to homeschooling and unschooling (student-led or self-directed learning).

http://www.mhla.org/HoltOrigins.htm

Link to article titled "John Holt and the Origins of Contemporary Homeschooling" by Patrick Farenga. Originally published in *Paths of Learning,* 1 (Spring 1999).

Online Magazines

Homefires: The Journal of Homeschooling Online Magazine
Web site: http://www.homefires.com/index.html

Homeschool Fun Online Magazine
Web site: http://www.homeschoolfun.com/

Educational Freedom Press
(formerly HELM: Home Education Learning Magazine)
P.O. Box 1175
Tallevast, FL 34270
Web site: http://www.EducationalFreedom.com
Published online six times a year
Rates: $7.95/yr.

Eclectic Homeschool Online
P.O. Box 50188
Sparks, NV 89435-0188
Web site: http://www.eho.org
e-mail: eclectic@eho.org
Rates: Yahoo-hosted e-mail newsletter sent to subscribers. Subscribe
   online

Homeschooling Teens

http://www.vegsource.com/homeschool/hischool/

High school homeschooling discussion board

http://www.vegsource.com/homeschool/hsteen/index.html

Teen homeschooling discussion board

Driver's Education

http://driversed.com

This complete, online course for driver's education is affiliated with the
well-known Web site, A to Z Home's Cool Homeschooling.

http://www.driveredtraining.com/

Site sells product titled "Driver Ed in a Box." Parent-led instruction
tools offered in multiple AV formats.

http://nebraskahs.unl.edu/

Driver's education offered as a course for credit from the University of
Nebraska-Lincoln Independent Study High School.

Distance Learning

http://home.calvertschool.org/

Calvert School, a nondenominational elementary school located in Baltimore, Maryland, offers instruction to English-speaking students worldwide through its Home Instruction Department.

http://www.clonlara.org/

One of the original distance learning schools for home educators. Offers programs through Grade 12; issues diplomas; assists families with record keeping.

http://www.keystonehighschool.com/

Students can earn a high school diploma or needed credits through independent study coursework. Keystone offers online or traditional correspondence formats.

http://www.citizenschool.com/

Citizens' High School is an accredited independent study high school that provides people who have not finished high school with an opportunity to earn their high school diploma.

http://www.laurelsprings.com/

Offers both text-based and online curricula for K-12 students, an honors program, and a special needs division. They will also customize an accredited program to fit student needs.

http://www.compuhigh.com/

The online division of Clonlara School. Provides year-round high school courses, issues a transcript and diploma accepted by universities and colleges.

http://www.utexas.edu/cee/dec/uths/index.shtml

The University of Texas Continuing and Extended Education department offers a high school diploma program through its Distance Education Center.

http://www.flvs.net/

The Florida Virtual School (FLVS) is a statewide, Internet-based, public high school offering curriculum online.

http://www.cdis.missouri.edu/MUHighSchool/HShome.htm

The University of Missouri-Columbia High School (MU High School) is a part of the University of Missouri Center for Distance and Independent Study. Through a variety of delivery methods, the university provides courses that complement traditional high school curricula, and provides an accredited diploma program for independent learners of all ages seeking an alternative to traditional high school attendance.

http://scs.indiana.edu

Established in 1999, Indiana University High School (IUHS) is a diploma program that can be completed entirely through distance education.

http://www.pachighschool.com/

Pacific High School offers a Distance Education Program that allows students to earn a high school diploma from home.

http://www.americanschoolofcorr.com/

Students can earn a diploma or take individual subjects from the American School through its High School Home Education Program.

http://www.distancecalculus.com/new/

Distance education offered by the computer science and math department of Suffolk University, Boston. High school students may enroll in these college-level courses to prepare for their AP calculus examinations and can receive fully transferable college credit while in high school.

http://nebraskahs.unl.edu/

Fully accredited, college prep high school coursework through the University of Nebraska-Lincoln Independent Study High School (ISHS).

http://www.jmhs.com/?code=E9920

James Madison High School offers accredited distance education program.

http://www.thejubileeacademy.org

The Jubilee Academy provides Bible-based curriculum to students in kindergarten through 12th grade.

http://www.hsi.edu/

Home Study International (HSI) is part of the Seventh-day Adventist school system and provides instruction through high school and beyond, including college degree programs.

http://www.e-tutor.com/et100/index.html

e-Tutor is a K-12 Internet education program for students, parents, and educators that is customizable and fully accessible through the Internet.

GED Online

http://www.gedonline.org/

Web site dedicated to helping students prepare online for the GED High School Equivalency Diploma Test.

http://www.getmyged.com/

Developed for adult students wishing to study privately at home, but could be used by homeschoolers.

Homeschoolers and College

http://www.collegeboard.com/

Links from this College Board homepage for information specific to homeschoolers, including Home-Schooled Students & College Admission and Home-Schooled Students and the SAT.

http://www.homeschoolteenscollege.net/

Web site maintained by Cafi and Terry Cohen, the go-to gurus on the topic of homeschooling teens and preparing them for college. Authors of *And What about College?* and *How Homeschooling Leads to Admissions to the Best Colleges and Universities,* 2nd ed.

http://www.rsts.net/colleges/

Lists "homeschool-friendly" colleges and universities in the United States and Canada. Also links to schools offering distance learning programs, and to sites for the U.S. Navy and West Point, both identified as receptive to homeschooled applicants.

Military Academy Admissions Information for Homeschoolers

http://www.usafa.af.mil/

Guidelines for homeschoolers interested in applying to the Air Force Academy.

http://www.usmma.edu/admissions/default.htm

General admissions information for the United States Merchant Marine Academy. Nothing specific regarding homeschoolers.

http://www.usna.edu/Admissions/sthome.htm

Guidelines for homeschoolers interested in applying to the United States Naval Academy.

http://www.usma.edu/admissions/

Admissions information for applying to the United States Military Academy at West Point. Nothing specific is mentioned about homeschoolers but site does list academic and other requirements.

http://www.cga.edu/default.htm

Admission information for homeschoolers who wish to attend the United States Coast Guard Academy is available through this link to admissions FAQs.

Supplies

http://www.scientificsonline.com/
http://www.radioshack.com/
http://www.homeschoolyellowpages.com/

The Homeschool Internet Yellow Pages is a primary source for home-school products and services, as well as companies owned and operated by homeschoolers. You will find contact information available about the companies and a description of their products and services. Also includes listings for homeschool vendors, state and local homeschool information, homeschooling articles, contests for homeschoolers, and homeschool convention information.

http://www.homeschoolbid.com/

Online auction site developed for homeschoolers. Both home-schooling and non-homeschooling items can be listed and sold here, such as used/new curriculum and computer hardware and software. Listings are free.

http://www.thehomeschoolsource.com/

Paid members have access to a homeschool Lending Library. Member-ship information available on Web site.

http://www.learningstreams.com/

Formerly Home School Products. Resource for buying supplies, books, and curriculum. Organized by grade level and topic.

http://theswap.com/

Homeschoolers' Curriculum Swap. Billed as the original and oldest second-hand curriculum site on the Web. Includes a handful of moderated forums including one on homeschooling teens.

http://www.standarddeviants.com

Free teaching, homework, and homeschool resources, including video clips, helpful cards, tests, games, and more.

STATEWIDE HOMESCHOOLING ORGANIZATIONS
Alabama

Home Educators of Alabama Round Table (HEART)
P.O. Box 1159, Tallevast, FL 34270
Phone: (941) 359-3628
E-mail: mirator@educationalfreedom.com
http://www.educationalfreedom.com/heart/

Alaska

Alaska Private & Home Educators Association (APHEA)
P.O. Box 141764, Anchorage, AK 99514
Contact: Marty van Diest
Phone: (907) 566-3450
Fax: (907) 272-2998
E-mail: networknews@gci.net
http://www.aphea.org

Christian Home Educators of Kodiak (CHEK)
12174 Gara Drive, Kodiak, AK 99615
Contact: Patty Heyes
Phone: (907) 487-2471
E-mail: chek@unforgettable.com
http://www.geocities.com/Heartland/Ranch/5447/

Arizona

Arizona Families for Home Education
P.O. Box 2035, Chandler, AZ 85244-2035
Phone: (602) 443-0612 or (800) 929-3927
E-mail: afhe@primenet.com
http://www.afhe.org

Covenant Home School Resource Center (CHSRC)
1117 E. Devonshire Avenue, Phoenix, AZ 85014
Contact: Holly Craw
Phone: (602) 277-3497
Fax: (602) 277-3497

E-mail: hsgrd@att.net
http://www.homeschoolresourcecenter.org

Arkansas

The Education Alliance
414 S. Pulaski Street, Ste. 2, Little Rock, AR 72201
Phone: (501) 375-7000
Fax: (501) 375-7040
E-mail: edu@familycouncil.org

Home Educators of Arkansas
P.O. Box 192455, Little Rock, AR 72219
E-mail: butchra@ipa.net
http://www.geocities.com/heartland/garden/4555/hear.html

Christian Home Educators Fellowship (CHEF)
Based in West Memphis, AR
Contact: Ken or Evelyn Nilsen
Phone: (870) 735-9806
E-mail: knilsen@classbydesign.com
http://www.chefhomeschool.org

California

Christian Home Educators Association of California
P.O. Box 2009, Norwalk, CA 90651-2009
Contact: Philip Trout
Phone: 1-800-564-2432
E-mail: mailto:cheaofca@aol.com
http://www.cheaofca.org

Homeschool Association of California (HSC)
P.O. Box 2442, Atascadero, CA 93423
Phone: (888) HSC-4440
http://www.hsc.org

California Homeschool Network
P.O. Box 55485, Hayward, CA 94545
Contact: Janis Stuart

Phone: (800) 327-5339
E-mail: chnmail@californiahomeschool.net
http://www.californiahomeschool.net

Association of Private Christian Educators
P.O. Box 66, Orangevale, CA 95662
Phone: (916) 989-8723
Fax: (916) 989-8723
E-mail: twig@mail.cwo.com

California Home Educators
10489 Sunland Boulevard, Sunland, CA 91040
Contact: Terry Neven
Phone: (800) 525-4419
Fax: (818) 951-5963
E-mail: scsandche@aol.com
http://www.home-schooling.org

Colorado

Christian Home Educators of Colorado (CHEC)
10431 South Parker Road, Parker, CO 80134
Phone: (720) 842-4852
Fax: (720) 842-4854
E-mail: office@chec.org
http://www.chec.org

Concerned Parents of Colorado
P.O. Box 547, Florissant, CO 80816
Phone: (719) 748-8360
Fax: (719) 748-8360
E-mail: treonelain@aol.com
http://members.aol.com/treonelain/

Connecticut

The Education Association of Christian Homeschoolers
282 Camp Street, Plainville, CT 06062
Fax: (860) 677-4677
E-mail: teach.info@pobox.com
http://www.teachct.org

Connecticut Home Educators Association (CHEA)
101 Mansfield Avenue, Waterbury, CT 06705
Phone: (203) 754-0004
Message Line: (203) 781-8569
E-mail: becherhomeschool@aol.com
http://www.cthomeschoolers.com

Connecticut Homeschool Network (CHN)
East Hampton, CT 06424
Contact: Diane Connors
Phone: (860) 267-6358
E-mail: cthmschlntwk@aol.com
http://www.cthomeschoolnetwork.org

Delaware

Delaware Home Education Association
500 N. Dual Highway, PMB 415, Seaford, DE 19973
Phone: (302) 337-0990
Fax: (302) 337-0990
E-mail: jcpoeii@juno.com
http://www.dheaonline.org

Florida

Florida Parent Educators Association (FPEA)
P.O. Box 50685, Jacksonville Beach, FL 32240-0685
Contact: David Frantz
Phone: 1-877-ASK-FPEA
E-mail: office@fpea.com
http://www.fpea.com

Florida Coalition of Christian Private School Adminstrators, Inc. (FCCPSA)
P.O. Box 13227, Fort Pierce, FL 34979-3227
Phone: (561) 344-2929
Fax: (561) 465-8012
E-mail: fccpsa@flhomeschooling.com
http://www.flhomeschooling.com

Christian Home Educators of Florida (CHEF)
P.O. Box 5393, Clearwater, FL 33758-5393
E-mail: chef@christianhomeeducatorsofflorida.com
http://www.christianhomeeducatorsofflorida.com

LIFE of Florida (Learning is for everyone)
E-mail: pubmail@tampabay.rr.com
http://www.lifeofflorida.org

Georgia

Georgia Home Education Association
141 Massengale Road, Brooks, GA 30205
Contact: Ken Patterson
Phone: (770) 461-3657
Fax: (770) 461-9053
E-mail: info@ghea.org
http://www.ghea.org

Home Education Information Resource (HEIR)
P.O. Box 2111, Roswell, GA 30077-2111
Phone: (404) 681-4347
E-mail: info@heir.org
http://www.heir.org

Hawaii

Christian Homeschoolers of Hawaii
91-824 Oama Street, Ewa Beach, HI 96706
Phone: (808) 689-6398
E-mail: chohinfo@aol.com
http://www.christianhomeschoolersofhawaii.org

Idaho

Christian Homeschoolers of Idaho State
P.O. Box 45062, Boise, ID 83711-5062
Phone: (208) 424-6685
E-mail: linda@chois.org
http://www.chois.org

Idaho Coalition of Home Educators
5415 Kendall Street, Boise, ID 83706
E-mail: listkeeper@iche-idaho.org
http://www.iche-idaho.org

NATHHAN
P.O. Box 39, Porthill, ID 83853
Phone: (208) 267-6246
E-mail: nathanews@aol.com
http://www.nathhan.com

NATional cHallenged Homeschoolers Associated Network. Newsletter and other resources for families with children who have special developmental or physical needs.

Illinois

Christian Home Educators Coalition (CHEC) of Illinois
P.O. Box 47322, Chicago, IL 60647-0322
Phone: (773) 278-0673
Fax: (773) 278-0673
E-mail: chec@chec.cc
http://www.chec.cc

Illinois Christian Home Educators
P.O. Box 775, Harvard, IL 60033
Phone: (815) 943-7882
Fax: (815) 943-7883
E-mail: info@iche.org
http://www.iche.org

Home Oriented Unique Schooling Experience (HOUSE)
c/o Stout, P.O. Box 216, Ashton, IL 61006
E-mail: illinois_house@hotmail.com
http://www.geocities.com/illinoishouse/

Indiana

Indiana Association of Home Educators
8106 Madison Avenue, Indianapolis, IN 46227
Contact: Sheila Nieten

Phone: (317) 859-1202
Fax: 317-859-1204
E-mail: iahe@inhomeeducators.org
http://www.inhomeeducators.org

Roman Catholic Home Educators of Indiana (RCHEI)
P.O. Box 858, Fishers, IN 46038
Phone: (317) 767-5217
E-mail: info@rchei.org
http://www.rchei.org

Iowa

Network of Iowa Christian Home Educators
P.O. Box 158, Dexter, IA 50070
Phone: (515) 830-1614 or (800) 723-0438
Fax: (515) 285-7468
E-mail: info@the-niche.org
http://www.the-niche.org

Kansas

Christian Home Educators Confederation of Kansas (CHECK)
P.O. Box 3968, Wichita, KS 67201-3968
Phone: (316) 945-0810
Fax: (316) 685-1617
E-mail: info@kansashomeschool.org
http://www.kansashomeschool.org

Kentucky

Christian Home Educators of Kentucky (CHEK)
691 Howardstown Road, Hodgenville, KY 42748
Phone: (270) 358-9270
Fax: (270) 358-9270
E-mail: chek@kvnet.org
http://www.chek.org

Kentucky Home Education Association
P.O. Box 81, Winchester, KY 40392-0081
Phone: (859) 737-3338

Fax: (859) 745-4466
E-mail: katy@mis.net
http://www.khea.8k.com

Bluegrass Home Educators
600 Shake Rag Road, Waynesburg, KY 40489-9759
E-mail: info@kyhomeschool.info
http://www.kyhomeschool.info

Louisiana

Christian Home Educators Fellowship (CHEF) of Louisiana
P.O. Box 74292, Baton Rouge, LA 70874-4292
Phone: (888) 876-2433
Fax: (504) 774-4114
E-mail: chefofla@hotmail.com
http://www.chefofla.org

Louisiana Home Education Network
PMB 700, 602 W. Prien Lake Road, Lake Charles, LA 70601
E-mail: webmaster@la-home-education.com
http://www.la-home-education.com

Maine

Homeschoolers of Maine
337 Hatchet Mountain Road, Hope, ME 04847
Phone: (207) 763-4251
Fax: (207) 763-4352
E-mail: homeschl@midcoast.com
http://www.homeschoolersofmaine.org

Maine Home Education Association
19 Willowdale Drive, Gorham, Maine 04038
E-mail: mainehomeed@yahoo.com
http://www.geocities.com/mainehomeed/

Maryland

Christian Home Educators Network, Inc. (CHEN)
P.O. Box 2010, Ellicott City, MD 21043
Contact: Chuck Johnson

Phone: (301) 474-9055

E-mail: chenmaster@chenmd.org

http://www.chenmd.org

Maryland Association of Christian Home Educators (MACHE)

P.O. Box 417, Clarksburg, MD 20871-0417

Phone: (301) 607-4284

E-mail: info@machemd.org

http://www.machemd.org

Massachusetts

Massachusetts Homeschool Organization of Parent Educators (Mass. HOPE)

5 Atwood Road, Cherry Valley, MA 01611-3332

Phone: (978) 544-7892

E-mail: info@masshope.org

http://www.masshope.org

Michigan

Information Network for Christian Homes (INCH)

4934 Cannonsburg Road, Belmont, MI 49306

Phone: (616) 874-5656

Fax: (616) 874-5577

E-mail: inch@inch.org

http://www.inch.org

Michigan Catholic Home Educators

P.O. Box 534, Dearborn Heights, MI 48127

Phone: (313) 565-6129

Fax: (313) 565-6129

E-mail: mch001@juno.com

http://www.rc.net/lansing/mch/

Minnesota

Minnesota Association of Christian Home Educators

P.O. Box 32308, Fridley, MN 55432-0308

Phone: (612) 717-9070

E-mail: mache@isd.net

http://www.mache.org

Minnesota Homeschoolers Alliance

P.O. Box 23072, Richfield, MN 55423

Phone: (612) 288-9662

E-mail: sleinen@pioneerplanet.infi.net

http://www.homeschoolers.org

Mississippi

Mississippi Home Educators Association (MHEA)

P.O. Box 855, Batesville, MS 38606

Phone: (662) 578-6432

Fax: (662) 563-0041

E-mail: mhea@mhea.net

http://www.mhea.net

Missouri

Missouri Association of Teaching Christian Homes (MATCH)

2203 Rhonda Drive, West Plains, MO 65775-1615

Phone: (815) 550-8641

Fax: (815) 550-8641

E-mail: match@match-inc.org

http://www.match-inc.org

Families for Home Education (FHE)

P.O. Box 800, Platte City, MO 64079-0800

Phone: (816) 767-9825

E-mail: 1983@fhe-mo.org

http://www.fhe-mo.org

Christian Home Educators Fellowship (CHEF)

St. Louis, Missouri

Contact: Jon and Candy Summers

Phone: (314) 521-8487

E-mail: jon.candy.summers@chef-missouri.com

http://www.chef-missouri.com

Montana

Montana Coalition of Home Educators
P.O. Box 43, Gallatin Gateway, MT 59730
Phone: (406) 587-6163
Fax: (406) 587-5630
E-mail: white@gomontana.com
http://www.mtche.org

Nebraska

Nebraska Christian Home Educators Association
P.O. Box 57041, Lincoln, NE 68505-7041
Contact: Kathleen Lenzen
Phone: (402) 423-4297
E-mail: nchea@alltel.net
http://www.nchea.org

Nevada

Nevada Homeschool Network (NHN)
2250 East Tropicana, Suite 19, Box 378, Las Vegas, NV 89119
Phone: (888) 842-2606
http://www.nevadahomeschoolnetwork.com

New Hampshire

Christian Home Educators of New Hampshire (CHENH)
P.O. Box 961, Manchester, NH 03105
Phone: (603) 569-2343
http://www.chenh.org

Homeschooling Friends
204 Brackett Road, New Durham, NH 03855-2330
E-mail: info@homeschoolingfriends.org
http://www.homeschoolingfriends.org

New Hampshire Home Schooling Resources
E-mail: nhhr@dimentech.com
http://nhhr.dimentech.com

New Jersey

Education Network of Christian Home Schoolers (ENOCH)
P.O. Box 308, Atlantic Highlands, New Jersey 07716
Phone: (732) 291-7800
Fax: (732) 291-5398
E-mail: office@enochnj.org
http://www.enochnj.org

New Mexico

Christian Association of Parent Educators—New Mexico (CAPE-NM)
P.O. Box 25046, Albuquerque, NM 87125
Phone: (505) 898-8548
E-mail: cape-nm@juno.com
http://www.cape-nm.org

New Mexico Family Educators (NMFE)
P.O. Box 92276, Albuquerque, NM 87199-2276
Contact: Darla McLeod, President
Phone: (505) 275-7053

Publishes newsletter ten times per year, The Connection. Membership
$20 per year, fee includes subscription.

New York

NYS Loving Education At Home (LEAH)
P.O. Box 438, Fayetteville, NY 13066-0438
Phone: (315) 637-4525
Fax: (315) 637-4525
E-mail: info@leah.org
http://www.leah.org

LEAH has over 150 chapters and 3700 families.

New York Home Educators' Network (NYHEN)
P.O. Box 24, Sylvan Beach, NY 13157
E-mail: membership@nyhen.org
http://nyhen.org

North Carolina

North Carolinians for Home Education
419 North Boylan Avenue, Raleigh, NC 27603-1211
Phone: (919) 834-6243
Fax: (919) 834-6241
E-mail: nche@mindspring.com

North Dakota

North Dakota Home School Association
P.O. Box 7400, Bismarck, ND 58507-7400
Contact: Gail Bilby
Phone: (701) 223-4080
E-mail: ndhsa@wdata.com

Ohio

Christian Home Educators of Ohio (CHEO)
117 W. Main Street, Ste. 103, Lancaster, OH 43130
Phone: (740) 654-3331
Fax: (740) 654-3337
E-mail: cheoorg@usa.net
http://www.cheohome.org

Ohio Home Educators Network
P.O. Box 38132, Olmsted Falls, OH 44138-8132
E-mail: ohen@ohiohomeeducators.net
http://www.ohiohomeeducators.net

Oklahoma

Christian Home Educators Fellowship (CHEF) of Oklahoma
P.O. Box 471363, Tulsa, OK 74147-1363
Contact: Larry Mason
Phone: (918) 583-7323
Fax: (801) 880-0205
E-mail: staff@chefok.org
http://www.chefok.org

Oklahoma Christian Home Educators Consociation, Inc. (OCHEC)

3801 Northwest 63rd Street, Building 3, Suite 236, Oklahoma City, OK 73116

Phone: (405) 810-0386

Fax: (405) 810-0386

E-mail: staff@ochec.com

http://www.ochec.com

Home Educator's Resource Organization (HERO) of Oklahoma

302 N. Coolidge, Enid, OK 73703-3819

E-mail: hero@oklahomahomeschooling.org

http://www.oklahomahomeschooling.org

Oregon

Oregon Christian Home Education Association Network (OCEAN)

17985 Falls City Road, Dallas, OR 97338

Phone: (503) 288-1285

E-mail: oceanet@oceanetwork.org

http://www.oceanetwork.org

Pennsylvania

Pennsylvania Homeschoolers

RR 2, Box 117, Kittanning, PA 16201

E-mail: richmans@pahomeschoolers.com

http://www.pahomeschoolers.com

Christian Homeschool Association of Pennsylvania (CHAP)

P.O. Box 115, Mount Joy, PA 17552-0115

Phone: (717) 661-2428

Fax: (717) 653-2454

E-mail: chap@chapboard.org

http://www.chapboard.org

Catholic Homeschoolers of Pennsylvania

101 South College Street, Myerstown PA 17067-1212

Contact: Larry and Ellen Kramer

Phone: (717) 866-5425
Fax: (717) 866-9383
E-mail: info@catholichomeschoolpa.org
http://www.catholichomeschoolpa.org

Pennsylvania Home Education Network
285 Allegheny Street, Meadville, PA 16335
Contact: Jessica Molek
Phone: (412) 922-8344
E-mail: pasage@juno.com
http://www.phen.org

Puerto Rico

The Caribbean Center of Home Education Resources (T'CHERs)
P.O. Box 867, Boqueron, PR 00622
Contact: Alison Martin
E-mail: rarcmartin@prw.net
http://www.geocities.com/tchers2001/

Rhode Island

Rhode Island Guild of Home Teachers (RIGHT)
Box 11, Hope, RI 02831
Phone: (401) 821-7700
E-mail: right_right@mailexcite.com

South Carolina

South Carolina Association of Independent Home Schools (SCAIHS)
930 Knox Abbott Drive, Cayce, SC 29033
Phone: (803) 454-0427
Fax: (803) 454-0428
E-mail: scaihs@scaihs.org
http://www.scaihs.org

South Carolina Home Educators Association (SCHEA)
P.O. Box 3231, Columbia, SC 29230-3231
Phone: (803) 772-2330

E-mail: schea1@aol.com
http://www.christianity.com/schea

Palmetto Independent Educators (PIE)
P.O. Box 2475, Aiken, SC 29802
Contact: Denise Merchant
Phone: (803) 643-0807
E-mail: mpielady@msn.com
http://www.homeschoolingwithpie.org

South Dakota

South Dakota Christian Home Educators (SDCHE)
P.O. Box 9571, Rapid City, SD 57709-9571
Voice Mail: (605) 348-2001
Fax: (605) 341-2447
E-mail: sdche@christianemail.com
http://www.sdche.org

Home Educators Are Real Teachers (HEART)
P.O. Box 528, Black Hawk, SD 57718

South Dakota Home School Association
P.O. Box 882, Sioux Falls, SD 57101

Tennessee

Tennessee Home Education Association
P.O. Box 681652, Franklin, TN 37068
Phone: (858) 623-7899

Texas

Home School Texas (HOST)
P.O. Box 29307, Dallas, TX 75229
Contact: Phillip and Betty May
Phone: (214) 358-5723
Fax: (214) 358-2996
E-mail: info@homeschooltexas.com
http://www.homeschooltexas.com

Minority Homeschoolers of Texas
P.O. Box 2322, Cedar-Hill, TX 75106
Phone: (972) 293-9209
Voicemail: (972) 354-2520 x7693
Fax: (972) 293-9209
E-mail: president@mhot.org
http://www.mhot.org

Texas Home School Coalition
P.O. Box 6747, Lubbock, TX 79493
Phone: (806) 744-4441
Fax: (806) 744-4446
E-mail: staff@thsc.org
http://www.thsc.org

Utah

Utah Christian Home School Association (UTCH)
P.O. Box 3942, Salt Lake City, UT 84110-3942
Voice Mail: (801) 296-7198
E-mail: utch@utch.org
http://www.utch.org

Utah Home Education Association
P.O. Box 737, Farmington, UT 84025
Contact: Jon Yarrington
E-mail: jyarrington@utah-uhea.org
http://www.utah-uhea.org

Vermont

Vermont Association of Home Educators (VAHE)
c/o Tim Terhune
1646 E. Albany Road, Barton, VT 05822
E-mail: vahemembership@together.net
http://www.vermonthomeschool.org

Virginia

Home Educators Association of Virginia (HEAV)
1900 Byrd Avenue, Suite 201, Richmond, VA 23230-0745

Phone: (804) 288-1608
Fax: (804) 288-6962
E-mail: heav33@aol.com
http://www.heav.org

Virginia Home Education Association
P.O. Box 5131, Charlottesville, VA 22905
Phone: (540) 832-3578
E-mail: vhea@vhea.org
http://www.vhea.org

Washington

Washington Association of Teaching Christian Homes (WATCH)
1026 224th Avenue NE, Sammamish, WA 98074
Phone: (206) 729-4804
E-mail: info@watchhome.org
http://www.watchhome.org

Washington Homeschool Organization (WHO)
6632 S. 191st Place, Suite E100, Kent, WA 98032-2117
Phone: (425) 251-0439
Fax: (425) 251-6984
E-mail: whooff99@foxinternet.net
http://www.washhomeschool.org

Washington Home Educators Network (WHEN)
E-mail: gardnfev.em@gte.net
List: when-subscribe@yahoogroups.com
http://www.homestead.com/WaHomeEdNet/WHENmain.html

West Virginia

Christian Home Educators of West Virginia (CHEWV)
P.O. Box 8770, S. Charleston, WV 25303-0770
Phone: (304) 776-4664
Fax: (304) 776-4664
E-mail: executivedirector@chewv.org
http://www.chewv.org

West Virginia Home Educators Association (WVHEA)
P.O. Box 3707, Charleston, WV 25337-3707

Phone: (800) 736-WVHE
E-mail: mgmiller@citynet.net
http://www.wvhea.org

Wisconsin

Wisconsin Christian Home Educators Association (WCHEA)
2307 Carmel Avenue, Racine, WI 53405
Contact: Al or Jan Gnascinski
Phone: (262) 637-5127
Fax: (262) 638-8127
E-mail: jang8@prodigy.net
http://www.wisconsinchea.com

Wyoming

Homeschoolers of Wyoming (HOW)
P.O. Box 3151, Jackson, WY 83001
Contact: Cindy Munger
Phone: (307) 883-0618
E-mail: contact@homeschoolersofwy.org
http://www.homeschoolersofwy.org

STATE DEPARTMENTS OF EDUCATION
Alabama

Alabama Department of Education
Gordon Persons Office Building
50 North Ripley Street
P.O. Box 302102
Montgomery, AL 36130-2101
Phone: (334) 242-9700
Fax: (334) 242-9708
Web site: http://www.alsde.edu/html/home.asp

Alaska

Alaska Department of Education and Early Development
Suite 200

801 West 10th Street
Juneau, AK 99801-1894
Phone: (907) 465-2800
Fax: (907) 465-4156
TTY: (907) 465-2800
Web site: http://www.eed.state.ak.us/

Arizona

Arizona Department of Education
1535 West Jefferson
Phoenix, AZ 85007
Phone: (602) 542-5460
Toll Free: (800) 352-8400
Fax: (602) 542-5440
Web site: http://www.ade.state.az.us/

Arkansas

Arkansas Department of Education
General Education Division
Room 304 A
Four State Capitol Mall
Little Rock, AR 72201-1071
Phone: (501) 682-4204
Fax: (501) 682-1079
Web site: http://arkedu.state.ar.us/

California

California Department of Education
P.O. Box 944272
Sacramento, CA 94244-2720
Phone: (916) 319-0791
Fax: (916) 657-2682
Web site: http://www.cde.ca.gov/

Colorado

Colorado Department of Education
201 East Colfax Avenue
Denver, CO 80203-1704
Phone: (303) 866-6646
Fax: (303) 866-6938
Web site: http://www.cde.state.co.us/

Connecticut

Connecticut Department of Education
Room 305
State Office Building
165 Capitol Avenue
Hartford, CT 06106-1630
Phone: (860) 713-6548
Fax: (860) 713-7001
Web site: http://www.state.ct.us/sde/

Delaware

Delaware Department of Education
John G. Townsend Building
P.O. Box 1402
Federal and Lockerman Streets
Dover, DE 19903-1402
Phone: (302) 739-4601
Fax: (302) 739-4654
Web site: http://www.doe.state.de.us/

District of Columbia

District of Columbia Public Schools
Union Square
825 North Capitol Street, NE
Washington, DC 20002
Phone: (202) 724-4222
Fax: (202) 442-5026
Web site: http://www.k12.dc.us/dcps/home.html

Florida

Florida Department of Education
Room PL 08
Capitol Building
Tallahassee, FL 32399-0400
Phone: (850) 487-1785
Fax: (850) 413-0378
Web site: http://www.fldoe.org

Georgia

Georgia Department of Education
2054 Twin Towers East
205 Jesse Hill Jr. Drive, SE
Atlanta, GA 30334-5001
Phone: (404) 656-2800
Toll Free: (800) 311-3627
Toll Free Restrictions: GA residents only
Fax: (404) 651-6867
Web site: http://www.doe.k12.ga.us/index.asp

Hawaii

Hawaii Department of Education
1390 Miller Street
Honolulu, HI 96813
Phone: (808) 586-3310
Fax: (808) 586-3320
Web site: http://www.k12.hi.us/

Idaho

Idaho Department of Education
Len B. Jordan Office Building
650 West State Street
P.O. Box 83720
Boise, ID 83720-0027
Phone: (208) 332-6800
Toll Free: (800) 432-4601

Toll Free Restrictions: ID residents only
Fax: (208) 334-2228
TTY: (800) 377-3529
Web site: http://www.sde.state.id.us/

Illinois

Illinois State Board of Education
100 North First Street
Springfield, IL 62777
Phone: (217) 782-4321
Toll Free: (866) 262-6663
Toll Free Restrictions: IL residents only
Fax: (217) 524-4928
TTY: (217) 782-1900
Web site: http://www.isbe.net/

Indiana

Indiana Department of Education
State House, Room 229
Indianapolis, IN 46204-2795
Phone: (317) 232-0808
Fax: (317) 233-6326
Web site: http://www.doe.state.in.us/

Iowa

Iowa Department of Education
Grimes State Office Building
East 14th and Grand Streets
Des Moines, IA 50319-0146
Phone: (515) 281-3436
Fax: (515) 281-4122
Web site: http://www.state.ia.us/educate/

Kansas

Kansas Department of Education
120 South East 10th Avenue

Topeka, KS 66612-1182
Phone: (785) 296-3201
Fax: (785) 296-7933
TTY: (785) 296-6338
Web site: http://www.ksde.org/

Kentucky

Kentucky Department of Education
19th Floor
500 Mero Street
Frankfort, KY 40601
Phone: (502) 564-3421
Toll Free: (800) 533-5372
Fax: (502) 564-6470
Web site: http://www.kentuckyschools.org/

Louisiana

Louisiana Department of Education
626 North Fourth Street
P.O. Box 94064
Baton Rouge, LA 70704-9064
Phone: (225) 342-4411
Toll Free: (877) 453-2721
Fax: (225) 342-7316
Web site: http://www.doe.state.la.us/lde/index.html

Maine

Maine Department of Education
23 State House Station
Augusta, ME 04333-0023
Phone: (207) 624-6600
Fax: (207) 624-6601
TTY: (207) 624-6800
Web site: http://www.state.me.us/education/homepage.htm

Maryland

Maryland Department of Education
200 West Baltimore Street
Baltimore, MD 21201
Phone: (410) 767-0100
Fax: (410) 333-6033
Web site: http://www.marylandpublicschools.org/MSDE

Massachusetts

Massachusetts Department of Education
Educational Improvement Group
350 Main Street
Malden, MA 02148
Phone: (781) 338-3000
Fax: (781) 338-3395
TTY: (800) 439-2370
Web site: http://www.doe.mass.edu/

Michigan

Michigan Department of Education
Hannah Building
Fourth Floor
608 West Allegan Street
Lansing, MI 48933
Phone: (517) 373-3324
Fax: (517) 335-4565
Web site: http://www.mi.gov/mde/

Minnesota

Minnesota Department of Children, Families, and Learning
1500 Highway 36 West
Roseville, MN 55113-4266
Phone: (651) 582-8200
Fax: (651) 582-8727

TTY: (651) 582-8201
Web site: http://cfl.state.mn.us/

Mississippi

Mississippi State Department of Education
Suite 365
359 North West Street
Jackson, MS 39201
Phone: (601) 359-3513
Fax: (601) 359-3242
Web site: http://www.mde.k12.ms.us/

Missouri

Missouri Department of Elementary and Secondary Education
P.O. Box 480
Jefferson City, MO 65102-0480
Phone: (573) 751-4212
Fax: (573) 751-8613
TTY: (800) 735-2966
Web site: http://www.dese.state.mo.us

Montana

Montana Office of Public Instruction
P.O. Box 202501
Helena, MT 59620-2501
Phone: (406) 444-2082
Toll Free: (888) 231-9393
Toll Free Restrictions: MT residents only
Fax: (406) 444-3924
Web site: http://www.opi.state.mt.us/

Nebraska

Nebraska Department of Education
301 Centennial Mall South

P. O. Box 94987
Lincoln, NE 68509-4987
Phone: (402) 471-2295
Fax: (402) 471-0117
TTY: (402) 471-7295
Web site: http://www.nde.state.ne.us/

Nevada

Nevada Department of Education
700 East Fifth Street
Carson City, NV 89701
Phone: (775) 687-9141
Fax: (775) 687-9111
Web site: http://www.nde.state.nv.us/

New Hampshire

New Hampshire Department of Education
101 Pleasant Street
State Office Park South
Concord, NH 03301
Phone: (603) 271-3495
Fax: (603) 271-1953
TTY: (800) 735-2964
Web site: http://www.ed.state.nh.us/

New Jersey

New Jersey Department of Education
P.O. Box 500
100 Riverview Place
Trenton, NJ 08625-0500
Phone: (609) 292-4469
Fax: (609) 777-4099
Web site: http://www.state.nj.us/education/

New Mexico

New Mexico State Department of Education
Education Building
300 Don Gaspar
Santa Fe, NM 87501-2786
Phone: (505) 827-6516
Fax: (505) 827-6588
TTY: (505) 827-6541
Web site: http://www.sde.state.nm.us/

New York

New York Education Department
Education Building
Room 111
89 Washington Avenue
Albany, NY 12234
Phone: (518) 474-5844
Fax: (518) 473-4909
Web site: http://www.nysed.gov/

North Carolina

North Carolina Department of Public Instruction
Education Building
6301 Mail Service Center
Raleigh, NC 27699-6301
Phone: (919) 807-3300
Fax: (919) 807-3445
Web site: http://www.ncpublicschools.org/

North Dakota

North Dakota Department of Public Instruction
11th Floor
Department 201
600 East Boulevard Avenue
Bismarck, ND 58505-0440

Phone: (701) 328-2260
Fax: (701) 328-2461
Web site: http://www.dpi.state.nd.us/

Ohio

Ohio Department of Education
25 South Front Street
Columbus, OH 43215-4183
Toll Free: (877) 644-6338
Fax: (614) 752-3956
Web site: http://www.ode.state.oh.us/

Oklahoma

Oklahoma State Department of Education
2500 North Lincoln Boulevard
Oklahoma City, OK 73105-4599
Phone: (405) 521-3301
Fax: (405) 521-6205
Web site: http://www.sde.state.ok.us/

Oregon

Oregon Department of Education
255 Capitol Street, NE
Salem, OR 97310-0203
Phone: (503) 378-3600
Fax: (503) 378-5156
TTY: (503) 378-2892
Web site: http://www.ode.state.or.us/

Pennsylvania

Pennsylvania Department of Education
333 Market Street
Harrisburg, PA 17126-0333
Phone: (717) 787-5820
Fax: (717) 787-7222

Web site: http://www.pde.state.pa.us/pde_internet/site/default.asp

Rhode Island

Rhode Island Department of Elementary and Secondary Education
255 Westminster Street
Providence, RI 02903-3400
Phone: (401) 222-4600, Ext. 2150
Fax: (401) 222-4044
TTY: (800) 745-5555
Web site: http://www.ridoe.net/

South Carolina

South Carolina Department of Education
1006 Rutledge Building
1429 Senate Street
Columbia, SC 29201
Phone: (803) 734-8492
Fax: (803) 734-3389
Web site: http://www.myscschools.com/

South Dakota

South Dakota Department of Education and Cultural Affairs
700 Governors Drive
Pierre, SD 57501-2291
Phone: (605) 773-3553
Fax: (605) 773-6139
TTY: (605) 773-6302
Web site: http://www.state.sd.us/deca/

Tennessee

Tennessee State Department of Education
Andrew Johnson Tower, Sixth Floor
710 James Robertson Parkway

Nashville, TN 37243-0375
Phone: (615) 741-2731
Fax: (615) 532-4791
Web site: http://www.state.tn.us/education/

Texas

Texas Education Agency
William B. Travis Building
1701 North Congress Avenue
Austin, TX 78701-1494
Phone: (512) 463-9050
Fax: (512) 475-3447
TTY: (512) 475-3540
Web site: http://www.tea.state.tx.us/

Utah

Utah State Office of Education
P.O. Box 144200
250 East 500 South
Salt Lake City, UT 84114-4200
Phone: (801) 538-7500
Fax: (801) 538-7521
Web site: http://www.usoe.k12.ut.us/

Vermont

Vermont Department of Education
120 State Street
Montpelier, VT 05620-2501
Phone: (802) 828-3135
Fax: (802) 828-3140
TTY: (802) 828-2755
Web site: http://www.state.vt.us/educ/

Virginia

Virginia Department of Education
P.O. Box 2120

101 North 14th Street
Richmond, VA 23218-2120
Phone: (804) 225-2020
Toll Free: (800) 292-3820
Toll Free Restrictions: VA residents only
Fax: (804) 371-2455
Web site: http://www.pen.k12.va.us/go/VDOE/

Washington

Office of Superintendent of Public Instruction (Washington)
Old Capitol Building
600 South Washington
P. O. Box 47200
Olympia, WA 98504-7200
Phone: (360) 725-6000
Fax: (360) 753-6712
TTY: (360) 664-3631
Web site: http://www.k12.wa.us/

West Virginia

West Virginia Department of Education
Building 6
1900 Kanawha Boulevard East
Charleston, WV 25305-0330
Phone: (304) 558-0304
Fax: (304) 558-2584
Web site: http://wvde.state.wv.us/

Wisconsin

Wisconsin Department of Public Instruction
125 South Webster Street
P.O. Box 7841
Madison, WI 53707-7841
Phone: (608) 266-3390
Toll Free: (800) 441-4563
Fax: (608) 267-1052

TTY: (608) 267-2427

Web site: http://www.dpi.state.wi.us/

Wyoming

Wyoming Department of Education

Hathaway Building

Second Floor

2300 Capitol Avenue

Cheyenne, WY 82002-0050

Phone: (307) 777-7675

Fax: (307) 777-6234

TTY: (307) 777-7744

Web site: http://www.k12.wy.us/

APPENDIX

ILLINOIS STATE LIBRARY
FY 2001 LIBRARY SERVICES AND TECHNOLOGY ACT
APPLICATION COVER SHEET

APPLICANT NAME AND LEGAL
ADDRESS
Johnsburg Public Library District
3000 W. Johnsburg Rd.
Johnsburg, IL 60050

PROJECT DIRECTOR
Maria Zawacki

PHONE NUMBER   815-344-0077

FAX NUMBER   815-344-3524

E-MAIL ADDRESS   mzawacki@johnsburglibrary.org

GRANT OFFERING PROGRAM
Model Or Innovative Grant Offering

PROJECT TITLE
"Establishing a Homeschool Resource Center at the Johnsburg Public Library"

LSTA GOALS - CHECK WHICH **ONE** GOAL YOUR APPLICATION ADDRESSES

_____Goal 1 - Ensure access to information by citizens by enabling all Illinois libraries to share resources in regional and statewide databases.

_____X_____Goal 2 - Ensure that Illinois libraries have access to all sources and formats of information.

_____Goal 3 - Enrich the quality of life for citizens of Illinois by advocating the pleasures of reading, the ability to read, and the importance of reading.

_____Goal 4 - Develop training methods and activities that will allow library personnel and Illinois citizens to become technologically literate and have full access to information available through libraries.

_____Goal 5 - Continue expanding the role of networks, consortia, and partnerships in library development.

County McHenry

Congressional District 16

Library System Northern Illinois Library System (NILS)

Taxpayer Identification Number (TIN)

Do not complete the information below. **To be completed by the Illinois State Library upon grant award**

Contract Dates:
_____

LSTA Amount:
_____

Contract Number:
_____

Obligation Number:
_____

ISL 4/19/00

A. PREPLANNING AND GROUND WORK

Johnsburg Public Library is located in northern McHenry County near the Wisconsin border. Johnsburg itself is a small, rural community where there are few large industries, some small business centers, much open farm area, and mostly single family homes. Based on the 1990 census, the library district services a population of almost 11,000. While McHenry County is one of the fastest growing counties in the state of Illinois, it still maintains a rural flavor as a whole. The preplanning for this grant began as a result of our library receiving a list of McHenry County homeschooling group contact names that was compiled by one of our library patrons, Ms. Kathy Wentz. Ms. Wentz homeschools her children and is the activity coordinator for one of the homeschool groups, as well as being on numerous Internet listservs and discussion groups for homeschoolers. She tutors students from the local school district and is a former science teacher. She took it upon herself to compile this list for reference purposes for the library. Some McHenry County homeschool groups are specifically denomination based, while others are non-denominational. Library staff was astounded to discover from this list that there are ten different homeschooling groups that specifically serve the needs of homeschoolers in McHenry County. There are no clear statistics on how many homeschool families exist in Johnsburg or McHenry County, but Ms. Wentz informed us that many homeschool families settle in the Johnsburg area oddly enough because of the school district. She said many school districts provide little cooperation with homeschool families. But the Johnsburg school district is well known in the homeschool community for its cooperation with homeschool families. This is a result of the school district's desire to provide children with the best education, whether it is in the schools or in the home. In discussing the library's astonishment regarding the number of homeschool groups that serve our library patrons, Ms. Wentz relayed that her dream some day was to have the public library provide an extensive homeschool resource center for the many homeschool families in the area. This would include such things as math manipulatives, science equipment such as microscopes, telescopes, and scales, educational board games, quality software, curriculum materials, and catalogs from a variety of homeschool suppliers. Ms. Wentz is not aware of any such resource center existing for homeschoolers in any public library in northern Illinois or southern Wisconsin. Thus, the idea for the Johnsburg Public Library's Homeschool Resource Center was born.

With limited funding available, it became clear that LSTA funds might be the perfect solution for finding monies to equip a Homeschool Resource Center at the library. The Johnsburg Public Library is a small library with total annual tax revenue of only $300,000. Extra funds for expensive special programs or services, such as a quality Homeschool Resource Center, simply are not available from within the library's budget. Providing this segment of our population with materials unique to homeschoolers needs, is clearly addressing LSTA Goal #2 by providing access to a variety of sources and formats of information. After realizing that LSTA funding might be a possibility, the next step was sending out a survey to homeschool families in the area to determine exactly what they would like to see in a Homeschool Resource Center. Ms. Wentz constructed a survey and was responsible for sending it to as many of her homeschool contacts as possible. There were 112 people who responded to the "Homeschoolers Library Usage Interest Survey". Certainly not all respondents were from the Johnsburg area, but the large number of respondents provides an excellent sample of what homeschool families in general would want in a Homeschool Resource Center at a public library.

Survey results show that 84% of the respondents plan on homeschooling through high school. This figure indicates that there is a significant long-term interest in homeschooling. When asked what subject area(s) concern them most about homeschooling, a large majority stated science. The next most frequently mentioned subjects, in order, were math, English, foreign language, history, reading, writing, computer science, music, social studies, and art. This illustrates that while there is a clear need in most homeschool families for science information, there is concern and interest in all curricular areas. When asked regarding their interest in basic homeschooling information, response choices were "very interested", "interested", and "not interested". There were 61% of the respondents who were "very interested" in being able to preview curriculum materials from a variety of publishers, with 56% being "very interested" in having access to catalogs from a wide variety of homeschool suppliers. Other requests for basic homeschooling information were for books and magazines supporting homeschooling, information on learning disabilities, homeschool convention videotapes, teacher materials from area museums, local field trip information, and lists of mentors and tutors. Regarding having access to manipulatives, 66% were "very interested" in math manipulatives such as fraction circles, tanagrams, algebra blocks, etc. There were 76% who were very interested in science equipment such as glassware, scales, and other non-consumables. 86% were "very interested" in having access to both microscopes and telescopes, with 90% being "very interested" in science kits on topics such as light, magnetism, rocks and minerals, anatomy, etc. Educational board games such as Fraction Action or Elemento were rated as "very interested" in having access to by 76%. Other manipulatives that respondents requested were geography puzzles.

In rating their interest for having quality software available, 56% were "very interested" in foreign languages. Only 36% were "very interested" in language arts software, with 49% being "interested". Regarding math software, 41% were "very interested" and 50% were "interested". Science software rated 54% as "very interested" and history software rated 51% "very interested". Other quality software requested by the respondents in order of frequency were geography, fine arts, music and anything at the high school level. The results of this survey clearly point to the fact that homeschoolers in our area do indeed have a real desire to have access to a variety of materials. The local public library is the ideal place to provide these resources for the many homeschool families that exist.

B. PROJECT PLAN

As demonstrated by the Homeschoolers survey we conducted, there is a definite need in this segment of the population for a variety of information and material that is desirable to successfully educate their children at home. Homeschooler needs and requests differ from other library patrons whose children do attend local schools, and thus have access to a variety of instructional formats and materials. More than likely, expense prevents many homeschool families from providing their children with a large variety of quality supplemental learning materials traditionally found in a school setting. If our library were able to establish a Homeschool Resource Center that would house these learning materials, they could be checked out and easily shared, much as other library materials currently are. These materials would include a large variety of books and magazines supporting homeschooling, subject area information for homeschoolers, curriculum materials to preview, homeschool supplier catalogs, quality educational software and games, and math and science manipulatives and equipment. The only materials that the library currently provides that is geared specifically for homeschoolers interests are a few books on that topic in the general collection. By providing this segment of the population with a Homeschool Resource Center we are clearly addressing LSTA Goal 2 by providing homeschoolers with access to all sources and formats of information. We anticipate that the Homeschool Resource Center would have an impact much beyond the local Johnsburg community. Out of necessity, homeschoolers do a great deal of networking. As word of our Homeschool Resource Center spreads, we fully expect that members of many of the homeschooling groups from throughout McHenry County would frequent it and take advantage of its resources.

With statistics that are available showing that the homeschool movement is becoming more and more popular, there are probably few libraries that currently exist that do not serve this segment of the population. Other libraries could contact their area homeschooling groups and conduct a survey similar to ours to find out what their particular needs and wants are and then work towards meeting those needs and wants. Just as other library materials are shared by all in the community, these homeschool resource materials can be cataloged and processed in a similar manner, housed in an area together, and made available to the homeschool population in their community.

C. PROJECT FEASIBILITY

In looking at where the library could set up a Homeschool Resource Center, it is clear that the library's existing study room would be an ideal location. With the numerous manipulatives and equipment that we hope to provide, the Homeschool Resource Center needs to be housed in an area accessible to the public, yet not on the regular open shelves. The study room is an enclosed room visible from the circulation desk and able to be locked if so desired. It is infrequently used and has ample room to house such a collection. Currently housed in the room are a small collection of telecourses from the local community college and a study table with chairs. Additional shelving is available in the library's basement and could be added to the study room to accommodate the components of the Homeschool Resource Center. All materials in the Homeschool Resource Center would be available for check out and added to the library's online catalog. To address the concern regarding the security of some of the more expensive materials, the library has a security system and all items in the Homeschool Resource Center would be tagged with a security strip. The library also employs the services of a collection agency to help retrieve overdue materials, should there be a concern regarding the return of expensive materials.

With funds requested from this grant we hope to supply the Homeschool Resource Center with the following items, based on the responses from the survey. Books and magazines supporting homeschooling that will be purchased have been selected from a recommended list in the book "The Librarian's Guide to Homeschooling Resources" by Susan G. Scheps, published by the American Library Association in 1998. All items selected were checked to make sure they are still in print and available for purchase. Grant funds would pay for 3-year subscriptions to 22 recommended homeschool magazines and newsletters. Following this 3-year subscription period, usage statistics would be analyzed to determine which of the more heavily used titles the library would pick up the subscription costs for. We would also purchase 247 recommended books. These books include general titles on homeschooling, as well as books on specific content areas of literature, math, social studies, and science. This list of 247 books does not provide a listing of recommended books for the specific subject areas of foreign language, computer science, music, or art. We would then purchase materials in these subject areas that are recommended in the book "The Complete Home Learning Source Book" by Rebecca Rupp and published by Three Rivers Press in 1998. This would include purchasing 25 of the recommended music items still in print, 16 books on computers, 37 foreign language items, and 37 books on art. Our purchases would also include textbook series from a variety of publishers covering the five main subject areas of reading, science, social studies, math, and spelling. With a textbook averaging $50, we would plan on supplying texts for all eight grade levels from ten different publishers. Ms. Wentz has also suggested purchasing 100 historical literature titles, at an average cost of $20 per book. She has a suggested list and has found that most homeschoolers are now using a literature-based approach to history, rather than a textbook approach. We will also purchase 59 other curriculum titles that are recommended in "The Complete Home Learning Source Book under the headings of "Curricula, Lesson Plans, and How-Tos" and "Reading Programs". All print materials to be purchased with these grant funds total 921 books and 22 magazine subscriptions, totaling $35,764 based on current prices.

Of the survey respondents, 66% were "very interested" in having math manipulatives available for checkout at the public library. We plan on purchasing 33 math games and hands-on activities that are recommended in "The Complete Home Learning Source Book" and suitable for repeated use in a library setting, as well as 40 science games and kits. In addition, as a former science teacher, Ms. Wentz has recommended that we purchase three different kinds of microscopes. These include a dissection microscope, a children's microscope, and one appropriate for high school age. In addition, she recommended purchasing a children's telescope and one appropriate for older children and adults. Other science equipment to be purchased includes 3 scales and other measuring devices. 76% of the survey respondents were "very interested" in educational board games. Again based on recommended lists in "The Complete Home Learning Source Book", we plan on purchasing 17 language arts games, 3 music games, 5 art games, and 8 history games suitable for repeated use. Grant funds would then allow us to purchase a total of 106 educational manipulatives, games, kits, and hands-on activities in all subject areas totaling $2,822. The recommended telescopes, microscopes and other science equipment total an additional $8, 438.

Specific software purchases will be selected again based on recommended lists in "The Complete Home Learning Source Book" and a foreign language set specifically recommended by Ms. Wentz based on homeschool family recommendations. These include 31 foreign language titles, 5 math titles, 15 science titles, 10 reading titles, 11 history titles, 7 geography titles, 3 music titles, and 5 art titles, for a total of 87 software titles at a cost of $7, 117. Existing library staff would be responsible for cataloging and processing all of the Homeschool Resource Center materials, as they do other library materials. Since we anticipate that many of the software titles and some educational manipulatives will need to be repackaged in studier containers to withstand circulations, we are also requesting an additional $1,000 for processing supplies. All items in the Homeschool Resource Center will have an extended checkout period. Should any items not be available for purchase at the time of ordering, we will request replacement suggestions from Ms. Wentz.

The library will absorb any costs for establishing a pamphlet file with materials of special interest to families who home school. This would include state regulations regarding homeschooling, homeschoolers support groups and local field trip information, as well as pamphlets of local area points of interest. The library would also absorb any costs associated with maintaining a collection of catalogs from homeschool suppliers, lists of which are available in many homeschool resource books. The Children's Librarian would be responsible for assembling and maintaining these files on a permanent basis. Regarding maintaining the resource center on a permanent basis, we will maintain it as we do any other collection in the library. New items on homeschooling that are reviewed in library journals will be added to the collection, based on the reviews. Recommendations from homeschool patrons regarding new acquisition requests will be taken into consideration for purchase. Worn or damaged items will be withdrawn as other library materials currently are.

Following grant notification, all items already selected for purchase from the recommended lists will be ordered. They will be cataloged and processed when they arrive. The library will assume all costs for publicizing the resource center after all items are received and in place. Information then will be sent to all ten of the McHenry County homeschool groups. In addition, information on the resource center will be included in the library's newsletter which is mailed to all households in the library district, in the village of Johnsburg's newsletter, in the library's local weekly newspaper column and in the Chicago newspapers, and added to the library web site.

D. PARTNERSHIPS & COMMUNITY INVOLVEMENT

The library's partners in this grant are the ten McHenry County homeschooling groups and their members. They have already contributed significantly by responding to our interest survey. It was their responses that formed the basis for what the Homeschool Resource Center should be. Since they are a countywide group, the impact of our resource center will reach much beyond the boundaries of Johnsburg. We fully expect many homeschool families from throughout the county to take advantage of the resource center. We will encourage and welcome their input regarding the resource center and any recommendations for it for the future.

ABSTRACT

The Johnsburg Public Library is providing services to the homeschool population by establishing a Homeschool Resource Center within the library. Items in the Resource Center that are available for checkout include curriculum materials, math manipulatives, science equipment such as microscopes and telescopes, educational board games and kits, quality software, homeschooling books and magazines, and catalogs from a variety of homeschool suppliers.

LSTA GRANT BUDGET SHEET

BUDGET CATEGORY	EXPLANATION	AMOUNT (in dollars only)
Library Materials	Books, non-print, software	$ 45,703
Capital Outlay *	Equipment valued over $500	$ 8,138
Professional Contracts *	Hiring an individual on contract	$
Contractual Services *	Hiring an agency on contract	$
Personnel	Salaries and benefits for additional agency staff	$
Travel and CE for Staff	Agency staff travel and meeting registrations	$
CE and Meetings for Others	Travel, registrations and honorariums for others	$
Public Relations	Advertising done by outside firm	$
Supplies, Postage and Printing	Equipment/supplies valued under $500	$ 1,300
Telephones and Telecommunications	Phone charges and rental	$
Equipment Rental, Repair, and Maintenance	Rental, repair, insurance and maintenance of equipment	$
	TOTAL	$ 55,141

LSTA GRANT BUDGET SHEET

Capital Outlay:

Zoom Stereo Dissection Microscope:	$1, 070
Video Zoom Microscope System	$3, 750
Phase-Contrast Trinocular Microscope	$1,575
Astroscan telescope and accessories	$ 750
Meade ETX Telescope	$ 993

LIBRARY'S LOCAL CONTRIBUTION BUDGET SHEET

BUDGET CATEGORY	EXPLANATION	AMOUNT (in dollars only)
Library Materials	Books, non-print, software	$
Capital Outlay	Equipment valued over $500	$
Professional Contracts	Hiring an individual on contract	$
Contractual Services	Hiring an agency on contract	$
Personnel	Salaries and benefits for additional agency staff	$
Travel and CE for Staff	Agency staff travel and meeting registrations	$
CE and Meetings for Others	Travel, registrations and honorariums for others	$
Public Relations	Advertising done by outside firm	$
Supplies, Postage and Printing	Equipment/supplies valued under $500	$ 1,000
Telephones and Telecommunications	Phone charges and rental	$
Equipment Rental, Repair, and Maintenance	Rental, repair, insurance and maintenance of equipment	$
	TOTAL	$ 1,000

LIST OF PARTICIPANTS and LETTERS OF ENDORSEMENT

Our partners in the grant are the ten McHenry County Homeschooling Groups. They are Apple Tree North, Apple Tree South, Cheer, Good Shepard Catholic Homeschooling Group, H.O.U.S.E. (Home Oriented Unique Schooling Experience) McHenry Co., ICHEA (Illinois Christian Home Educators Association) Chain of Lake Chapter, Pillar Tillers, Society of St. Scholastica Homeschoolers, Wonder Kids, and Northern Illinois Christian Home Educators Assoc.

LETTERS OF ENDORSEMENT

This is the text of an e-mail received from Kathy Wentz regarding actual comments made on our survey, in support of our Homeschool Resource Center. (Please note there are some respondents that do not live in Johnsburg and therefore are not referring to our library in particular when making comments).

From: Kathy Wentz [kwentz@mc.net]
Sent: Monday, August 28, 2000 12:23 AM
To: Maria Zawacki
Subject: survey comments + mine

Here are some of the comments that were attached to the surveys when I got them back. Some of the comments have had individual names removed, but otherwise remain largely unedited. Yes, mine is the last - and you may attach my name to it if you feel that is appropriate. :-)

Kathy

1)

This is a wonderful idea! I've passed out several surveys in hopes you'll get them back. Please let me know if I can help you in any way. I know Maria Zawacki, she is wonderful and helpful, so this type of program should work very nicely. Thanks for all your hard work on this project!

2)

hope this helps!
we use our library so much that i'm happy to help any chance this may be able to be used for other areas?

i miss the library we had in Cleveland, that had software and magazines! but i'm just happy we have one that has videos! ;)

3)   (on an out of state reply)

Hey, you forgot a comments section!<g> When this paradise exists, let me know. My dear husband is a librarian and I have found relatively little help locally for homeschooling. This particular library is under

financial stress and the collection is way out of date. I keep sending
in purchase requests and I
hear nothing back. My guess is they view homeschoolers as too small a
group to be concerned about their needs. They do have a toy lending
library at the main branch, but otherwise that's it.

4)
(In response to the final line on the survey: "Thank you for your time!
I know how valuable it is!"

Yes, but well worth it, doing things like this (filling out surveys
about homeschooling and library usage) will probably not help me, but be
of enormous help to those who follow in our steps.

5)
Thank you for giving me the opportunity to participate in this survey.
We love our library but has so little to offer homeschoolers. Wouldn't
it be nice if we could reroute the tax dollars we pay to schools to the
public library to be used for these resources. Have a wonderful day

6)
I would like to add a comment. I am very fortunate in that I belong to
a
group that supplies classes. Therefore I am less interested in the
library supplying that need. It would be a different story if I did not
have
that group. Having the availability of scientific materials would be
wonderful, however! I hope this helps.

7)
Let us know the outcome. Hope they get the grant!!!!

8)
Generally speaking I think all of these are great ideas and would be
great resources for homeschoolers. The items/areas about which I am
less enthusiastic in the survey have to do more with my personal
needs and the materials we already have available to us (i.e., the kids
and I can already program, so no need for computer classes, and we
have a microscope and telescope, so while I'd be vaguely interested I
am not enthusiastic about these items).

Good luck with the survey.

9)
All of the above would be great! Items like what I mentioned above -
learning kits, audio books, CD's, board games, teacher resource guides,
videos. Make it very much like a lending library, only specialized for
homeschoolers. You could even include items like posters, instruments
and music books - anything that people might like to try out for a
period of time to determine whether it would be a worthwhile investment
for them to purchase it personally.

10)

What a wonderful resource for homeschoolers (and schoolers interested in
more or different materials!) a resource center such as this could be!
What a great idea! It is so very difficult for homeschoolers, who are
generally one income families, to provide more than a few of the vast
wealth of educational materials available.
I have spoken to many homeschooling families who have shared the same
set of experiences. We have all found ourselves buying an expensive
set of materials only to find they are not appropriate for the
curriculum or are not useful to the child they were bought for. It is
so frustrating to have spent all that money just to have the materials
sitting on a shelf - and then try to resell them for a tenth of what you
paid for them! This type of loan program would eliminate most if not
all of those purchasing mistakes, saving homeschoolers thousands of
dollars each and helping them truly get the best programs and materials
to meet each of their children's individual needs.

All parents want the best educational resources and materials for their
children's needs. With the wonderful inter-library loan system in this
area, I can only envision these materials being used so much they will
never be on the shelf for me! (Hey, can you buy two of everything???
<g>)

Thanks for your hard work!

INDEX

A to Z Home's Cool Homeschooling
  Web Site, 178
ACT programs, 110
Administration, support of, 33–34
Adolescent development: early, 14,
  16–17; late, 14, 17–18. *See also*
  Developmental assets; Develop-
  mental needs
Adolescent Psychological Development:
  Rationality, Morality, and Identity, 23
Advertisements: classified, 155; dis-
  play, 155; paid, 155–56; pricing,
  155–56
After Homeschool: Fifteen Homeschoolers
  Out in the Real World, 173
Allies for providing services to home-
  schoolers, 31
American Academy of Child and
  Adolescent Development, 16
American Association of School
  Librarians (AASL), 101
American Red Cross, 125
And What about College? How Home-
  schooling Can Lead to Admissions to

the Best Colleges and Universities,
  164, 184
Art exhibits, 109
Art prints, included in a homeschool-
  ing collection, 60
Art programs, 109–10
Art resources, vendors, 81
Association for Educational Commu-
  nications and Technology (AECT),
  101
Association of College and Research
  Libraries (ACRL), 100
Audio materials, included in a home-
  schooling collection, 59–60;
  unabridged, vendors, 80–81
Award winning books, Web sites, 107–8

Babysitting programs, 125
Basic Young Adult Services Handbook,
  109
Bears' Guide to Earning Degrees by
  Distance Learning, 172
The Beginner's Guide to Homeschooling,
  167

Berkowitz, Mike, 101
Beyond Survival: A Guide to Abundant Life Homeschooling, 171–72
The Big Book of Home Learning. Volume Three: Junior High to College, 84, 179
Big6 ™, 101
Bingo, 96
Board game programs, 118
Boise Public Library, Idaho, 47
Book discussion groups, 101–4; cooperative (*see* Literature circles); resources, 103–4; title selection, 104; with children's literature, 103
Book fairs, 44
Book review forms, 125
Book reviewing projects for homeschoolers on Teen Advisory Board, 124
Book sales, 44
Booktalks, 95, 106–7
Bridging Generations: Adults Discuss Children's Books, 102–3
Brown bag lunch programs, 102, 106
Budget, 29
Budgeting programs, 126
Bushnell, Tom, 9

Car care courses, 125
Cardiff, Chris, 1–2
Career fairs, 110
Career guidance, 18
Career programs, 110–11
Catholic Home School Network of America, 177
Catholic Home Schooling: A Handbook for Parents, 167
Certificates of program completion, 94
Challenges: to collections by homeschooling families, 60–63; to special services for homeschoolers, 35–36
Chess clubs, 118
Childhood and Society, 16
Children's literature, in book discussion groups, 103
Christian collections, developing, 84
Christian Home Educators' Curriculum Manual: Junior/Senior High, 172
Christian publishers, 79–80

Clubs, 118–19
Cockett, Lynn, 123
Coffeehouse programs, 117–18
Cohen, Cafi and Terry, 184
Colfax, David and Micki, 4, 10
Collection connections, to programs, 91–92
Collection development policies, 63
Collections for homeschoolers. *See* Homeschooling collections
College guidance, 18
College preparation materials, included in a homeschooling collection, 56
College programs: college application process, 111; college preparation, 110–11; searching for colleges online, 111
Communication: with library administration, 33–34; with library staff, 34–35; with other libraries, 35
Community calendar, 154
Competition for libraries, 132–34, 136–37
The Complete Guide to Homeschooling, 170–71
The Complete Home Learning Source Book: The Essential Resource Guide for Homeschoolers, Parents, and Educators Covering Every Subject from Arithmetic to Zoology, 166
The Complete Idiot's Guide to Homeschooling, 171
The Complete Idiot's Guide to Volunteering for Teens, 168
Compulsory attendance laws, 5
Computer software, included in a homeschooling collection, 60
Confidentiality concerns of homeschooling families, 96
Connecting Young Adults and Libraries: A How-to-do-it Manual, 36
Contests, 126–27
Core collection for homeschooled teens, 164–66
A Core Collection for Young Adults, 84
Correspondence schools. *See* Distance learning institutions

Creative Home Schooling for Gifted Children: A Resource Guide, 171
Creative writing programs, 108
Curriculum catalogs, included in a homeschooling collection, 65–66
Curriculum exchanges, 43–44
Curriculum guides, included in a homeschooling collection, 56
Curriculum publishers, 66–71
Customers, library patrons as, 133

Dating, Christian resources, 15–16
Debate night programs, 112
Departments of Education, 204–18
Deschooling, 3
Designing Your Own Classical Curriculum, A Guide to Catholic Home Education, 167
Developing Christian Fiction Collections for Children and Adults: Selection Criteria and a Core Collection, 84
Developmental assets, 22–23
Developmental needs, 20–22
Display space, homeschoolers use of, 42
Distance learning institutions, 2, 71–75; Web sites, 181–83
Do it Right: Best Practices for Serving Young Adults in School and Public Libraries, 37
Dorman, Gayle, 20–22
Drama programs, 112–14
Driver safety course, 125
Driver's education, Web sites, 180
Dunn, Jim, 8

Eclectic Homeschool Online, 178
Economics programs, 126
Educational Travel on a Shoestring: Frugal Family Fun and Learning Away from Home, 166–67
Edwards, Kirsten, 109
Eisenberg, Mike, 101
E-lists, as promotional tool, 150
E-mail, as promotional tool, 150
Employment opportunities for homeschooling teens, 123
Entertainment programs, 115–18
Environmental scan, 26–27

Erikson, Erik, 16
Evaluation: of library services, 37; of marketing, 137; of programs, 92
Excellence in Library Services to Young Adults (1994), 128
Excellence in Library Services to Young Adults (1997), 128
Excellence in Library Services to Young Adults (2000), 102, 128

Fairfield Public Library, Connecticut, 43
Falmouth Public Library, Massachusetts, 42
Family board game night, 118
Family math night, 114–15
Family programs, 94, 114–15, 118
Family Unschoolers Network, 179
Federal Communications Commission (FCC), 153
Fiction, included in a homeschooling collection, 56
Financial aid night, 111
First aid programs, 125
Focus groups, 40; as marketing tool, 146–49; as program evaluation tool, 93
Foreign language clubs, 121
Free (and Almost Free) Adventures for Teenagers, 173
Freedom Challenge: African American Homeschoolers, 169–70
Friends organizations, teen volunteers, 122
From Homeschool to College and Work: Turning Your Homeschooled Experiences into College and Job Portfolios, 173
Funding, 61–62; for collections, 64–65; for services, 50–51
Fundraising, 30, 64; teen volunteers, 122–23

GED Web sites, 183
Getting Started on Home Learning: How and Why to Teach Your Kids at Home, 171
Goal setting, 28–29; measurable, 137

Grants, 29–30, 65; Johnsburg Public
  Library District grant, 220–33;
  resources for obtaining, 51, 65
Great Books Foundation, 104
Growing Without Schooling, 6
*Guerrilla Learning: How to Give Your
  Kids a Real Education With or With-
  out School*, 170
*The Guidance Manual for the Christian
  Home School: A Parent's Guide for
  Preparing Home School Students for
  College or Career*, 167
A Guide to Homeschooling for Librarians,
  164

*Help for the Harried Homeschooler: A
  Practical Guide to Balancing Your
  Child's Education with the Rest of
  Your Life*, 167–68
Helping Teenagers into Adulthood, 23
Hobby programs, 109–10
*Hold Them in your Heart: Successful
  Strategies for Library Services to At-
  Risk Teens*, 37
Holt, John, 5–6, 8, 10, 179
Home Education Magazine, 177, 179
Home Learning Year by Year: How to
  Design a Homeschool Curriculum
  from Preschool Through High
  School, 171
Home School Foundation, 176
Home School Legal Defense Associa-
  tion, 6, 176; 1997 study, xvi
*The Home School Manual: Plans, Point-
  ers, Reasons, and Resources*, 166
The Home School Source Book, 166
Homeschool Internet Yellow Pages,
  185
Homeschool Open House, 169
*Homeschool Your Child for Free: More
  Than 1,200 Smart, Effective, and
  Practical Resources for Home Edu-
  cation on the Internet and Beyond*, 168
Homeschool.com, 177
Homeschooled teenagers, resources:
  books, 172–73; Web sites, 180
Homeschooler task force, as part of a
  Teen Advisory Board, 124

Homeschoolers: college-bound, 10;
  college-bound, Web sites, 183–84;
  disabled, 9; diversity of, 7–9; grade
  levels of, 14; number of, xvi, 7;
  performance on standardized tests,
  9–10; Use of the public library, xvi
*Homeschoolers' College Admissions
  Handbook: Preparing your 12– to
  18–Year-Old for a Smooth Transition*,
  164
*The Homeschooler's Guide to Portfolios
  and Transcripts*, 165
Homeschoolers' Success Stories: 15
  Adults and 12 Young People Share
  the Impact That Homeschooling
  Has Made on Their Lives, 165
Homeschooling: history, 5–7; legal
  issues, 6–7; parental roles, 8
Homeschooling advocates, 48–49
*Homeschooling All the Way Through
  High School*, 173
Homeschooling Almanac 2002–2003, 165
Homeschooling collections, 54; art
  prints, 60; audio materials, 59–60;
  college preparation materials, 56;
  computer software, 60; core collection for homeschooled teens,
  164–66; curriculum catalogs, 65–66;
  curriculum guides, 56; elements of,
  55; fiction, 56; homeschooling cur-
  ricula, 55–56; nonfiction, 56; scien-
  tific equipment, 44–45, 60; space
  considerations, 63; textbooks, 55;
  videos, 60
Homeschooling curricula, included in
  a homeschooling collection, 55–56
Homeschooling for Excellence, 4, 164–65
*Homeschooling for Success: How Parents
  Can Create a Superior Education for
  Their Child*, 169
The Homeschooling Handbook, 168
Homeschooling handbooks, main-
  tained by library, 45–46
*Homeschooling High School: Planning
  Ahead for College Admission*, 172
Homeschooling magazines, 56–59;
  Web sites, 179–80
Homeschooling on a Shoestring, 170

Homeschooling Our Children, Unschooling Ourselves, 170
Homeschooling resource centers, 47–49, 55
Homeschooling resources: articles, 173–76; books, 166–72; distributors, 83–84; listed on library Web site, 46, 49; organizations, statewide, 186–204; supply Web sites, 185; Web sites, 176–79
Homeschooling the Teen Years, 164
Homeschooling Today, 176
Homeschooling: Untangling the Web of Confusion, 172
Hooking Teens with the 'Net', 127
How Children Fail, 168–69
How Children Learn, 168–69
How Homeschooling Leads to Admissions to the Best Colleges and Universities, 184

I Learn Better by Teaching Myself, 169
Identity, 23; in early adolescence, 16–17; in later adolescence, 17–18
Independence, 16–17
Independent learning schools. *See* Distance learning institutions
Information literacy, 100–101; courses, 100–101
Instruction programs, 97–101
Interest clubs, 118–19
International night, 121
Internet for Educators and Homeschoolers, 169
Interview skills programs, 111
Interviews: as program evaluation tool, 93; in marketing, 146

Jackson County Library Services, Oregon, 46
Jewish Home Educator's Network, 178
Job fair program, 110–11
Johnsburg Public Library District, Illinois, 47–49, 220–33
Jon's Homeschool Resource Page, 177
Junior Great Books Club, 104

King County Library System, Washington, 102
Kingdom of Children: Culture and Controversy in the Homeschooling Movement, 171
Kleiner, Carolyn, 7–8
Koontz, Christie, 134

Language clubs, 121
Language programs, 121–22
Lead time for library promotions, 154–55
Leadership opportunities for homeschooled teens, 123
The Librarian's Guide to Homeschooling Resources, 166
Library administration, support of, 33–34
Library bingo, 96
Library instruction programs, 97–101
Library management, market-oriented, 133
Library open house programs, 94–96
Library orientation programs, 94–96
Library research instruction, 41
Library Services and Technology Act (LSTA), 51–52; grants, 49, 220–33
Library tours, 41, 95, 96–97
Likert scale, 143, 145
Lines, Patricia, 7, 8
Literature circles, 104–6; resources, 106; roles for participants, 104–5
Literature-based programming, 101–8
Lock-ins, 119–21; activities, 120; chaperones, 119–20
Loneliness, 20
Lord, Mary, 8
LSTA. *See* Library Services and Technology Act (LSTA)
Lunch 'n' Lit program, 102

Mailing lists, 96; electronic, 150
Managing Young Adult Services, A Self-Help Manual, 37
Market plan checklist, 138
Market-oriented library management, 133

Marketing: audits, 137; defined, 133; online resources, 160–61; plans, 134–38

Marketing: A How-To-Do-It Manual for Librarians, 159

Marketing and Libraries Do Mix: A Handbook for Libraries and Information Centers, 159

Marketing and Public Relations for Libraries, 159

Marketing Concepts for Libraries and Information Services, 158

Marketing Information Products and Services: A Primer for Librarians and Information Professionals, 158

Marketing Library Services, 134, 159

Marketing/Planning Library and Information Services, 159–60

Math programs, 114–15

Math resources, vendors, 81–83

The McGraw-Hill Homeschooling Companion, 166

Media directories, 154–55

Media outlets, 154

Medlin, Richard G., 19

Meeting rooms, 41–42; policies, 42

The Middle Grades Assessment Program User's Guide, 20–22

Military academies, Web sites, 184

Mission, tied to programming, 91

Mission statement, in marketing plan, 135; review of, 27–28

Money management programs, 126

Moore, Dorothy, 6

Moore, Raymond, Dr., 6

Morning by Morning: How We Home-Schooled our African-American Sons to the Ivy League, 170

Motion Picture Licensing Corporation, 116

Movie night, 115–17

Multnomah County Library, Oregon, 46–47

Murder mystery programs, 114

Museum passes, 42–43

Muslim Homeschool Network, 178

Mystery programs, 114

National Challenged Homeschoolers Association (NATHHAN), 9, 177

National Home Education Network (NHEN), 176

National Home Education Research Institute, xvi, 176

New Directions for Library Service to Young Adults, 37

Newsletters for teenagers, as promotional tool, 150

Nonfiction, as included in a home-schooling collection, 56; publishers, 75–79

Nutrition programs, 125

Objectionable content, concerns for book discussion groups, 102

Observations, as program evaluation tool, 93

101+ Teen Programs that Work, 128

Online schools. *See* Distance learning institutions

Online searching programs, 99–100

Open house programs, 94–96

The Organized Home Schooler, 167

Orientation programs, 94–96

Output Measures and More: Planning and Evaluating Public Library Services for Young Adults, 37

Outstanding Books for the College Bound, 84

Overnight programs. *See* Lock-ins

Pappas, Marjorie, 101

Participation programs, teen, 122–24

Passive reading programs, 107

Pathways to Knowledge®, 101

Pathways to Knowledge® and Inquiry Learning, 101, 128–29

Patrick Henry College, Virginia, 10

Pen pal programs, 109–10

Physical education, 167

Plugged In: Helping Parents and Youth Leaders Guide Teens through the World of Popular Youth Culture, 60

Poetry clubs, 108

Portfolios of homeschooling teens, 94, 101, 165

Powerful Public Relations: A How-To Guide for Libraries, 158–59

Practical Homeschooling, 179

Press releases, 152–55; sample 152

Program ideas, 87, 91. *See also specific program ideas*

Program incentives/benefits for homeschooling teens, 93–94

Program planning checklists, 86, 89–90

Program planning worksheets, 86–88

Program portfolios, 86

Promotion strategies, 136; lead time, 154–55; marketing, 149–51; schedules, 155

Puberty, 14–15

Public performance rights, 115–16

Public relations, defined, 133

Public service announcements, 152–55; sample, 153

Puppet shows, 112

Purdy, Jedediah, 9, 10

Quaqua Society, Inc., 178

The Question is College: On Finding and Doing Work You Love, 173

Ray, Brian D., xvi

Readers' theatre, 112–14; resources, 113–14

Reading circles. *See* Literature circles

Reading programs, passive, 107

Reading Programs for Young Adults: Complete Plans for 50 Theme-Related Units for Public, Middle School and High School Libraries, 129

Real Lives: Eleven Teens Who Don't Go to School, 165–66

Real-Life Homeschooling: The Stories of 21 Families Who Teach Their Children at Home, 164

Reference source scavenger hunt, 97–99

Reporters, speaking to, 154; working with, 156–57

Research instruction, 41, 97–101

Research journals, 101

Resource lists, prepared for home-schoolers, 45, 54

SAT programs, 110

Scavenger hunts, 97–99

Science fairs, 115

Science programs, 115

Science resource vendors, 81–83

Scientific equipment, included in a homeschooling collection, 44–45, 60

Search Institute, 22, 23

Selling it checklist, 151

A Sense of Self: Listening to Homeschooled Adolescent Girls, 17

Sexuality, Christian resources, 15–16

Sign language workshops, 121–22

Sizzling Summer Reading Programs, 128

Skills programs, 124–26

Skokie Public Library, Illinois, 102

Socialization, 18–20

Something Funny Happened at the Library: How to Create Humorous Programs for Children and Young Adults, 129

Space considerations, 32; for collections, 63

Speech programs, 112

Staff: negativity, 31–32, 35; promoting events, 157; time, 30–31; training, 35

Statistics, 92–93

Still Teaching Ourselves, 169

Story hours, using homeschoolers as volunteers, 112, 122

Strategic planning, 134

Strengths of Their Own, Home Schoolers Across America: Academic Achievement, Family Characteristics, and Longitudinal Traits, 171

Suggestion box, 93

Summer Pen Pal Letter Exchange, 109–10

Summer reading clubs, 107

Survey questions: qualitative, 145; quantitative, 145

Surveys, 40, 138–46; as program evaluation tool, 93; customer satisfaction, 142; design, 142–43, 145; organization of instrument, 145–46;

samples, 140–41, 143–44; telephone, 139; written, 139–42

Target market, 135
Teach Your Own, 6, 10
Teacher loan cards, 40–41
Teen advisory boards, 123–24; assisting with mystery programs, 114; homeschooler task force, 124; officers, 123; school quotas, 123
Teen Library Events: A Month-by-Month Guide, 109, 128
Teen participation programs, 122–24
Teen Read Week, 107
Teen Spaces: The Step-by-Step Library Makeover, 159
The Teenage Liberation Handbook, 11
The Teenagers' Guide to School Outside the Box, 173
Teens.library: Developing Internet Services for Young Adults, 127–28
Television coverage of events, 157
Tepe, Ann, 101
Test proctoring, 49; space considerations, 32
Textbooks, included in a homeschooling collection, 55
Things We Wish We'd Known, 172
Thorsen, Gail, 9
Times of programs, weekday programming, 94
Timetable, 33
Tours, 41, 95, 96–97

The Ultimate Homeschool Physical Education Game Book, 167
Umbrella schools. *See* Distance learning institutions
University of Nebraska-Lincoln (UNL) Independent Study High School, test proctoring, 49

The Unofficial Guide to Homeschooling, 11
Unschoolers, 6; defined, 2–3
The Unschooling Handbook: How to Use the Whole World as Your Child's Classroom, 168

Videos, included in a homeschooling collection, 60; vendors, 81
Volunteers, 30–31, 50; space considerations, 32; homeschooling teen volunteers, 122–23

Wadsworth Public Library, Ohio, 142–44
Web sites, as promotional tool, 150–51; homeschoolers assistance with, 124
The Well-Trained Mind: A Guide to Classical Education at Home, 172
Wentz, Kathy, 48–49, 50
What Kids Need to Succeed, 23
Word-of-mouth promotion, 151
Working with Adolescents: Constructing Identity, 23

Young Adults and Public Libraries: A Handbook of Materials and Services, 37, 123
You're Going to do What? Helping You Understand the Homeschool Decision, 165
Youth Advisory Boards. *See* Teen advisory boards
The Youth Cybrarian's Guide to Developing Instructional, Curriculum-related, Summer Reading, and Recreational Programs, 128
Youth Participation in School and Public Libraries: It Works, 128

Zawacki, Maria, 48

About the Author

MAUREEN T. LERCH is a Reference/Outreach Librarian at the University of Akron Wayne College Library. She has served homeschooled teen patrons in the communities of Findlay, Louisville, and Orrville, Ohio.

JANET WELCH is Marketing and Public Relations Coordinator at Wadsworth Ella M. Everhard Public Library in Wadsworth, Ohio. A homeschooling mom, Welch is convinced that the public library is the greatest resource a homeschooler can have.